The transition at the end of compulsory full-time education

Marina Trebbels

The transition at the end of compulsory full-time education

Educational and future career aspirations of native and migrant students

Marina Trebbels
Universität Hamburg, Deutschland

Zugl. Dissertation an der Universität Hamburg, 2014

ISBN 978-3-658-06240-8   ISBN 978-3-658-06241-5 (eBook)
DOI 10.1007/978-3-658-06241-5

Die Deutsche Nationalbibliothek verzeichnet diese Publikation in der Deutschen Nationalbibliografie; detaillierte bibliografische Daten sind im Internet über http://dnb.d-nb.de abrufbar.

Springer VS
© Springer Fachmedien Wiesbaden 2015
Das Werk einschließlich aller seiner Teile ist urheberrechtlich geschützt. Jede Verwertung, die nicht ausdrücklich vom Urheberrechtsgesetz zugelassen ist, bedarf der vorherigen Zustimmung des Verlags. Das gilt insbesondere für Vervielfältigungen, Bearbeitungen, Übersetzungen, Mikroverfilmungen und die Einspeicherung und Verarbeitung in elektronischen Systemen.

Die Wiedergabe von Gebrauchsnamen, Handelsnamen, Warenbezeichnungen usw. in diesem Werk berechtigt auch ohne besondere Kennzeichnung nicht zu der Annahme, dass solche Namen im Sinne der Warenzeichen- und Markenschutz-Gesetzgebung als frei zu betrachten wären und daher von jedermann benutzt werden dürften.

Gedruckt auf säurefreiem und chlorfrei gebleichtem Papier

Springer VS ist eine Marke von Springer DE. Springer DE ist Teil der Fachverlagsgruppe Springer Science+Business Media.
www.springer-vs.de

Contents

Figures.. 6

Tables... 7

1 Introduction... 9

2 Educational attainment of migrants in Germany............ 19
   2.1 Data to explain the attainment gap........................ 19
   2.2 Evidence from the German Microcensus 24

3 The concept of educational aspirations 37

4 Models of educational aspirations and choice 47
   4.1 The Wisconsin model of status attainment.................. 48
   4.2 Rational choice theories of educational attainment.......... 53
   4.3 Empirical evidence: Socialization or individual choice?...... 57

5 Educational aspirations, expectations and choices of migrants....... 65
   5.1 Explaining background-adjusted ethnic differentials in education ... 66
   5.2 Empirical evidence and discussion......................... 69

6 Research objective and contribution to the field 79

7 Study design... 83

8 Sample description 87
   8.1 Sociodemographic composition 87

8.2 Language use and test scores 89
8.3 Aspirations in general education............................... 93
8.4 Expectations in general education 96
8.5 Future educational aspirations 99
8.6 Occupational aspirations 104
8.7 Comparing future educational and occupational aspirations 113

9 Explaining students' educational aspirations 119
9.1 Primary effects of social and ethnic origin 121
9.2 Future career aspirations 126
    9.2.1 Future educational aspirations 127
    9.2.2 Occupational aspirations 132
    9.2.3 Considerations of uncertainty............................ 134
9.3 Social-psychological correlates 141

10 Explaining students' educational expectations 153
10.1 Primary effects of social and ethnic origin 155
10.2 Future career aspirations 158
10.3 Social-psychological correlates 164

11 Conclusions 171
11.1 Distribution and construction of educational aspirations 171
11.2 Distribution and construction of educational expectations......... 174
11.3 Future career aspirations: cause or consequence? 175
11.4 Meaning of respondent-reported career plans 180
11.5 Applicability of traditional approaches to explain ethnic
      differentials in education 183
11.6 Measurement of aspirations................................... 185
11.7 Secondary effects of ethnic origin.............................. 186
11.8 Limitations and prospects for future research 193

Glossary 201

Figures
Figure 2.1: Track of secondary education 2008-2010, natives 26
Figure 2.2: Track of secondary education 2008-2010, migrants 26
Figure 2.3: Educational attainment 2005-2010, natives 28
Figure 2.4: Educational attainment 2005-2010, migrants................... 29
Figure 2.5: Professional qualifications 2010 30

Figure 4.1: Wisconsin model of status attainment, original specification..... 48
Figure 4.2: Wisconsin model of status attainment, revised specification 50
Figure 8.1: Language acquisition and use in migrant families............... 91
Figure 8.2: Language use between students and parents 92
Figure 8.3: Aspirations in general education 94
Figure 8.4: Motives for aspirations in general education 96
Figure 8.5: Expected probabilities of success, by educational aspiration...... 97
Figure 8.6: Expected probabilities of success, by migration background 98
Figure 8.7: Future educational aspirations 100
Figure 8.8: Motives for future educational aspirations.....................102
Figure 8.9: Certainty of career aspirations, by choice motive 104
Figure 8.10: Number of occupational aspirations 105
Figure 8.11: Formal entry requirements
 for idealistic occupational aspirations 106
Figure 8.12: Formal entry requirements
 for realistic occupational aspirations 106
Figure 8.13: Importance of adoption mechanisms.........................109
Figure 8.14: Importance of imitation mechanisms 110
Figure 8.15: Importance of societal valuation............................110
Figure 8.16: Importance of income prospects............................111
Figure 8.17: Importance of prospects for job promotion....................112
Figure 8.18: Importance of labor market demand in country of origin.......113
Figure 8.19: Realistic occupational aspirations and VET 114
Figure 8.20: Realistic occupational aspirations and higher education........116

Tables
Table 8.1: Sociodemographic composition 88
Table 8.2: Language test scores 90
Table 9.1: Summary of variables, students' educational aspirations..........120
Table 9.2: Educational aspirations, primary effects (one migrant dummy)....122
Table 9.3: Educational aspirations, primary effects (two migrant dummies) ..124
Table 9.4: Educational aspirations, future career aspirations................128
Table 9.5: Educational aspirations, considerations of uncertainty 136
Table 9.6: Educational aspirations, considerations of uncertainty,
 changed reference group......................................139
Table 9.7: Educational aspirations, parental aspirations...................143
Table 9.8: Educational aspirations, self-efficacy beliefs....................148
Table 10.1: Summary of variables used for analysis of students'
 educational expectations......................................154

Table 10.2: Educational expectations, primary effects
(one migrant dummy) 156
Table 10.3: Educational expectations, primary effects
(two migrant dummies) 157
Table 10.4: Educational expectations, future career aspirations 161
Table 10.5: Educational expectations, parental aspirations
and self-efficacy beliefs 166

Introduction 1

Despite some improvement in the educational situation of migrants in the last decades, empirical data points to substantially lower attainments of persons with a migration background in many western countries. In Germany, students with a migration background attend more prestigious tracks of secondary education and obtain qualifications that provide access to higher education less often than their native peers, they drop out of the general educational system more often without any formal qualification and experience less successful transitions into the vocational education and training (VET) system (Autorengruppe Bildungsberichterstattung 2014; Behörde für Schule und Berufsbildung 2011). While ethnic differentials in education are not a fundamentally new phenomenon, they have been more seriously considered in the face of a shrinking population, the struggle with skilled labor shortage and an increasing share of young persons with a migration background (Söhn and Özcan 2007; Stanat and Christensen 2006a). According to the National Report on Education 20% of the total population in Germany have a migration background. The share among children aged younger than five is as high as 36% (Autorengruppe Bildungsberichterstattung 2014, p. 14).

In view of the overrepresentation of migrants in lower socioeconomic positions, micro-level approaches have modeled ethnic differentials in educational attainment[1] as a function of the systematically unequal distribution of resources that leads to less favorable preconditions for educational success in migrant families. Indeed, differences in parental level of education and occupation are consistently found to explain a significant proportion of the attainment gap. Yet, available evidence also points to variations in the background-adjusted transition

---

1 The present study uses the term educational attainment as defined by the United States Census Bureau, i.e., the highest level of education an individual has completed (United States Census Bureau 2013).

and attainment patterns across different groups of immigrants (e.g., Heath and Brinbaum 2007). While some immigrant groups even outperform their native peers when the family's socioeconomic position is taken into account, significant gaps remain in the case of others. Following these observations, more recent approaches explicitly take into account the existence of conditions that specifically affect the educational outcomes of migrant students *net* of social origin (Heath and Brinbaum 2007; Lehmann et al. 2002; van der Werfhorst and van Tubergen 2007). Based on Boudon's (1974) approach to explain social disparities in educational attainment, the current literature discusses ethnic differentials in educational attainment as a two-component process that involves different preconditions for educational success in native and migrant families on the one hand, and their educational decisions net of their probabilities of success on the other hand (Heath and Brinbaum 2007; Kristen and Dollmann 2010).

The increased interest in educational belief-formation and decision-making processes as a potential explanation for the emergence and persistence of ethnic disparities in educational attainment is not least reflected in the rapidly growing body of transitions studies (R. Becker and Schubert 2011; Brinbaum and Cebolla-Boado 2007; Diefenbach 2010; Kristen and Dollmann 2010; van der Werfhorst and van Tubergen 2007). Yet, so far empirical applications of models to explain the attainment gap in Germany have almost exclusively been confined to the investigation of subjective data in the form of respondent-reported educational aspirations and expectations. This body of studies not only points to a clear pattern of significantly higher background-adjusted aspirations and expectations in migrant families, but also shows the educational aspirations, and sometimes expectations, of migrants to exceed those of their native counterparts when background characteristics are not taken into account (Heath and Brinbaum 2007; Stanat and Christensen 2006a). In view of the significantly lower attainment levels of migrants, several researchers have taken these patterns to indicate that it is not lower levels of ambition but primarily features of the opportunity structure that hinder migrants to translate their high aspirations into attainment and matter most to the persistence of the attainment gap (e.g., Gresch et al. 2012, p. 65; Klieme et al. 2010, p. 202).

While longitudinal studies indeed point to significant correlations between expressed aspirations, expectations and attainment levels (e.g., Beal and Crockett 2010; Buriel and Cardoza 1988; Jacob and Wilder 2010; Domina et al. 2011; Mau and Bikos 2000; Ou and Reynolds 2008; Rojewski and Kim 2003; Zhang et al. 2011), both the assumption of a causal effect from aspirations on attainment levels and the value of subjective data to predict later attainment outcomes are discussed controversially. Considerations that have been brought forward in this vein include the concern that respondent-reported aspirations may be vague preferences that have no salience to students' everyday behavior (Alexander and Cook 1979; Coleman et al. 1966), that expressed aspirations do not represent value orientations as much as students' perceptions of the opportunity structure (Alexander and Cook 1979; Bourdieu 1973; Jencks et al. 1983; Kerckhoff 1976), and that subjective beliefs may result from inaccurate or lacking information about the educational system and/or unrealistic self-appraisals (Coleman et al. 1966; Kerckhoff 1977; Kerckhoff and Campbell 1977; Rosenbaum 1976, 1978, 1980).

Empirical findings such as an increasing gap between respondent-reported aspirations and expectations and eventual attainment outcomes in many western countries certainly call for the relevance of these considerations in the interpretation of subjective data (e.g., Domina et al. 2011; Goyette 2008; J. Reynolds et al. 2006; J. R. Reynolds and Johnson 2011; Rosenbaum 1976, 1978, 1980, 2001; Schneider and Stevenson 1999). In view of the concern that migration-specific conditions may be associated with a lack of knowledge about the educational system that leads to more unrealistic appraisals of students' educational potential in the migrant population (Diefenbach 2010; Gresch 2012; Relikowski et al. 2010), the observation of comparatively large gaps between expressed aspirations, expectations and attainment levels in the migrant population further suggests that the considerations above may be particularly relevant to better understand the emergence of ethnic disparities in education. Yet, they have received little attention in empirical studies that attempt to identify the micro-mechanisms that generate ethnic differentials in educational attainment.

Also, the literature discusses a variety of mechanisms to theoretically explain systematically different investments in education in native and migrant families but provides little direct evidence on individual belief-formation and decision-making processes (Diefenbach 2010; Kristen and Dollmann 2010). Available data sets typically allow for the investigation of the distribution of aspirations, expectations and/or transitions but contain little or no information on the mechanisms by which they are shaped (Kristen and Dollmann 2010). The great majority of empirical studies in Germany further investigate parental aspirations, and sometimes decisions, at the transition from primary into secondary education (Beck et al. 2010; Maaz et al. 2010). These studies not only attest higher aspirations in migrant families, but also point to more favorable background-adjusted transitions of migrant students into secondary education (e.g., R. Becker and Schubert 2011; Relikowski et al. 2010). Yet, it is also well-documented that the type of secondary education attended is a rough indicator for students' eventual attainment outcomes only, and that track changes mostly occur in the direction of lower tracks (Stubbe et al. 2012). Besides, while parents are conceived of as the primary decision makers when children are still fairly young, it is widely acknowledged that students' own motivation becomes increasingly important with increasing age and that educational decisions are taken more and more personally by students themselves in the course of their educational careers (B. Becker 2013a, p. 435; Erikson and Jonsson 1996, p. 54; Henz and Maas 1995, p. 610).

Following these considerations, it appears that both the role of students' educational aspirations in the explanation of the attainment gap and the mechanisms that shape systematically different educational aspirations and decisions in native and migrant families remain to be empirically investigated.

The present study attempts to add a further dimension to the understanding of how native and migrant students orient themselves toward the future by investigating the educational and future career aspirations and expectations of several hundred 9th- and 10th-graders in Hamburg. At this point of the educational career, students reach the end of compulsory full-time education and face the decision to continue in general education to obtain higher qualifications or to leave the general educational system and pursue a career in the VET system. In view of the significance of the highest level of general education in determining students' future career opportunities not only by means of providing access to an academic career but also by means of determining their chances of a successful transition into the VET system (Autorengruppe Bildungsberichterstattung 2014; Bundesministerium für Bildung und Forschung 2013), a particular concern at this stage of the educational career is that students unnecessarily or overly restrict their future opportunities due to a lack of motivation to obtain higher general educational qualifications, insufficient or incorrect information about the full spectrum of career opportunities, the misperception of the opportunity structure or their failure to deal effectively with anticipated or experienced barriers (Gottfredson 1981, 1996, 2005; Morgan 2005).

In consideration of the mechanisms that are discussed in the literature to explain social and ethnic disparities in educational attainment, a first research objective is to provide insight into the dimensions along which students construct their educational and future career aspirations as well as into the barriers they perceive in implementing their aspirations. A first focus is the identification of systematic differences in these patterns between native and migrant students. A second focus is to shed light on the nature of the association between students' future career aspirations and their aspirations and expectations in general education. While the impact of educational qualifications on later labor market opportunities is without controversy, several researchers have brought forward arguments and empirical evidence to support the notion that students' future career aspirations may be conceived of as a cause rather than the consequence of their aspirations and expectations in general education (Goyette 2008; Looker and McNutt 1989; Shapira 2009). Following the consideration that it may not be objective possibilities of achieving significant labor market returns but the extent to which students' life plans will allow them to take full advantage of high educational qualifications that matter most to their educational choices (G. Becker 1993; Gambetta 1987), and that the likelihood that aspirations are translated into attainment depend on dimensions such as the strength of preference for a given career alternative and the extent to which aspirations are clear and specific (Gambetta 1987; Gottfredson 1981, 2005; Haller and Miller 1963; Lent et al. 1994), the study investigates whether there is evidence to support the notion that students construct their aspirations and expectations in general education in consideration of the entry requirements for their future career aspirations. A second research objective is to provide insight into the theoretical meaning of respondent-reported educational aspirations, and into their role in the explanation of ethnic disparities in educational attainment.

The remainder of the study is organized as follows: Chapter 2 provides an overview over available data sources that allow to empirically investigate the micro-mechanisms that shape ethnic differentials in educational attainment in Germany as well as an empirical description of the educational situation of natives and migrants based on data from the German Microcensus. Chapter 3 outlines the controversy surrounding the meaning of respondent-reported aspirations and discusses the value of subjective data to investigate disparities in educational attainment. The fourth chapter provides the theoretical framework of the empirical study and discusses two research traditions that are commonly used as a point of departure for models of educational aspirations, expectations and choice. Both the Wisconsin model of status attainment and rational choice theories of educational attainment were originally developed to explain social disparities in education but have in more recent years been increasingly drawn on to explain the attainment gap between natives and migrants. The suitability of traditional approaches to explain social disparities in education to investigate the emergence of ethnic differentials in educational attainment, and extensions that explicitly consider the existence of conditions that specifically affect the educational outcomes of migrants, are discussed in chapter 5. Chapters 6 and 7 outline the research objective and the study design. Chapter 8 provides a descriptive analysis of the data. Chapters 9 and 10 develop models to explain the variation in students' probability to plan to attain the highest level of general education and in their expected probability to accomplish their high aspirations. Chapter 11 starts off with a brief summary and discussion of the key findings of the study in relation to previous research and the questions posed in chapter 6. It further provides a discussion of the theoretical, methodological and interpretative implications the present findings give rise to at a more general level and concludes the study by pointing out its limitations and prospects for future research.

References

Alexander, K. L., & Cook, M. A. (1979). The Motivational Relevance of Educational Plans: Questioning the Conventional Wisdom. *Social Psychology Quarterly, 42*(3), 202-213.
Autorengruppe Bildungsberichterstattung (2014). *Bildung in Deutschland 2014. Ein indikatorengestützter Bericht mit einer Analyse zur Bildung von Menschen mit Behinderungen.* Bielefeld: Bertelsmann.
Beal, S. J., & Crockett, L. J. (2010). Adolescents' Occupational and Educational Aspirations and Expectations: Links to High School Activities and Adult Educational Attainment. *Developmental Psychology, 46*(1), 258-265.
Beck, M., Jäpel, F., & Becker, R. (2010). Determinanten des Bildungserfolgs von Migranten. In G. Quenzel & K. Hurrelmann (Eds.), *Bildungsverlierer: Neue Ungleichheiten* (Vol. 1, pp. 313-337). Wiesbaden: VS Verlag für Sozialwissenschaften.
Becker, B. (2013a). Eltern von Vorschulkindern und ihre Bildungsaspirationen. In M. Stamm & D. Edelmann (Eds.), *Handbuch frühkindliche Bildungsforschung* (pp. 435-446). Wiesbaden: Springer.
Becker, G. (1993). *Human Capital: A Theoretical and Empirical Analysis, with Special Reference to Education* (3rd ed.). Chicago: University of Chicago Press.
Becker, R., & Schubert, F. (2011). Die Rolle von primären und sekundären Herkunftseffekten für Bildungschancen von Migranten im deutschen Schulsystem. In R. Becker (Ed.), *Integration durch Bildung: Bildungserwerb von jungen Migranten in Deutschland* (pp. 161-194). Wiesbaden: VS Verlag für Sozialwissenschaften.
Behörde für Schule und Berufsbildung (2011). *Bildungsbericht. Hamburg 2011.* Hamburg. Retrieved October 29, 2013, from http://www.bildungsmonitoring.hamburg.de/index.php/bildungsbericht2011
Boudon, R. (1974). *Education, Opportunity and Social Inequality: Changing Prospects in Western Society.* New York: Wiley.
Bourdieu, P. (1973). Cultural Reproduction and Social Reproduction. In R. K. Brown (Ed.), *Knowledge, Education, and Cultural Change: Papers in the Sociology of Education* (pp. 71-112). London: Tavistock.
Brinbaum, Y., & Cebolla-Boado, H. (2007). The School Careers of Ethnic Minority Youth in France: Success or Disillusion? *Ethnicities, 7*(3), 445-474.
Bundesministerium für Bildung und Forschung (2013). *Berufsbildungsbericht 2013.* Retrieved October 30, 2013, from http://www.bmbf.de/pub/bbb_2013.pdf
Buriel, R., & Cardoza, D. (1988). Sociocultural Correlates of Achievement Among Three Generations of Mexican American High School Seniors. *American Educational Research Journal, 25*(2), 177-192.
Coleman, J. S., Campbell, E. Q., Hobson, J. C., McPartland, J., Mood, A. M., Weinfeld, F. D., & York, R. L. (1966). *Equality of Educational Opportunity.* Washington, D.C.: U.S. Government Printing Office.

References

Diefenbach, H. (2010). *Kinder und Jugendliche aus Migrantenfamilien im deutschen Bildungssystem: Erklärungen und empirische Befunde* (3rd ed.). Wiesbaden: VS Verlag für Sozialwissenschaften.

Domina, T., Conley, A., & Farkas, G. (2011). The Link between Educational Expectations and Effort in the College-for-all Era. *Sociology of Education, 84*(2), 93-112.

Erikson, R., & Jonsson, J. O. (1996). Explaining Class Inequality in Education: The Swedish Test Case. In R. Erikson & J. O. Jonsson (Eds.), *Can Education Be Equalized? The Swedish Case* (pp. 1-63). Stockholm: Westview Press.

Gambetta, D. (1987). *Were They Pushed Or Did They Jump? Individual Decision Mechanisms in Education*. Cambridge: Cambridge University Press.

Gottfredson, L. S. (1981). Circumscription and Compromise: A Developmental Theory of Occupational Aspirations. *Journal of Counseling Psychology Monograph, 28*(6), 545-579.

Gottfredson, L. S. (1996). Gottfredson's Theory of Circumscription and Compromise. In D. Brown & L. Brooks (Eds.), *Career Choice and Development* (3 ed., pp. 179-232). San Francisco: Jossey–Bass.

Gottfredson, L. S. (2005). Applying Gottfredson's Theory of Circumscription and Compromise in Career Guidance and Counseling. In S. D. Brown & R. W. Lent (Eds.), *Career Development and Counseling: Putting Theory and Research to Work* (pp. 71-100). New Jersey: Wiley.

Goyette, K. A. (2008). College for Some to College for All: Social Background, Occupational Expectations, and Educational Expectations over Time. *Social Science Research, 37*(2), 461-484.

Gresch, C. (2012). *Der Übergang in die Sekundarstufe I: Leistungsbeurteilung, Bildungsaspiration und rechtlicher Kontext bei Kindern mit Migrationshintergrund*. Wiesbaden: VS Verlag für Sozialwissenschaften.

Gresch, C., Maaz, K., Becker, M., & McElvany, N. (2012). Zur hohen Bildungsaspiration von Migranten beim Übergang von der Grundschule in die Sekundarstufe: Fakt oder Artefakt? In P. Pielage, L. Pries & G. Schultze (Eds.), *Soziale Ungleichheit in der Einwanderungsgesellschaft: Kategorien, Konzepte, Einflussfaktoren* (pp. 56-67). Bonn: Friedrich-Ebert-Stiftung.

Haller, A. O., & Miller, I. W. (1963). *The Occupational Aspiration Scale: Theory, Structure and Correlates* (AES-TB No. 288). Retrieved September 9, 2011, from http://files.eric.ed.gov/fulltext/ED016712.pdf

Heath, A. F., & Brinbaum, Y. (2007). Guest Editorial: Explaining Ethnic Inequalities in Educational Attainment. *Ethnicities, 7*(3), 291-304.

Henz, U., & Maas, I. (1995). Chancengleichheit durch die Bildungsexpansion? *Kölner Zeitschrift für Soziologie und Sozialpsychologie, 47*(4), 605-633.

Jacob, B. A., & Wilder, T. (2010). *Educational Expectations and Attainment* (NBER Working Paper No. 15683). Retrieved January 26, 2013, from http://www.nber.org/papers/w15683

Jencks, C., Crouse, J., & Mueser, P. (1983). The Wisconsin Model of Status Attainment: A National Replication with Improved Measures of Ability and Aspiration. *Sociology of Education, 56*(1), 3-19.

Kerckhoff, A. C. (1976). The Status Attainment Process: Socialization or Allocation? *Social Forces, 55*(2), 368-381.

Kerckhoff, A. C. (1977). The Realism of Educational Ambitions in England and the United States. *American Sociological Review, 42*(4), 563-571.

Kerckhoff, A. C., & Campbell, R. T. (1977). Social Status Differences in the Explanation of Educational Ambition. *Social Forces, 5*(3), 701-714.

Klieme, E., Artelt, C., Hartig, J., Jude, N., Köller, O., Prenzel, M., Schneider, W., & Stanat, P. (2010). *PISA 2009: Bilanz nach einem Jahrzehnt.* Münster: Waxmann.

Kristen, C., & Dollmann, J. (2010). Sekundäre Effekte der ethnischen Herkunft: Kinder aus türkischen Familien am ersten Bildungsübergang. In B. Becker & D. Reimer (Eds.), *Vom Kindergarten bis zur Hochschule: Die Generierung von ethnischen und sozialen Disparitäten in der Bildungsbiographie* (pp. 117-144). Wiesbaden: VS Verlag für Sozialwissenschaften.

Lehmann, R. H., Peek, R., Gänsfuß, R., & Husfeldt, V. (2002). *LAU 9 – Aspekte der Lernausgangslage und der Lernentwicklung – Klassenstufe 9: Ergebnisse einer längsschnittlichen Untersuchung in Hamburg.* Hamburg: Behörde für Schule, Jugend und Berufsbildung/ Behörde für Bildung und Sport.

Lent, R. W., Brown, S. D., & Hackett, G. (1994). Monograph: Toward a Unifying Social Cognitive Theory of Career and Academic Interest, Choice, and Performance. *Journal of Vocational Behavior, 45*, 79-122.

Looker, D. E., & McNutt, K. L. (1989). The Effect of Occupational Expectations on the Educational Attainments of Males and Females. *Canadian Journal of Education, 14*(3), 352-367.

Maaz, K., Baumert, J., & Trautwein, U. (2010). Genese sozialer Ungleichheit im institutionellen Kontext der Schule: Wo entsteht und vergrößert sich soziale Ungleichheit? In H.-H. Krüger, U. Rabe-Kleberg, R.-T. Kramer & J. Budde (Eds.), *Bildungsungleichheit Revisited: Bildung und soziale Ungleichheit vom Kindergarten bis zur Hochschule* (pp. 69-102). Wiesbaden: VS Verlag für Sozialwissenschaften.

Mau, W.-C., & Bikos, L. H. (2000). Educational and Vocational Aspirations of Minority and Female Students: A Longitudinal Study. *Journal of Counseling & Development, 78*(2), 186-194.

Morgan, S. L. (2005). *On the Edge of Commitment: Educational Attainment and Race in the United States.* Stanford, CA: Stanford University Press.

Ou, S.-R., & Reynolds, A. J. (2008). Predictors of Educational Attainment in the Chicago Longitudinal Study. *School Psychology Quarterly, 23*(2), 199-229.

Relikowski, I., Schneider, T., & Blossfeld, H.-P. (2010). Primäre und sekundäre Herkunftseffekte beim Übergang in das gegliederte Schulsystem: Welche Rolle spielen soziale Klasse und Bildungsstatus in Familien mit Migrationshintergrund? In T. Beckers, K. Birkelbach, J. Hagenah & U. Rosar (Eds.), *Komparative empirische Sozialforschung* (pp. 143-167). Wiesbaden: VS Verlag für Sozialwissenschaften.

Reynolds, J., Stewart, M., MacDonald, R., & Sischo, L. (2006). Have Adolescents Become Too Ambitious? High School Seniors' Educational and Occupational Plans, 1976 to 2000. *Social Problems, 53*(2), 186-206.

Reynolds, J. R., & Johnson, M. K. (2011). Change in the Stratification of Educational Expectations and Their Realization. *Social Forces, 90*(1), 85-110.

Rojewski, J. W., & Kim, H. (2003). Career Choice Patterns and Behavior of Work-Bound Youth During Early Adolescence. *Journal of Career Development, 30*(2), 89-108.

Rosenbaum, J. E. (1976). *Making Inequality: The Hidden Curriculum of High School Tracking.* New York: Wiley.

Rosenbaum, J. E. (1978). The Structure of Opportunity in School. *Social Forces, 57*(1), 236-256.

References

Rosenbaum, J. E. (1980). Track Misperceptions and Frustrated College Plans: An Analysis of the Effects of Tracks and Track Perceptions in the National Longitudinal Survey. *Sociology of Education, 53*(2), 74-88.

Rosenbaum, J. E. (2001). *Beyond College-for-all: Career Paths for the Forgotten Half.* New York: Russell Sage Foundation.

Schneider, B. L., & Stevenson, D. (1999). *The Ambitious Generation: America's Teenagers, Motivated but Directionless.* New Haven: Yale University Press.

Shapira, M. (2009). Trends in the Impact of Post-compulsory Educational Qualifications and Experience on the Occupational Attainments of Young People in England and Scotland, 1986-2001. In A. Hadjar & R. Becker (Eds.), *Expected and Unexpected Consequences of the Educational Expansion in Europe and USA: Theoretical Approaches and Empirical Findings in Comparative Perspective* (pp. 179-200). Bern: Haupt Verlag.

Söhn, J., & Özcan, V. (2007). Bildungsdaten und Migrationshintergrund: Eine Bilanz. In Bundesministerium für Bildung und Forschung (Ed.), *Migrationshintergrund von Kindern und Jugendlichen: Wege zur Weiterentwicklung der amtlichen Statistik* (pp. 117-128). Berlin.

Stanat, P., & Christensen, G. (2006a). *Schulerfolg von Jugendlichen mit Migrationshintergrund im internationalen Vergleich: Eine Analyse von Voraussetzungen und Erträgen schulischen Lernens im Rahmen von PISA 2003.* Berlin: Bundesministerium für Bildung und Forschung.

Stubbe, T. C., Bos, W., & Euen, B. (2012). Der Übergang von der Primar- in die Sekundarstufe. In W. Bos, I. Tarelli, A. Bremerich-Vos & K. Schwippert (Eds.), *IGLU 2011: Lesekompetenzen von Grundschulkindern in Deutschland im Internationalen Vergleich* (pp. 210-226). Münster: Waxmann.

United States Census Bureau (2013). Retrieved June 23, 2013, from www.census.gov/hhes/socdemo/education/

van der Werfhorst, H. G., & van Tubergen, F. (2007). Ethnicity, Schooling, and Merit in the Netherlands. *Ethnicities, 7*(3), 416-444.

Zhang, Y., Haddad, E., Torres, B., & Chen, C. (2011). The Reciprocal Relationships Among Parents' Expectations, Adolescents' Expectations, and Adolescents' Achievement: A Two-Wave Longitudinal Analysis of the NELS Data. *Journal of Youth and Adolescence, 40*(4), 479-489.

Educational attainment of migrants in Germany

2

This chapter comprises an overview over available data sources that provide information on the educational situation of natives and migrants in Germany and a brief discussion of their suitability to investigate the micro-mechanisms that generate ethnic differentials in educational attainment. It further provides an empirical description of the educational situation of young persons with and without a migration background based on time series data from the German Microcensus.

2.1 Data to explain the attainment gap

Data on level of educational attainment in Germany can be obtained from official statistics and population surveys. Yet, data that allows for the systematic investigation of the micro-mechanisms that generate the observed educational differentials between natives and migrants is scarce. Partly, this situation is attributable to the change in the concept of 'migrants', who were identified based on the criterion of citizenship until several years ago but are now generally identified by country of birth (Haug 2009; Söhn and Özcan 2006). According to the Federal Statistical Office, the migrant population consists of "[…] all persons who have immigrated into the territory of today's Federal Republic of Germany after 1949, and of all foreigners born in Germany and all persons born in Germany who have at least one parent who immigrated into the country or was born as a foreigner in Germany" (Statistisches Bundesamt 2013c). Following the naturalization of foreigners and the immigration of ethnic German repatriates in the last decades, the identification of migrants based on their citizenship leads to a severe underestimation of the migrant population (Diefenbach 2010; Haug 2009). In 2010, slightly more than 19% of the total population in Germany had a migration background according to the definition above, but only 9% were foreigners (Autorengruppe Bildungsberichterstattung 2012).

While official statistics are advantageous in that they constitute full population surveys, they allow the identification of migrants based on their citizenship only and will lead to a biased assessment of their educational situation. Level of educational integration will be underestimated as the group of natives also includes migrants who are disadvantaged with respect to aspects such as majority language skills, and overestimated as educationally successful migrants are not classified as foreigners. Also, official statistics provide aggregate-level data only and limited information on relevant background data such as familial conditions and migration-specific circumstances (Halbhuber 2007; Herwartz-Emden 2007; Söhn and Özcan 2007).

Population surveys that are designed to be representative allow the identification of migrants based on their own and family members' country of birth, and to draw inference about the wider population based on individual-level data. The largest German population survey is the Microcensus, a rotating panel with four-year intervals that comprises one percent of all households in Germany and provides a variety of economic, demographic and education data since 1957.[2] A particular advantage is the fact that the participation in the survey is a legal obligation, so that unit non-response rates are very low (Jäger and Schimpl-Neimanns 2012). Yet, its usefulness for the investigation of the micro-mechanisms that generate ethnic disparities in education is limited by the fact that the census is designed to cover a broad range of topics and provides little information on background variables that are discussed in the literature as potential influences of students' educational success (Diefenbach 2010).

A particularly popular survey to explain ethnic differentials in education is the German Socio-Economic Panel Study (SOEP), which is the longest-running longitudinal survey of Germany and collects representative micro data on persons, households and families since 1984 (Haisken-DeNew and Frick 2005).[3] Besides the main topic of labor market activities, it provides detailed information on various life areas such as health, education and social participation. The longitudinal design enables the observation of early transitions and track changes as parents provide information on their children's educational participation given they are younger than 17 years of age. Since 2000, the survey comprises an additional youth questionnaire for adolescents who are 17 years of age that includes ques-

---

2 https://www.destatis.de/EN/Homepage.html (accessed Oct. 1, 2013).
3 http://www.diw.de/soep (accessed Oct. 19, 2013).

2.1 Data to explain the attainment gap

tions on a variety of educationally relevant aspects, such as parental support and the participants' future career aspirations, as well as retrospective information on their educational careers (Frick and Söhn 2007; Haisken-DeNew and Frick 2005; Scheller 2011; SOEP Group 2001). Data on the participants' country of birth was not included in the Microcensus until 2005 and in the SOEP until 2008, but links can be made between parents' and their children's data to retroactively identify a large proportion of naturalized migrants and ethnic German immigrants (Jäger and Schimpl-Neimanns 2012). The SOEP is particularly suited to address questions of ethnic differentials as the oversampling of distinct migrant groups allows for subgroup analyses.

Besides actual attainment data, information on the track of secondary education attended is commonly used to assess and compare the educational situation of native and migrant students (Diefenbach 2010). In Germany, after four years of primary education students are traditionally selected into three different tracks of secondary education that are related to distinct leaving certificates and provide access to different types of vocational and post-secondary education. *Hauptschule* ('lower secondary education') traditionally leads to the lowest qualification after nine years of general education, *Realschule* ('intermediate secondary education') leads to a medium-level qualification after ten years of general education, and *Gymnasium* ('higher secondary education') leads to a qualification that provides access to higher education after 12 or 13 years of general education (Lohmar and Eckhardt 2011a, 2011b). Apart from the most demanding track, which in fact constitutes the only constant in the educational system across the federal states (*Länder*), this traditional division has been progressively replaced over the last years by schools that offer several or all tracks of secondary education (Stubbe et al. 2012).

Data on the track of secondary education attended is provided by several surveys, including the SOEP, the Microcensus and various assessment studies (e.g., IGLU/PIRLS, TIMSS, PISA, KESS, DESI, LAU).[4] The latter mostly do not provide longitudinal data, and if so they typically do not follow students until the end of their careers in the general educational system (exceptions are for example the KESS and LAU study for students in Hamburg). Yet, due to their focus on the explanation of social and ethnic disparities, assessment studies collect detailed individual-level background information. Also, they provide information on aspects

---

4   IGLU/PIRLS, TIMSS: http://timssandpirls.bc.edu/ (accessed Oct. 19, 2013). PISA http://www.oecd.org/pisa/ (accessed Oct. 19, 2013). KESS: http://bildungsserver.hamburg.de/bildungsqualitaet/ (accessed Oct. 19, 2013). LAU: http://bildungsserver.hamburg.de/lau/ (accessed October 19, 2013).

like level of demonstrated performance as indicated by teacher-assigned grades and performance test scores. The fact that they are often embedded in an international context allows for cross-country comparisons, and their cyclical nature further enables the investigation of the effects of changes at the institutional level (Diefenbach 2010). However, empirical data shows that the track of secondary education attended constitutes a rough indicator for students' eventual attainment outcomes only. As track changes in the course of students' educational careers mostly occur in the direction of lower tracks, information on the type of secondary education attended will overestimate eventual attainment levels (Stubbe 2009; Stubbe et al. 2012).

Also, there are several studies that specifically focus on the transition from general education into the VET system and provide detailed information on students' educational and occupational orientations. Popular examples are the BIBB School Graduate Surveys (investigation of students aged 14 years and older who just left the general educational system or vocational schools), the BIBB Transition Survey (a retrospective longitudinal cohort survey of the educational and occupational biographies of young adults aged 18 to 24 years), and the DJI Transition Panel (which follows students who are in their last year in the lowest track of general education through their careers in the VET system).[5] These studies allow for the identification of migrants by their (family members') country of birth and provide valuable insight into how students orient themselves toward the future. However, they typically do not allow for a more fine-grained analysis of the mechanisms that generate ethnic disparities in education due to their focus on particular groups of students and the limited provision of background information, such as familial and migration-specific conditions and measures of students' educational potential. An exception with respect to the latter aspect is the ULME survey in Hamburg, a longitudinal study that focuses on the transition into and continued careers in the VET system of students who leave the general educational system after grade 9.[6] As a parallel survey to the last phase of the LAU survey, which focuses on the development and learning processes of students in Hamburg throughout their general educational careers, the study provides information on students' performance in different educational domains as well as on various background variables.

---

[5] BIBB School Graduate Surveys: http://www.bibb.de/en/50124.htm (accessed Sept. 12, 2013). BIBB Transition Survey: http://www.bibb.de/en/50124.htm (accessed Sept. 12, 2013). DJI Transition Panel: http://www.dji.de/cgi-bin/projekte/output.php?projekt=723 (accessed Sept. 12, 2013).

[6] http://bildungsserver.hamburg.de/lau/ (accessed Oct. 19, 2013).

The National Educational Panel Study (NEPS), which has recently released its first scientific use files, explicitly considers the drawbacks of available data sets and will open up new research opportunities for the analysis of educational processes from early childhood to late adulthood.[7] The NEPS has been set up to provide longitudinal data on individuals' competence development in different domains, on educational processes, decisions and returns to education in different contexts over the entire life span, and has a separate pillar which focuses on the educational careers of persons with a migration background. The survey is based on a multi-cohort sequence design with six starting cohorts, of which each comprises several thousand participants, to cover the different stages of individuals' educational careers as well as their transitions into the labor market. To allow for a more fine-grained analysis of the migrant population, students of Turkish origin and repatriates from the Former Soviet Union – two large immigrant groups that are disadvantaged in the German educational system – are oversampled. Based on the increased acknowledgment that majority language skills constitute a prerequisite for a successful educational career, the NEPS further assesses receptive language skills in German and (if applicable) Turkish and Russian (Blossfeld et al. 2011a; Blossfeld et al. 2011b; Chlosta and Ostermann 2007).

As regards the assessment of the educational situation of migrants, the interpretation of empirical results requires considerable caution not least due to the rather wide variety of classification criteria that are used to identify migrants. While the identification criterion of country of birth has become widely accepted, there is no common definition of the concept 'migration background' (Diefenbach 2010; Haug 2009). A large part of empirical studies define migrants as persons who were born abroad themselves or who have at least one parent born abroad, and several studies further distinguish different 'generations' of immigrants (e.g., Klieme et al. 2010; Schwippert et al. 2003). The first generation typically refers to persons who migrated to Germany themselves. The second generation refers to persons who were born in Germany but whose parents were born abroad, and the third generation refers to persons who themselves and whose parents were born in Germany but whose grandparents were born abroad. Questions regarding the number of parents and grandparents who have to be born abroad for a person to be classified as a migrant, and whether the third generation should be classified as migrants or natives, are discussed controversially (Haug 2009). Quite often, studies further differentiate the migrant population by whether both parents were born abroad or one parent only, and the latter are sometimes referred to as the '2.5 generation' (Kristen and Dollmann 2010). Also, several studies use identification

---

7   https://www.neps-data.de/ (accessed Oct. 19, 2013).

criteria according to which persons are not classified as migrants if they were born abroad but migrated at an early age and went to school in the receiving country (Kristen and Dollmann 2010). Following the increased interest in processes of language acquisition and majority language skills as determinants of a successful educational career, which have been shown to predict the educational outcomes of both natives and migrants but are assumed to affect the latter particularly strongly as their first language(s) often differ(s) from the language of instruction in school, some studies classify students by whether German is (among) their first language(s) or not (Chlosta and Ostermann 2007; DESI-Konsortium 2006).

In sum, while the current data situation does not allow for a detailed investigation of the micro-level processes that generate ethnic disparities in educational attainment in Germany, significant advances have been made to develop data sets that allow for such analyses. Besides the extension of existing population surveys to collect data on the participants' migration biographies and various conditions that are assumed to specifically affect the educational outcomes of students from migrant families, several projects were funded in more recent years and are being planned to develop rich longitudinal data sets that will provide opportunities for more fine-grained analyses of the micro-mechanisms that shape educational differentials between natives and migrants (e.g., the NEPS as a national example or the Norface Research Programme on Migration as an example for a large-scale international project).[8] Also, the increasing number of smaller-scale studies will contribute to a better understanding of the emergence and persistence of educational disparities. While they do not allow inference about the wider population, they often focus on groups of students with similar migration biographies and can thus contribute to the explanation of variations in the educational success across different groups of immigrants. Further, they provide important data that cannot be collected and processed by large-scale surveys for reasons of cost and time, such as productive language data (e.g., LiMA Panel Study as an example for productive heritage and majority language data from students of Vietnamese, Russian, Turkish and German origin).[9]

2.2 Evidence from the German Microcensus

The analysis below provides information on the distribution of natives and migrants across the different tracks of secondary education as well as on the highest educational and professional qualifications completed based on data from the

---

8   http://www.norface-migration.org/ (accessed Oct. 19, 2013).
9   http://www.lima.uni-hamburg.de/ (accessed Sept. 30, 2013).

2.2 Evidence from the German Microcensus

German Microcensus. Data on level of educational attainment is available since 2005, and on the track of secondary education students attend since 2008. The Microcensus distinguishes persons with a migration background 'in the narrow sense', referring to all persons who migrated to Germany themselves and to foreigners who were born in Germany, and persons with a migration background 'in the broader sense', referring to migrants as identified by the definition of the Federal Statistical Office outlined above. In line with the procedure of the Statistical Office, the analysis includes migrants 'in the narrow sense' only as this type of data is available for each year. Migrants 'in the broader sense' can be identified in four-year intervals only provided respondents do not live in a household with their parents (Statistisches Bundesamt 2013c).[10] Only younger age groups are considered to take into account the increased educational integration across generations.

Figures 2.1 and 2.2 provide information on the distribution of natives and migrants under the age of 20 (who were still in the general educational system at the time of data collection) across the different tracks of secondary education from 2008 to 2010. As regards native students, the data points to a relatively stable pattern over the years. Almost every other native student attended the highest type of secondary education (*Gymnasium*) in all three years. This share slightly increased from 2008 to 2010 by two percentage points. Less than one third of native students attended the intermediate type of secondary education (*Realschule*), and a comparatively small share attended the lowest type of school (*Hauptschule*). The share of students who attended the intermediate track remained stable over the years, whereas the share who attended the lowest track decreased from 14% in 2008 to 11% in 2010.

---

10 The share of persons with a migration background based on the narrow definition is always smaller compared to the broader definition (about 2% in 2009, cf. Statistisches Bundesamt 2013b). A reanalysis of the data for the years 2005 and 2009, where migrants 'in the broader sense' can be identified, did not reveal results that significantly differ from those presented below.

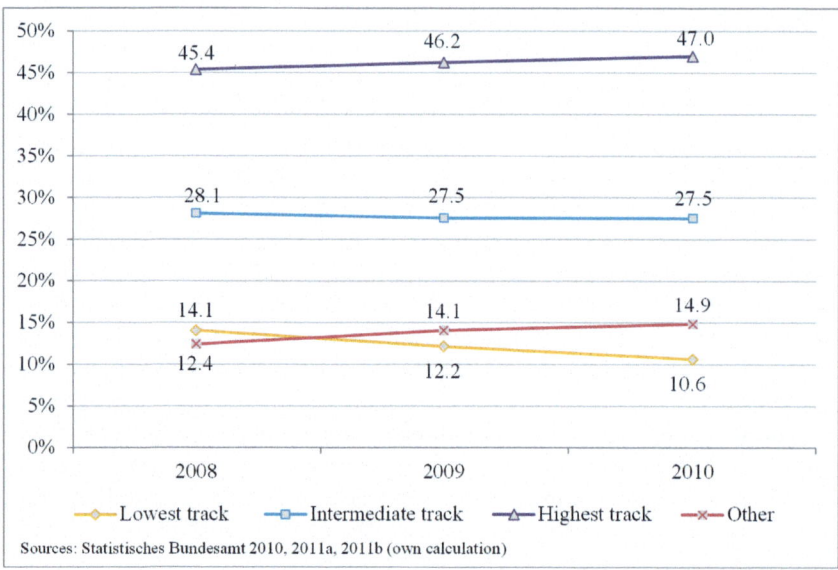

Figure 2.1 Track of secondary education 2008-2010, natives

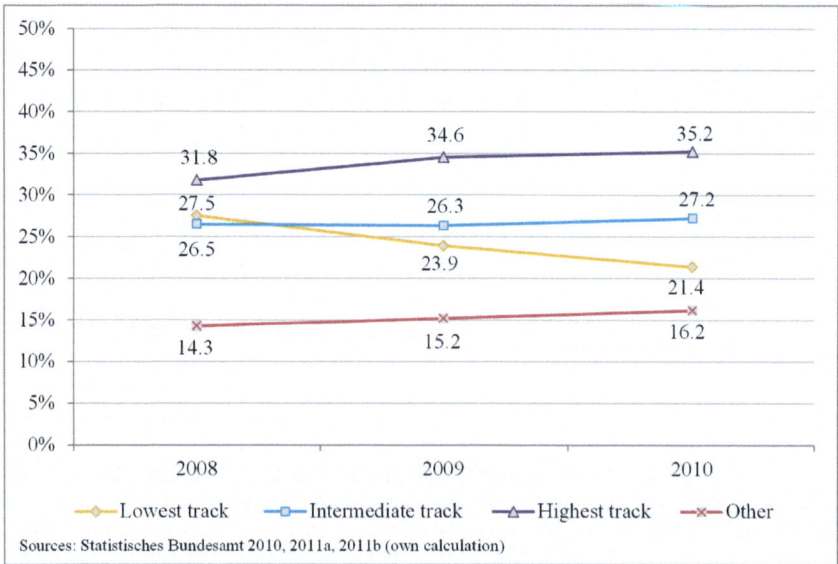

Figure 2.2 Track of secondary education 2008-2010, migrants

2.2 Evidence from the German Microcensus

Figure 2.2 reveals a clear pattern of a less advantageous positioning of migrants. Only every third migrant attended the highest type of secondary education in all three years. The share slightly increased to a similar extent as among natives from 32% in 2008 to 35% in 2009 but remained stable thereafter. Striking changes can be observed with respect to the distribution of migrants across the lower tracks of secondary education. In 2008, the share of migrants who attended the lowest track was nearly as high as the share who attended the highest track, and slightly exceeded the share who attended the intermediate track. Following a comparatively strong decrease in the share who attended the lowest track by as much as six percentage points from 2008 to 2010, and a slight increase in the share who attended the intermediate type of secondary education, this pattern reversed over the years. In 2010, the share of migrants who attended the intermediate track was as much as six percentage points higher than the share who attended the lowest track (27% and 21%, respectively) and comparable to the corresponding share among natives. The growing share of students who attended 'other types' of secondary education, which increased to a comparable extent in both groups but is slightly higher in the group of migrants, can be explained by the growing number of schools which offer several or all tracks of secondary education instead of a single one only that leads to a specific qualification.

Figure 2.3 provides information on the highest level of general education completed by natives aged 15 to under 25 years (who were not in the general education system anymore at the time of data collection) from 2005 to 2010. The majority of natives obtained an intermediate certificate from the general educational system in all six years. While this share slightly decreased from 41% in 2005 to 39% in 2010, an increase can be observed in the share who obtained certificates that provide full or restricted access to higher education (*allgemeine Hochschulreife* and *Fachhochschulreife*). The share who completed the highest level of education slightly exceeded the share who obtained the lowest qualification in 2005. Following a slight increase in the share who obtained full access to higher education and a decrease in the share who completed the lowest level by four percentage points, a considerable difference of nine percentage points can be observed between these shares in 2010. The data further points to a slight increase in the share who left the general educational system without any formal qualification from 3% in 2005 to almost 5% in 2010.

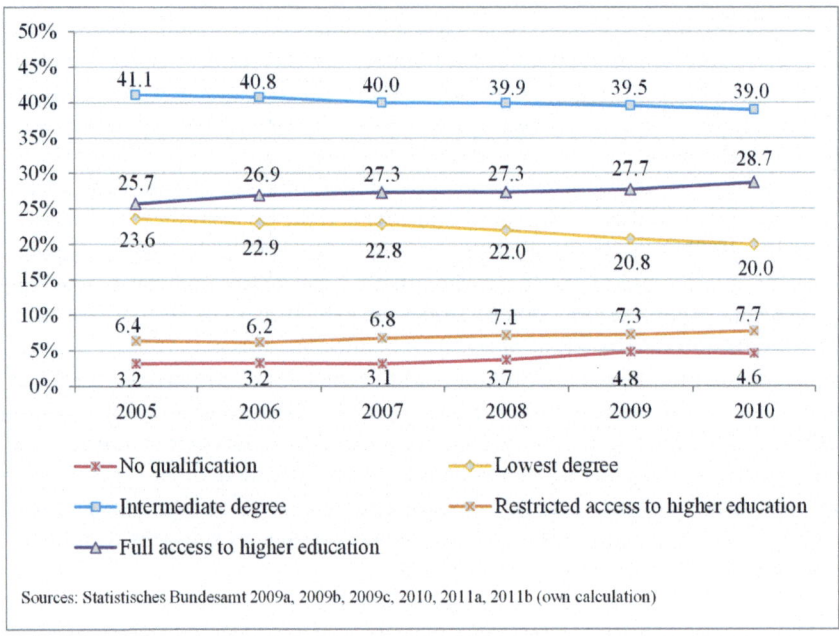

Figure 2.3 Educational attainment 2005-2010, natives

An entirely different pattern can be observed in the migrant population (figure 2.4). Until 2009, the great majority of migrants obtained the lowest certificate from the general education system. While the share who obtained the intermediate qualification was as much as eight percentage points smaller than the share who obtained the lowest degree in 2005, this difference slowly but steadily reduced over the years through a decrease in the share who completed the lowest level by as much as eight percentage points and a slight increase in the share who obtained the intermediate qualification. Accordingly, the share of migrants who completed the intermediate level exceeded the share who obtained the lowest certificate in 2010. The share who completed the highest level of general education is much smaller among migrants compared to natives. It slightly increased from 20% in 2005 to 22% in 2007 but remained stable thereafter. The share who obtained restricted access to higher education is comparable to the corresponding share among natives and increased to a similar extent over the years. Further, the data reveals a slight increase in the share who left the educational system without any formal qualification, which was as high as 10% in 2010 and thus about twice as high as the corresponding share among natives.

2.2 Evidence from the German Microcensus

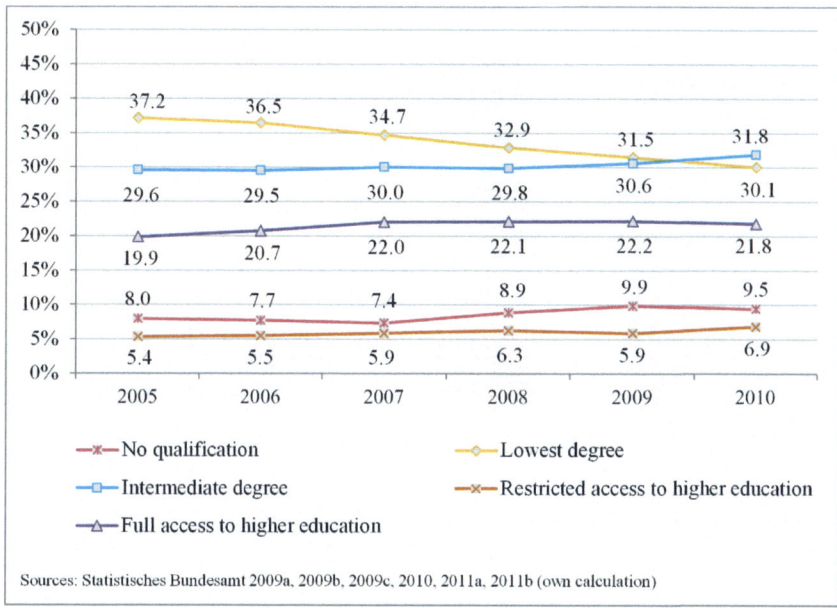

Figure 2.4 Educational attainment 2005-2010, migrants

Figure 2.5 provides information on the highest professional qualifications obtained by natives and migrants aged 25 to under 35 in 2010. In Germany, after leaving the general educational system adolescents can enter higher education (provided they have completed the required level of general education) or enter the VET system, which is divided into three sectors and includes all non-academic career paths: the dual VET system, full-time school-based VET (*Schulberufssystem*), and the transition system (*Übergangssystem*). The transition system involves pre-vocational training that aims to better qualify adolescents and to thereby increase their chances to find a position in the dual or school-based VET system. Opposed to the former two career paths, it partly allows students to obtain general educational qualifications but not to obtain formal professional qualifications (Bundesministerium für Bildung und Forschung 2013; Lohmar and Eckhardt 2011a; Siemon 2010).

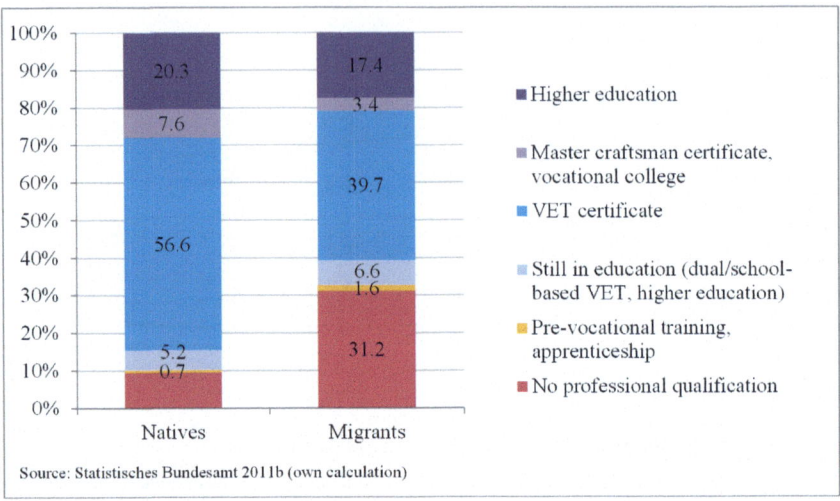

Figure 2.5 Professional qualifications 2010

A first striking observation is the high share of almost one third of migrants who had not obtained any professional qualification from the VET system or completed higher education compared to only 10% of natives. As regards the remainder, the great majority of both natives and migrants obtained a qualification in the VET system. In line with the high share of migrants without any professional qualifications, the share of natives who successfully completed a career in the VET system drastically exceeds the corresponding share among migrants (57% among natives and 40% among migrants). The share who obtained a master craftsman certificate or a vocational college degree (*Meister-/ Techniker-/Fachschlue, Berufsakademie*) is comparatively small in both groups but as much as four percentage points smaller among migrants. An even smaller share of both natives and migrants aged 25 to under 35 attended pre-vocational education when the data was collected.

Partly, the extremely large difference in the share of natives and migrants who successfully completed a career in the VET system can be attributed to the lower general educational qualifications obtained by migrants. While careers in the dual VET system are not associated with any formal educational prerequisites, and careers in school-based vocational education do for the most part not require the highest general educational qualification, students' actual transition probabilities and the level of prestige associated with the VET positions that are realistically attainable are strongly related to the qualifications they obtain in the general

2.2 Evidence from the German Microcensus

educational system. Since 2000, about two thirds of persons in the dual VET system and as much as four fifths in full-time school-based vocational education had completed the intermediate or higher levels of general education. Also, the share of students who start but fail to successfully complete a career in VET is much higher among students with lower general educational qualifications (Autorengruppe Bildungsberichterstattung 2014; Bundesinstitut für Berufsbildung 2011). Yet, there is also evidence that migrants experience significantly less successful transitions into the VET system even if their educational backgrounds are comparable to those of their native peers (Bundesinstitut für Berufsbildung 2011). Conditions that are discussed to explain this observation, as well as variations in the transition propensities across different groups of immigrants, include differential job preferences and contextual aspects such as the regional labor market situation and selection processes in recruitment (Bundesinstitut für Berufsbildung 2013; Bundesministerium für Bildung und Forschung 2013).

In contrast to the substantial differences in the share of natives and migrants who successfully completed a career in the VET system, the data shows that about one fifth of both groups had completed higher education in 2010. In view of the fact that migrants obtain educational qualifications that provide access to higher education much less often than natives, this observation indicates that migrants tend to favor higher education more often than their native peers provided they have successfully obtained the entry qualification in the general educational system. This pattern in turn suggests that a central matter in the explanation of the observed educational and labor market differentials is whether migrants manage to obtain high certificates in general education or not (Autorengruppe Bildungsberichterstattung 2012; Kristen and Granato 2007). A small share of 5% of natives and 7% of migrants aged 25 to under 35 were still in education (dual/ school-based VET or higher education) when the survey was carried out.

In sum, the data points to an overall increase in the share of students who attend more prestigious types of secondary education as well as in the levels of education completed both in the group of natives and migrants. While the share who attend more prestigious tracks and complete high levels of general education increased slightly only, the share who attend the lowest track and obtained the respective qualification strongly decreased in favor of more prestigious tracks and higher qualifications in both groups, and to a comparatively strong extent among migrants. Further, the data confirms the notion that the type of secondary education may be closely related to the attainment levels achieved by students who attend lower tracks of secondary education, but that it does not as well predict the educational outcomes of students in higher tracks. Even though the data presented on track attendance and students' attainment levels is not directly comparable, the figures above clearly show that the share who eventually complete the highest general qualification strongly falls short of the share who attend the most demanding track of secondary education both in the group of natives and migrants (Stubbe 2009). As regards the ethnic attainment gap, the data points to a slow but steady convergence in the share of native and migrant students who attend the lowest and intermediate track of secondary education. However, despite these favorable trends the difference in the share of natives and migrants who obtain the highest level of general education appears to remain relatively stable. Also, migrants can be found to leave the educational system without any formal qualification much more often than their native peers.

References

Autorengruppe Bildungsberichterstattung (2012). *Bildung in Deutschland 2012: Ein indikatorengestützter Bericht mit einer Analyse zur kulturellen Bildung im Lebenslauf.* Bielefeld: Bertelsmann.

Autorengruppe Bildungsberichterstattung (2014). *Bildung in Deutschland 2014. Ein indikatorengestützter Bericht mit einer Analyse zur Bildung von Menschen mit Behinderungen.* Bielefeld: Bertelsmann.

Blossfeld, H.-P., Maurice, J. v., & Schneider, T. (2011a). *Grundidee, Konzeption und Design des Nationalen Bildungspanels für Deutschland* (NEPS Working Paper No. 1). Retrieved September 20, 2013, from www.unibamberg.de/fileadmin/inbil/Publikationen/Working-Papers/WP_I.pdf

Blossfeld, H.-P., von Maurice, J., & Schneider, T. (2011b). The National Educational Panel Study: Need, Main Features, and Research Potential. *Zeitschrift für Erziehungswissenschaft, 14*(2), 5-17.

Bundesinstitut für Berufsbildung (2011). *BIBB Report. Forschungs- und Arbeitsergebnisse aus dem Bundesinstitut für Berufsbildung.* Retrieved September 12, 2013, from www.bibb.de/de/60272.htm

Bundesinstitut für Berufsbildung (2013). *Datenreport zum Berufsbildungsbericht 2013: Informationen und Analysen zur Entwicklung der beruflichen Bildung.* Retrieved October 30, 2013, from http://datenreport.bibb.de/media2013/BIBB_Datenreport_2013.pdf

Bundesministerium für Bildung und Forschung (2013). *Berufsbildungsbericht 2013.* Retrieved October 30, 2013, from http://www.bmbf.de/pub/bbb_2013.pdf

Chlosta, C., & Ostermann, T. (2007). Warum fragt man nach der Herkunft, wenn man die Sprache meint? Ein Plädoyer für eine Aufnahme sprachbezogener Fragen in demographische Untersuchungen. In Bundesministerium für Bildung und Forschung (Ed.), *Migrationshintergrund von Kindern und Jugendlichen: Wege zur Weiterentwicklung der amtlichen Statistik* (pp. 55-65). Berlin.

DESI-Konsortium (2006). *Unterricht und Kompetenzerwerb in Deutsch und Englisch: Zentrale Befunde der Studie Deutsch-Englisch-Schülerleistungen-International (DESI).* Frankfurt: Deutsches Institut für Internationale Pädagogische Forschung.

References

Diefenbach, H. (2010). *Kinder und Jugendliche aus Migrantenfamilien im deutschen Bildungssystem: Erklärungen und empirische Befunde* (3rd ed.). Wiesbaden: VS Verlag für Sozialwissenschaften.

Frick, J. R., & Söhn, J. (2007). Das Sozio-oekonomische Panel (SOEP) als Grundlage für Analysen zur Bildungslage von Personen mit Migrationshintergrund. In Bundesministerium für Bildung und Forschung (Ed.), *Migrationshintergrund von Kindern und Jugendlichen: Wege zur Weiterentwicklung der amtlichen Statistik* (pp. 81-90). Berlin.

Haisken-DeNew, J. P., & Frick, J. R. (2005). *Desktop Companion to the German Socio-Economic Panel Study (SOEP)*. German Institute for Economic Research (DIW). Berlin. Retrieved October 23, 2011, from http://www.diw.de/de/diw_02.c.222846.de/

Halbhuber, W. (2007). Die Schulstatistik der Kultusministerkonferenz. In Bundesministerium für Bildung und Forschung (Ed.), *Migrationshintergrund von Kindern und Jugendlichen: Wege zur Weiterentwicklung der amtlichen Statistik* (pp. 67-74). Berlin.

Haug, S. (2009). *Migration and Statistics* (RatSWD Working Paper No. 101). German Council for Social and Economic Data. Berlin. Retrieved July 3, 2013, from http://www.ratswd.de/publikationen/working-papers/2009?page=1

Herwartz-Emden, L. (2007). Migrant/-innen im deutschen Bildungssystem. In Bundesministerium für Bildung und Forschung (Ed.), *Migrationshintergrund von Kindern und Jugendlichen: Wege zur Weiterentwicklung der amtlichen Statistik* (pp. 7-24). Berlin.

Jäger, D., & Schimpl-Neimanns, B. (2012). *Typisierung des Migrationshintergrundes in den Mikrozensus Scientific-Use-Files 2005-2009* (GESIS-Technical Reports 2012|08). Retrieved July 3, 2013, from http://www.ssoar.info/ssoar/handle/document/32066

Klieme, E., Artelt, C., Hartig, J., Jude, N., Köller, O., Prenzel, M., Schneider, W., & Stanat, P. (2010). *PISA 2009: Bilanz nach einem Jahrzehnt*. Münster: Waxmann.

Kristen, C., & Dollmann, J. (2010). Sekundäre Effekte der ethnischen Herkunft: Kinder aus türkischen Familien am ersten Bildungsübergang. In B. Becker & D. Reimer (Eds.), *Vom Kindergarten bis zur Hochschule: Die Generierung von ethnischen und sozialen Disparitäten in der Bildungsbiographie* (pp. 117-144). Wiesbaden: VS Verlag für Sozialwissenschaften.

Kristen, C., & Granato, N. (2007). The Educational Attainment of the Second Generation in Germany: Social Origins and Ethnic Inequality. *Ethnicities, 7*(3), 343-366.

Lohmar, B., & Eckhardt, T. (2011a). *Das Bildungswesen in der Bundesrepublik Deutschland 2010/2011: Darstellungen der Kompetenzen, Strukturen und bildungspolitischen Entwicklungen für den Informationsaustausch in Europa*. Sekretariat der ständigen Konferez der Kultusminister der Länder in der Bundesrepublik Deutschland. Bonn. Retrieved July 13, 2012, from http://www.kmk.org/fileadmin/doc/Dokumentation/Bildungswesen_pdfs/dt-2012.pdf

Lohmar, B., & Eckhardt, T. (2011b). *The Education System in the Federal Republic of Germany 2010/2011: A Description of the Responsibilities, Structures and Developments in Education Policy for the Exchange of Information in Europe*. Sekretariat der ständigen Konferez der Kultusminister der Länder in der Bundesrepublik Deutschland. Bonn. Retrieved July 13, 2012, from http://www.kmk.org/fileadmin/doc/Dokumentation/Bildungswesen_en_pdfs/en-2012.pdf

Scheller, F. (2011). *Bestimmung der Herkunftsnationen von Teilnehmern des Sozio-oekonomischen Panels (SOEP) mit Migrationshintergrund* (SOEPpapers on Multidisciplinary Panel Data Research No. 407). Retrieved Januar 18, 2007, from http://www.diw.de/documents/publikationen/73/diw_01.c.388707.de/diw_sp0407.pdf

Schwippert, K., Bos, W., & Lankes, E.-M. (2003). Heterogenität und Chancengleichheit am Ende der vierten Jahrgangsstufe im internationalen Vergleich. In W. Bos, E.-M. Lankes, M. Prenzel, K. Schwippert, G. Walther & R. Valtin (Eds.), *Erste Ergebnisse aus IGLU: Schülerleistungen am Ende der vierten Jahrgangsstufe im internationalen Vergleich* (pp. 265-302). Münster: Waxmann.

Siemon, J. (2010). Berufsausbildung in der Wissensgesellschaft. In A. Liesner & I. Lohmann (Eds.), *Gesellschaftliche Bedingungen von Bildung und Erziehung* (pp. 216-227). Stuttgart: Kohlhammer.

SOEP Group. (2001). The German Socio-Economic Panel (GSOEP) after More than 15 Years – Overview. *Vierteljahrshefte zur Wirtschaftsforschung, 70*(1), 7-14.

Söhn, J., & Özcan, V. (2006). The Educational Attainment of Turkish Migrants in Germany. *Turkish Studies, 7*(1), 101-124.

Söhn, J., & Özcan, V. (2007). Bildungsdaten und Migrationshintergrund: Eine Bilanz. In Bundesministerium für Bildung und Forschung (Ed.), *Migrationshintergrund von Kindern und Jugendlichen: Wege zur Weiterentwicklung der amtlichen Statistik* (pp. 117-128). Berlin.

Statistisches Bundesamt (2009a). *Bevölkerung und Erwerbstätigkeit: Bevölkerung mit Migrationshintergrund: Ergebnisse des Mikrozensus 2005* (Series 1, 2.2). Wiesbaden. Retrieved June 6, 2013, from https://www.destatis.de/DE/Publikationen/Thematisch/Bevoelkerung/AlteAusgaben/MigrationshintergrundAlt.html

Statistisches Bundesamt (2009b). *Bevölkerung und Erwerbstätigkeit: Bevölkerung mit Migrationshintergrund: Ergebnisse des Mikrozensus 2006* (Series 1, 22). Wiesbaden. Retrieved June 6, 2013, from https://www.destatis.de/DE/Publikationen/Thematisch/Bevoelkerung/AlteAusgaben/MigrationshintergrundAlt.html

Statistisches Bundesamt (2009c). *Bevölkerung und Erwerbstätigkeit: Bevölkerung mit Migrationshintergrund: Ergebnisse des Mikrozensus 2007* (Series 1, 2.2). Wiesbaden. Retrieved June 6, 2013, from https://www.destatis.de/DE/Publikationen/Thematisch/Bevoelkerung/AlteAusgaben/MigrationshintergrundAlt.html

Statistisches Bundesamt (2010). *Bevölkerung und Erwerbstätigkeit: Bevölkerung mit Migrationshintergrund: Ergebnisse des Mikrozensus 2008* (Series 1, 2.2). Wiesbaden. Retrieved June 6, 2013, from https://www.destatis.de/DE/Publikationen/Thematisch/Bevoelkerung/AlteAusgaben/MigrationshintergrundAlt.html

Statistisches Bundesamt (2011a). *Bevölkerung und Erwerbstätigkeit: Bevölkerung mit Migrationshintergrund: Ergebnisse des Mikrozensus 2009* (Series 1, 2.2). Wiesbaden. Retrieved June 6, 2013, from https://www.destatis.de/DE/Publikationen/Thematisch/Bevoelkerung/AlteAusgaben/MigrationshintergrundAlt.html

Statistisches Bundesamt (2011b). *Bevölkerung und Erwerbstätigkeit: Bevölkerung mit Migrationshintergrund: Ergebnisse des Mikrozensus 2010* (Series 1, 2.2). Wiesbaden. Retrieved June 6, 2013, from https://www.destatis.de/DE/Publikationen/Thematisch/Bevoelkerung/AlteAusgaben/MigrationshintergrundAlt.html

Statistisches Bundesamt (2013b). Retrieved October, 14, 2013, from https://www.destatis.de/DE/ZahlenFakten/GesellschaftStaat/Bevoelkerung/MigrationIntegration/Migrationshintergrund/Aktuell.html

Statistisches Bundesamt (2013c). Retrieved October 14, 2013, from https://www.destatis.de/EN/FactsFigures/SocietyState/Population/MigrationIntegration/PersonsMigrationBackground/Current.html

References

Stubbe, T. C. (2009). *Bildungsentscheidungen und sekundäre Herkunftseffekte: Soziale Disparitäten bei Hamburger Schülerinnen und Schülern der Sekundarstufe I*. Münster: Waxmann.

Stubbe, T. C., Bos, W., & Euen, B. (2012). Der Übergang von der Primar- in die Sekundarstufe. In W. Bos, I. Tarelli, A. Bremerich-Vos & K. Schwippert (Eds.), *IGLU 2011: Lesekompetenzen von Grundschulkindern in Deutschland im Internationalen Vergleich* (pp. 210-226). Münster: Waxmann.

The concept of educational aspirations 3

Educational aspirations have been studied intensively by different disciplines to explain educational disparities, including psychological, social-psychological, sociological and economic perspectives (Domina et al. 2011; Rojewski 2005). Yet, despite the frequent use of the term 'educational aspirations', which is generally used to refer to the educational goals students set for themselves, there is no single and universally accepted definition or common agreement as to what the term means (Lent et al. 1994; Quaglia and Cobb 1996; Rojewski 2005). A variety of terms like plans, decisions or preferences are commonly used – sometimes interchangeably – as they are all essentially viewed as goal terms that primarily differ along dimensions such as the degree of specificity and proximity to the choice implementation (Lent et al. 1994; Rojewski 2005). For instance, career goals have often been referred to as aspirations when they are assessed remotely in time from the decision situation and do not demand commitment or reality considerations, whereas terms like expressed choices, plans or decisions are more frequently used when goals are assessed near or at the point of transition (Lent et al. 1994, p. 85).

The importance ascribed to student aspirations derives from the acknowledgment that human behavior is not only regulated by external influences but that it is also extensively motivated by self-influence. While aspirations may be concrete or vague, the essence of the idea is that desired future events will direct and motivate effort in the present and thereby increase students' chances to succeed in the educational system (Bandura 1986, 1991; Caprara et al. 2008; Lent et al. 1994; Quaglia and Cobb 1996; Rojewski 2005). To take into account that expressed aspirations may not necessarily reflect the outcomes an individual realistically expects to achieve, the literature makes a clear theoretical distinction between idealistic and realistic aspirations, which are also referred to as aspirations and expectations in the international literature (Hanson 1994; Rojewski 2005; Spenner and Featherman 1978). Idealistic aspirations refer to desired attainment levels, which are not limited by constraints such as level of educational performance and the family's financial resources (Hauser and Anderson 1991, p. 270; Rojewski 2005, p. 133). Realistic aspirations relate to the perceived likelihood of success and reflect the level of education students realistically expect to complete (Haller 1968, p. 484; Rojewski 2005, p. 133).

Besides the use of subjective data to predict later attainment outcomes, student aspirations are frequently assessed to provide information on their belief-formation and decision-making processes, which cannot be investigated by means of the analysis of objective transition data (Jæger 2007; Manski 2004). For instance, data on students' idealistic and realistic aspirations is commonly collected to provide information on the congruence or discrepancy between the two, and to thereby obtain insight into students' views toward their particular circumstances, abilities, and the likely effects of perceived barriers and future opportunities (Gottfredson 1981; Ma and Wang 2001; Rojewski 2005).

While data on educational aspirations is comparatively easily accessible, there is no common agreement as to how the concept should be measured. Most commonly, survey participants are asked to choose between different educational alternatives in response to questions of the following form to collect information on their idealistic and realistic aspirations:

> "If it were up to you: What would you prefer to do after 9th grade? I would prefer..." and "And when you think realistically: What do you think will you really do after 9th grade? I probably will..." (NEPS questionnaire for 9th-graders)[11]

> "As things stand now, what is the highest level of education you think you will get?" and "What is the highest level of education you would like to get?" (YITS questionnaire for 15-year-olds)[12]

> "What is the highest grade or level of school you expect to complete?" (PISA questionnaire for 9th-graders)[13]

The small selection of questions above already points to the difficulties that are inherent to the measurement of aspirations and the interpretation of subjective data. First, the use of different phrasings and response categories severely limits the

---

11 https://www.neps-data.de/Portals/0/NEPS/Datenzentrum/Forschungsdaten/SC4/1-1-0/SC4_1-1-0_Q_w1_2_en.pdf (accessed Oct. 19, 2013).

12 http://www23.statcan.gc.ca/imdb/p3Instr.pl?Function=assembleInstr&Item_Id=75581&a=0&lang=en&db= imdb&adm=8&dis=2#qb98510 (accessed Oct. 19, 2013).

13 http://nces.ed.gov/surveys/pisa/pdf/MS12_StQ_FormA_ENG_USA_final.pdf (accessed Oct. 19, 2013).

comparability of results obtained from different studies. Second, interpretative difficulties may arise from the use of ambiguous expressions that do not clearly indicate whether questions refer to idealistic or realistic aspirations:

> "What is the highest level school leaving degree you *wish* to obtain?" (SOEP youth questionnaire, emphasis added)[14]
>
> "In the following questions, the point is what your parents *expect you* to achieve in school and in your future professional career. What is the highest school-leaving qualification your parents *would like* you to obtain?" (NEPS questionnaire for 9th-graders, emphasis added)[15]

Evidently, the use of inconsistent and ambiguous nomenclature, along with the fact that it is often not made explicit by researchers how aspirations were measured and conceptualized, may easily lead to an inaccurate view of the role of student aspirations in the explanation of attainment differentials (Rojewski 2005).

Even though longitudinal studies consistently point to considerable correlations between various measures of respondent-reported aspirations and level of educational performance and attainment (e.g., Beal and Crockett 2010; Buriel and Cardoza 1988; Jacob and Wilder 2010; Domina et al. 2011; Mau and Bikos 2000; Ou and Reynolds 2008; Rojewski and Kim 2003; Zhang et al. 2011), both the causal interpretation of the association between aspirations and future attainments and the predictive value of subjective data have been challenged by several researchers. Arguments that have been brought forward in this context range from the consideration that expressed aspirations are conditioned by students' perceptions of the opportunity structure and reflect their perceived chances to succeed in the educational system rather than index motivation (Alexander and Cook 1979; Bourdieu 1973; Jencks et al. 1983; Kerckhoff 1976), to the concern that respondent-reported aspirations may be the product of lacking or inaccurate information about the educational system and/or unrealistic self-appraisals (Coleman et al. 1966; Kerckhoff 1977; Kerckhoff and Campbell 1977; Rosenbaum 1976, 1978, 1980) or constitute "vague preferences" or "flights of fancy conjured up on the spur of the moment" (Alexander and Cook 1979, p. 202) that have no true salience to adolescents in their everyday lives as they fail to commit to and/

---

14 http://panel.gsoep.de/soepinfo2011/quests/pdf/en/q2001youth_en.pdf (accessed Oct. 19, 2013).

15 https://www.neps-data.de/Portals/0/NEPS/Datenzentrum/ Forschungsdaten/SC4/1-1-0/SC4_1-1-0_Q_w1_2_en.pdf (accessed Oct. 19, 2013).

or to take effective action to realize their aspirations (Alexander and Cook 1979; Coleman et al. 1966; Jencks et al. 1983; Kerckhoff 1976; Rosenbaum 1976, 1980).

As a matter of fact, several studies have brought forward evidence to support the relevance of these considerations. For example, empirical studies have revealed that students not only gradually adjust their realistic aspirations to aspects such as actual and perceived level of ability (Gottfredson 1981, 2005; Hanson 1994), but that they also tend to shift their idealistic aspirations in the direction of their realistic aspirations over time (Armstrong and Crombie 2000; Gottfredson 1981, 2005; for Germany, e.g., Heckhausen and Tomasik 2002). Also, there is a large body of evidence that not only shows students' idealistic but also their realistic aspirations to frequently exceed attainment outcomes, that the gap between realistic aspirations, student effort and attainment levels has increased over the last decades, and that this gap systematically varies across population subgroups (e.g., Domina et al. 2011; Goyette 2008; J. Reynolds et al. 2006; J. R. Reynolds and Johnson 2011; Rosenbaum 1976, 1978, 1980, 2001; Schneider and Stevenson 1999). For instance, migrants are consistently shown to have both comparatively high idealistic and realistic aspirations, whereas children from migrant families are characterized by systematically lower levels of educational attainment than natives even when background characteristics are taken into account (e.g., Heath and Brinbaum 2007; Diefenbach 2010).

Also, the assumption of a universal meaning of educational aspirations has been challenged on the ground that students may differentially weight their preferences against their perceived probability of success when constructing their educational aspirations. In consideration of the rapidly increasing realistic educational aspirations (expectations) that could be observed in the United States over the last decades, Goyette (2008) raised the presumption that low-performing students who are unlikely to eventually attend college but who face pressure from their significant others may not lower but "inflate" their realistic aspirations (cf. also Becker 2010; Morgan 2002):

> "Educational expectations are thought to measure both a student's desire to attain a particular level of education and that student's assessment of the likelihood of achieving that level of education. For this reason, researchers have argued that educational expectations are better predictors of attainment than are educational aspirations, which are presumed to measure only desires for further education. However, it is unclear how students weigh their desires to attain a level of education against the assessment of their chances when answering questions about educational expectations. For some students, educational expectations may reflect their goals of achievement, while for others they may be a realistic assessment of their chances of being accepted, financing, and completing a four-year degree" (Goyette 2008, pp. 446f.).

These considerations, in turn, call the comparability of expressed aspirations across students into question. Besides the consideration that respondent-reported aspirations may be biased themselves, a methodological concern is that aspirations are potentially endogenous measures that will produce biased estimates of the causal effect from aspirations on later attainment outcomes (Jæger 2007; Morgan 1998).[16]

Despite the legitimacy of the considerations above, strong arguments have been put forward to show that neither the conceptualization of aspirations as perceptions of the opportunity structure nor as the result of lacking or inaccurate information and unrealistic self-appraisals is inconsistent with a causal claim. If students' perceptions of the opportunity structure – including beliefs about their capabilities and their subjective probability to successfully complete a given educational alternative – are systematically incorrect, they may be self-fulfilling prophecies that compel students to pursue courses of action they would not have pursued if their expectations had been correct, and thereby constrain or promote educational development and advancement (Lent 2005; Morgan 2004, 2005). For instance, psychologists have found students who underestimate their capabilities to tend to avoid challenges that are within their competence range, and modest over-confidence to encourage students to take on challenges that promote the acquisition of skills (Lent et al. 1994). Also, even though there is evidence that students' idealistic aspirations frequently exceed their realistic aspirations, and that the latter often exceed the levels of education students will eventually complete, high aspirations may preclude early drop-outs that are not related to the opportunity structure but that result from a lack of motivation to continue in school (Rojewski 2005).

In spite of the increased interest in the role of student aspirations in the explanation of attainment differentials, little effort has been made to explicitly model the causal effect from aspirations on later attainment outcomes. With few exceptions, which in fact suggest the existence of a causal effect from educational as-

---

16 In regression models a variable is endogenous when it is correlated with the error term. For instance, the problem of endogeneity occurs if aspirations are correlated with omitted background variables that also determine attainment outcomes. This is a plausible assumption as both aspirations and attainment outcomes are assumed to be influenced by background characteristics that are not fully captured by proxy measures such as the family's socioeconomic position. Then, both the estimate and standard error of the influence of aspirations on attainment will be biased using standard inference methods. Popular methods to overcome this problem include instrumental variable regression and the Heckman selection correction. Yet, the applicability of these methods is often limited by a lack of relevant variables that can be used as instruments or to specify a selection equation (Wooldridge 2010).

pirations on later attainments (Domina et al. 2011), hardly any empirical studies use methods such as instrumental variable estimators or panel data approaches to explicitly take into account the potential endogeneity of subjective data on the one hand, and the consideration that aspirations are a dynamic phenomenon on the other hand. Therefore, the questions to what extent respondent-reported aspirations can predict attainment outcomes, and whether the association between aspirations and later attainment levels can be given a causal interpretation, remain controversial. As regards evidence for Germany, this situation is not least attributable to a lack of combined data on student aspirations and later attainment levels. In sum, while there is no irrefutable evidence that student aspirations are causal for the levels of education they complete, the considerations above strongly suggest that they may neither be given a universally causal nor a universally non-causal interpretation (Morgan 2005, p. 87).[17]

References

Alexander, K. L., & Cook, M. A. (1979). The Motivational Relevance of Educational Plans: Questioning the Conventional Wisdom. *Social Psychology Quarterly, 42*(3), 202-213.

Armstrong, P. I., & Crombie, G. (2000). Compromises in Adolescents' Occupational Aspirations and Expectations from Grades 8 to 10. *Journal of Vocational Behavior, 56*(1), 82-98.

Bandura, A. (1986). Human Agency in Social Cognitive Theory. *American Psychologist, 44*(9), 1175-1184.

Bandura, A. (1991). Social Cognitive Theory of Self-Regulation. *Organizational Behavior and Human Decision Processes, 50*(2), 248-287.

Beal, S. J., & Crockett, L. J. (2010). Adolescents' Occupational and Educational Aspirations and Expectations: Links to High School Activities and Adult Educational Attainment. *Developmental Psychology, 46*(1), 258-265.

Becker, B. (2010). *Bildungsaspirationen von Migranten: Determinanten und Umsetzung in Bildungsergebnisse* (MZES Working Paper No. 137). Retrieved Febuary 5, 2012, from http://www.mzes.unimannheim.de/publications/wp/wp-137.pdf

Bourdieu, P. (1973). Cultural Reproduction and Social Reproduction. In R. K. Brown (Ed.), *Knowledge, Education, and Cultural Change: Papers in the Sociology of Education* (pp. 71-112). London: Tavistock.

---

17 Due to the inconsistent use of the term aspirations in the literature, unless indicated otherwise the remainder of the theoretical part of the study uses the term educational aspirations as an umbrella term for different measures that do not explicitly ask for the careers students *expect* to complete. The latter are referred to as educational expectations. See glossary for terminology as used in my empirical analysis.

References

Buriel, R., & Cardoza, D. (1988). Sociocultural Correlates of Achievement Among Three Generations of Mexican American High School Seniors. *American Educational Research Journal, 25*(2), 177-192.

Caprara, G. V., Fida, R., Vecchione, M., Del Bove, G., Vecchio, G. M., Barbaranelli, C., & Bandura, A. (2008). Longitudinal Analysis of the Role of Perceived Self-efficacy for Self-regulated Learning in Academic Continuance and Achievement. *Journal of Educational Psychology, 100*(3), 525-534.

Coleman, J. S., Campbell, E. Q., Hobson, J. C., McPartland, J., Mood, A. M., Weinfeld, F. D., & York, R. L. (1966). *Equality of Educational Opportunity*. Washington, D.C.: U.S. Government Printing Office.

Diefenbach, H. (2010). *Kinder und Jugendliche aus Migrantenfamilien im deutschen Bildungssystem: Erklärungen und empirische Befunde* (3rd ed.). Wiesbaden: VS Verlag für Sozialwissenschaften.

Domina, T., Conley, A., & Farkas, G. (2011). The Link between Educational Expectations and Effort in the College-for-all Era. *Sociology of Education, 84*(2), 93-112.

Gottfredson, L. S. (1981). Circumscription and Compromise: A Developmental Theory of Occupational Aspirations. *Journal of Counseling Psychology Monograph, 28*(6), 545-579.

Gottfredson, L. S. (2005). Applying Gottfredson's Theory of Circumscription and Compromise in Career Guidance and Counseling. In S. D. Brown & R. W. Lent (Eds.), *Career Development and Counseling: Putting Theory and Research to Work* (pp. 71-100). New Jersey: Wiley.

Goyette, K. A. (2008). College for Some to College for All: Social Background, Occupational Expectations, and Educational Expectations over Time. *Social Science Research, 37*(2), 461-484.

Haller, A. O. (1968). On the Concept of Aspiration. *Rural Sociology, 33*(4), 484-487.

Hanson, S. L. (1994). Lost Talent: Unrealized Educational Aspirations and Expectations among U.S. Youths. *Sociology of Education, 67*(3), 159-183.

Hauser, R. M., & Anderson, D. K. (1991). Post-High School Plans and Aspirations of Black and White High School Seniors: 1976-86. *Sociology of Education, 64*(4), 263-277.

Heath, A. F., & Brinbaum, Y. (2007). Guest Editorial: Explaining Ethnic Inequalities in Educational Attainment. *Ethnicities, 7*(3), 291-304.

Heckhausen, J., & Tomasik, M. J. (2002). Get an Apprenticeship Before School is Out: How German Adolescents Adjust Vocational Aspirations When Getting Close to a Developmental Deadline. *Journal of Vocational Behavior, 60*, 199-219.

Jacob, B. A., & Wilder, T. (2010). *Educational Expectations and Attainment* (NBER Working Paper No. 15683). Retrieved January 26, 2013, from http://www.nber.org/papers/w15683

Jæger, M. M. (2007). Economic and Social Returns to Educational Choices: Extending the Utility Function. *Rationality and Society, 19*(4), 451-483.

Jencks, C., Crouse, J., & Mueser, P. (1983). The Wisconsin Model of Status Attainment: A National Replication with Improved Measures of Ability and Aspiration. *Sociology of Education, 56*(1), 3-19.

Kerckhoff, A. C. (1976). The Status Attainment Process: Socialization or Allocation? *Social Forces, 55*(2), 368-381.

Kerckhoff, A. C. (1977). The Realism of Educational Ambitions in England and the United States. *American Sociological Review, 42*(4), 563-571.

Kerckhoff, A. C., & Campbell, R. T. (1977). Social Status Differences in the Explanation of Educational Ambition. *Social Forces, 5*(3), 701-714.

Lent, R. W. (2005). A Social Cognitive View of Career Development and Counseling. In S. D. Brown & R. W. Lent (Eds.), *Career Development and Counseling: Putting Theory and Research to Work* (pp. 101-127). New Jersey: Wiley.

Lent, R. W., Brown, S. D., & Hackett, G. (1994). Monograph: Toward a Unifying Social Cognitive Theory of Career and Academic Interest, Choice, and Performance. *Journal of Vocational Behavior, 45*, 79-122.

Ma, X., & Wang, J. (2001). A Confirmatory Examination of Walberg's Model of Educational Productivity in Student Career Aspiration. *Educational Psychology, 21*(4), 443-453.

Manski, C. F. (2004). Measuring Expectations. *Econometrica, 72*(5), 1329-1376.

Mau, W.-C., & Bikos, L. H. (2000). Educational and Vocational Aspirations of Minority and Female Students: A Longitudinal Study. *Journal of Counseling & Development, 78*(2), 186-194.

Morgan, S. L. (1998). Adolescent Educational Expectations: Rationalized, Fantasized, or Both? *Rationality and Society, 10*(2), 131-162.

Morgan, S. L. (2002). Modeling Preparatory Commitment and Non-Repeatable Decisions: Information-Processing, Preference Formation and Educational Attainment. *Rationality and Society, 14*(4), 387-429.

Morgan, S. L. (2004). Methodologist as Arbitrator: Five Models for Black-White Differences in the Causal Effect of Expectations on Attainment *Sociological Methods & Research, 33*(1), 3-53.

Morgan, S. L. (2005). *On the Edge of Commitment: Educational Attainment and Race in the United States*. Stanford, CA: Stanford University Press.

Ou, S.-R., & Reynolds, A. J. (2008). Predictors of Educational Attainment in the Chicago Longitudinal Study. *School Psychology Quarterly, 23*(2), 199-229.

Quaglia, R. J., & Cobb, C. D. (1996). Toward a Theory of Student Aspirations. *Journal of Research in Rural Education, 12*(3), 127-132.

Reynolds, J., Stewart, M., MacDonald, R., & Sischo, L. (2006). Have Adolescents Become Too Ambitious? High School Seniors' Educational and Occupational Plans, 1976 to 2000. *Social Problems, 53*(2), 186-206.

Reynolds, J. R., & Johnson, M. K. (2011). Change in the Stratification of Educational Expectations and Their Realization. *Social Forces, 90*(1), 85-110.

Rojewski, J. W. (2005). Occupational Aspirations: Constructs, Meanings, and Application. In S. D. Brown & R. W. Lent (Eds.), *Career Development and Counseling: Putting Theory and Research to Work* (pp. 131-154). New Jersey: Wiley.

Rojewski, J. W., & Kim, H. (2003). Career Choice Patterns and Behavior of Work-Bound Youth During Early Adolescence. *Journal of Career Development, 30*(2), 89-108.

Rosenbaum, J. E. (1976). *Making Inequality: The Hidden Curriculum of High School Tracking*. New York: Wiley.

Rosenbaum, J. E. (1978). The Structure of Opportunity in School. *Social Forces, 57*(1), 236-256.

Rosenbaum, J. E. (1980). Track Misperceptions and Frustrated College Plans: An Analysis of the Effects of Tracks and Track Perceptions in the National Longitudinal Survey. *Sociology of Education, 53*(2), 74-88.

Rosenbaum, J. E. (2001). *Beyond College-for-all: Career Paths for the Forgotten Half*. New York: Russell Sage Foundation.

References

Schneider, B. L., & Stevenson, D. (1999). *The Ambitious Generation: America's Teenagers, Motivated but Directionless*. New Haven: Yale University Press.

Spenner, K. I., & Featherman, D. L. (1978). Achievement Ambitions. *Annual Review of Sociology, 4*, 373-420.

Wooldridge, J. M. (2010). *Econometric Analysis of Cross Section and Panel Data* (2nd ed.). Cambridge: MIT Press.

Zhang, Y., Haddad, E., Torres, B., & Chen, C. (2011). The Reciprocal Relationships Among Parents' Expectations, Adolescents' Expectations, and Adolescents' Achievement: A Two-Wave Longitudinal Analysis of the NELS Data. *Journal of Youth and Adolescence, 40*(4), 479-489.

4 Models of educational aspirations and choice

The following sections present two research traditions that are often used as a point of departure for models of educational aspirations, expectations and choice (Konczal and Haller 2008; Lloyd et al. 2008; Morgan 2002) and constitute the theoretical basis of the empirical study. The concept of educational aspirations experienced its breakthrough in the sociology of education in the context of the development of the celebrated Wisconsin model (Sewell et al. 1969; Sewell et al. 1970; cf. Paulus and Blossfeld 2007), which emerged in the status attainment literature in the late 1960s and constitutes one of the first attempts to introduce social-psychological variables into earlier models of intergenerational mobility. The model adopts a socialization perspective and conceptualizes students' attainment outcomes primarily as the outcome of their educational aspirations and how these are conditioned by the expectations of their significant others. A second research tradition that has gained increased attention in the educational literature in the last decades adopts a quite different perspective and models attainment outcomes as the aggregate consequence of individuals' rational responses to the costs and benefits that are associated with different educational alternatives at the successive points of transition (Boudon 1974; Jæger 2007; Morgan 1998). Following a brief outline of the key assumptions and findings of both types of approaches, the chapter concludes with a discussion of the extent to which results derived from empirical applications can be conceived of as conflicting or complementary, and whether there is evidence to claim supremacy of one perspective over the other. In this context, the question of the value of subjective data to obtain insight into the processes that shape attainment differentials is reconsidered.

4.1 The Wisconsin model of status attainment

The Wisconsin model of status attainment constitutes an extension of the Blau-Duncan model (Blau and Duncan 1967), which was a first crucial contribution in terms of systematizing the causal relationships through which the family's social origin influences their children's educational and later occupational attainments. Besides the observation that the father's educational and occupational position directly influence the statuses achieved by the son, as had been shown by much previous research, the most fundamental finding of Blau and Duncan's work was that occupational attainment is most fully influenced by educational attainment, and that the latter constitutes the central mobility factor that mediates the relation between social origin and later occupational attainment (Blau and Duncan 1967; Haller and Portes 1973; Kerckhoff 1976). Following the lack of identification of the finer mediating processes through which status attainment takes place, Sewell et al. (1969) added several variables to the Blau-Duncan model to examine the causal mechanisms at a more specific social-psychological level. Figure 4.1 illustrates the original specification of the path model that was derived from the analysis of longitudinal questionnaire data from male high school seniors in Wisconsin in 1957 and a follow up study in 1964 (Sewell et al. 1969). The straight solid lines stand for the causal links that were theoretically expected, the black dotted lines for possible but theoretically debatable causal links, and the orange dotted lines for correlations that were not assigned causal priority and left unanalyzed.

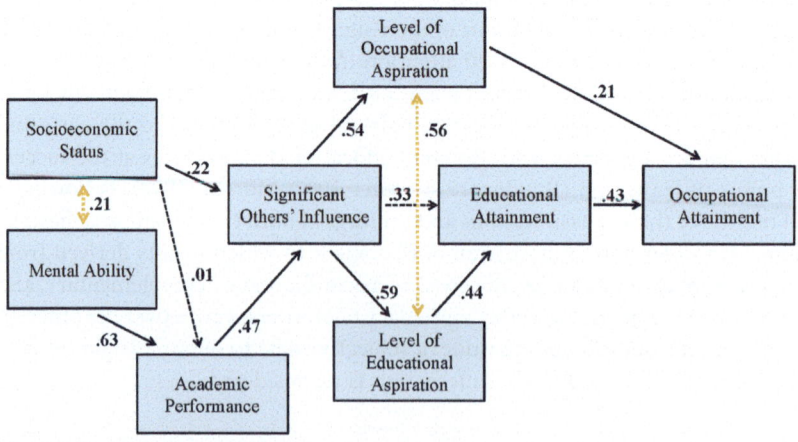

Source: Sewell et al. 1969, p. 85 (simplified depiction)

Figure 4.1 Wisconsin model of status attainment, original specification

4.1 The Wisconsin model of status attainment

The family's socioeconomic position and mental ability precede all other variables in the model. Level of educational performance, the influence of significant others and students' educational and occupational aspirations were added as variables that mediate the effects from family origin and mental ability on students' attainment outcomes. Educational performance is directly influenced by mental ability and influences the expectations of students' significant others, which implies that the latter are not only influenced by social origin but that they also adapt their expectations to level of demonstrated ability. Students' educational and occupational aspirations mediate the effect from significant others' influence on the respective attainment variable, and educational attainment directly predicts later occupational attainment.

Educational aspirations were measured as students' plans to go to college, and educational attainment by whether they had at least received some college education or not in the follow up study. The influence of significant others, referring to those persons from whom students obtain their level of aspiration either because they communicate to them their expectations ('adoption' processes) or because they serve as role models ('imitation' processes), was measured as a compound index of the perceived encouragement from parents and teachers to go to college and friends' college plans. The former was thought of as a normative reference group, and the plans of peers to shape students' aspirations by means of exercising pressure toward conformity and by serving as a cognitive comparison with similar others (Sewell et al. 1969, p. 87).

The influence of significant others, and most specifically students' compliance with the expectations of their significant others, was identified as the key mechanism in the attainment process. Apart from the effect from mental ability on academic performance, the strongest effects were exerted from significant others' influence on students' educational and occupational aspirations. Also, considerably strong associations were observed between level of performance and significant others' influence, and between students' educational and occupational aspirations and the respective attainment variable. As student aspirations were found to mediate most of the influence of the antecedent variables on educational and occupational attainment, they were conceived of as the "strategic center" of the model (Haller and Portes 1973, p. 68). As concerns the association between student aspirations and later attainment levels, the authors assumed the internalization of achievement aspirations to promote higher levels of educational attainment by means of converting ambition into motivation and effort:

> "Embedded in a mass of approximately consistent and mutually reinforcing cognitions, they [aspirations] come to have an inertia of their own and are expressed in

corresponding behavior [...] They guide one's selection among status opportunities encountered and determine activities toward which one's energies will be directed" (Haller 1982, p. 6).

As the model specification was derived based on a relatively homogenous sample with respect to social origin, the model was reestimated using data from a questionnaire survey of all high school seniors in different types of schools in Wisconsin in 1957 and a follow-up study in 1964-65 to test its adequacy with respect to a more diverse population (Sewell et al. 1970). Based on the new estimation results several paths were added to the original model (red lines in figure 4.2): A direct effect was added from mental ability on significant others' influence, from level of educational performance on student aspirations, and from academic performance and significant others' influence on educational attainment.

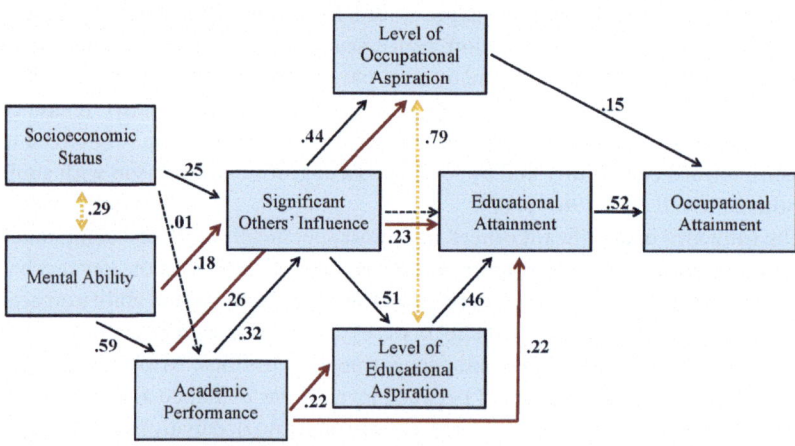

Source: Sewell et al. 1970, p. 1023 (simplified depiction)
Figure 4.2 Wisconsin model of status attainment, revised specification

The relationships that were identified in the original model were essentially confirmed by the results of the revised model specification. Yet, the finding of a strong direct effect from academic performance on both aspiration variables and on level of educational attainment had strong implications with respect to the critical role the authors had originally attributed to the influence of significant others. Based on the original estimation results, they concluded that student aspirations are primarily formed through imitation and, most importantly, adoption mechanisms.

4.1 The Wisconsin model of status attainment

The observation of a direct path from level of educational performance to student aspirations, however, revealed that students not only adopt the expectations and imitate the behavior of their significant others but that they also adjust their aspirations to level of past performance ('self-reflection' processes). This observation, along with a decrease in the magnitude of the effect from significant others' influence on both aspiration variables and educational attainment, led the authors to conclude that "the youth normally has a fairly adequate perception of the objective requirements for status attainment and to some extent independently gauges his ability to compete by assessing his grades relative to those of others" (Sewell et al. 1970, p. 1024), and that academic performance has an even more central role in the attainment process than had been thought originally. As the effects exerted from significant others' influence on students' aspirations were still much stronger than the effect from educational performance on these variables, however, the authors maintained that significant others' influence, and in particular the expectations students adopt from their significant others, constitute the key mechanism in the attainment process:

> "Perhaps the most important single finding in the latter report is the critical role of significant others' influence in the status attainment process. The present report confirms this but adds that academic performance has effects on aspirational and attainment variables that are not mediated by significant others' influence. We take this to mean that the individual is not wholly dependent upon his significant others (as identified herein) for guidance in the status aspects of his career decisions" (Sewell et al. 1970, p. 1025).

In view of the observation that the strong association between aspirations and attainment in the original model estimation had remained relatively stable, that significant others' influence and student aspirations were found to mediate quite a large proportion of the effect from social origin on later attainment levels, and that both models explained the variation in attainment outcomes significantly better than the Blau-Duncan model, the authors concluded that the inclusion of social-psychological dynamics significantly contributes to the understanding of the status attainment process. In consideration that the model explained a comparatively large amount of the variation in educational attainment, which was in turn found to largely explain level of occupational attainment, the authors further acknowledged that the model is an effective system to explain educational rather than occupational attainment (Sewell et al. 1970, pp. 1022f.).

The results of the Wisconsin model could be replicated by several subsequent studies that were based on more representative samples (e.g., Alexander et al. 1975; Jencks et al. 1983; cf. also Alexander and Cook 1979, p. 202), and both the influence of significant others and students' educational aspirations have been widely acknowledged to significantly contribute to the explanation of educational differentials across the population. Yet, several researchers challenged the theoretical position on which the model was based. In the previous chapter, the question of the theoretical meaning of respondent-reported aspirations was shown to be discussed controversially. In the context of the Wisconsin model, the concern that students' educational aspirations may constitute expectations that are formed based on students' perceptions of the opportunity structure was reinforced by the measurement of aspirations as *plans* close to an important transition, where students are assumed to become more realistic with respect to their future courses of action (Alexander and Cook 1979; Kerckhoff 1976, 1977). This concern was supported by several empirical findings, including the observation that college plans are not only conditioned by significant others' influence but also directly influenced by past performance experiences (Sewell et al. 1969; Sewell et al. 1970; cf. also Morgan 1998).

These considerations not only challenged the assumption that educational aspirations influence attainment levels but also the key finding of a causal effect from significant others' influence on student aspirations: If college plans are reconceptualized as reality-based expectations, the possibility remains that the association between significant others' influence and students' college plans is the mere result of the simultaneous perception and evaluation of external influences on the part of students and their significant others (Kerckhoff and Huff 1974; Kerckhoff 1976; Morgan 1998). Indeed, this notion was supported by empirical findings. For instance, student aspirations and significant others' influence were found to have the same antecedents in the Wisconsin model (Kerckhoff 1976; Kerckhoff and Huff 1974). In a retrospective account, the principal social psychologist Haller (1982) wrote about the model:

> "At the time of its appearance […] its authors appear to have seen it as an explanation for the influence of origin statuses on status attainments and nothing more. Only later […] was it recognized explicitly that most of the effects of the aspirations and of significant others have as yet unknown sources having nothing to do with the statuses of the parents of the subjects. As of the time of this writing, it appears that this important lacuna remains unfilled by empirical data" (Haller 1982, p. 10).

Besides the consideration that the association between significant others' influence and student aspirations may be the product of the omission of variables that simultaneously influence both students' own evaluations of the opportunity structure and their significant others' aspirations and expectations, the validity of the model was challenged by its failure to fully mediate the association between social origin and attainments on the one hand, and as it could explain the variation in the attainments of Blacks less well than that of Whites on the other hand. Attempting to increase the explanatory power of the model, subsequent attainment models gradually shifted their focus toward the role of structural constraints and allocation processes, and empirically demonstrated the potential explanatory value of the inclusion of aspects of the institutional structure, demographic effects and variations in resources other than measures of the family's socioeconomic position (cf. Morgan 2005, p. 59 and literature therein). As regards the unresolved question of Black-White differences in the estimates of the correspondence between aspirations and attainment outcomes, popular explanations refer to the neglect of externally imposed constraints that are faced by certain groups only and influence their view of the opportunity structure, such as experienced and anticipated discrimination (Alexander and Eckland 1975; Alexander et al. 1978; Coleman et al. 1966; Kerckhoff 1977; Mickelson 1990; Portes and Wilson 1976; Kerckhoff and Campbell 1977). While the explicit consideration of these conditions certainly added to the understanding of the attainment process, most subsequent attainment models did not provide insight into the micro-mechanisms with which prior status socialization models were concerned. Eventually, the Wisconsin model has undergone little change since its first tested versions and has remained a popular approach in the current literature, regarding both the causal interpretation of the association between significant others' influence and student aspirations and – as was outlined in the previous chapter – the assumption of a causal effect from aspirations on later attainment levels (Morgan 2005).

4.2 Rational choice theories of educational attainment

In contrast to the conception of students' educational aspirations and attainment levels as the outcome primarily of socialization mechanisms, rational choice theories shift the focus to the evaluations of students themselves, who are assumed to maximize individual utility by making educational choices in consideration of the costs and benefits that are associated with a given educational alternative (Morgan 1998). Rational choice theory has long been the dominant paradigm in economics to address questions of social and educational differentials, probably most well-known in the form of Becker's human capital theory (G. Becker 1964; 1993, 3rd ed.). Becker proposed a fundamental theoretical analysis of micro investment in human capital, which in essence constitutes a modified application of a framework traditionally used to analyze investment in other capital to human capital. The basic assumptions are that investments in human capital, most important education and training, raise the productivity of individuals by imparting knowledge and skills, and thereby their well-being by raising future incomes. The amounts invested in education are modeled as rational responses in terms of an individual's comparisons of the monetary and psychic costs and benefits of an additional investment in education. Money terms refer to benefits such as future earnings, to direct expenditures such as tuition fees and school supplies, and to opportunity costs in terms of foregone earnings. Psychic benefits include dimensions such as the prestige associated with a particular occupation and the extent to which an occupation meets an individual's interests and preferences. Psychic costs refer to aspects such as the value an individual places on the time and effort required to accumulate additional human capital.

Variations in the total amount invested in human capital across the population are explained by systematic differences in the abilities and opportunities of students from different social backgrounds. Students from families in higher social positions have the opportunity to invest more than others primarily due to the accessibility of financial resources, and students with higher abilities can produce a larger number of units of human capital from a given monetary investment. Also, opportunities are assumed to vary with level of demonstrated ability. For instance, students with higher abilities are more likely to receive scholarships than students with lower abilities. The rational decision is the selection of the investment strategy that maximizes the present value of the difference between the benefits and costs that are associated with an additional investment in education, so that students who have more favorable opportunities and higher abilities will invest larger amounts in themselves than students from lower social backgrounds.

Human capital theory has received strong empirical support and contributed considerably to the explanation of individual attainment decisions by integrating several influences into a coherent theoretical framework (Reder 1967; Xiao 2002). As regards its relatively strong assumptions, such as the "representative" (G. Becker 1993, p. 109) and hyperrational decision-maker who is able to calculate lifetime earnings, Becker presented several specific applications of his general theory and ways in which these assumptions can be relaxed and how further parameters, such as uncertainty or human capital of different quality, can be formally incorporated into his theoretical framework.

In consideration of the strong focus of empirical applications of human capital theory on monetary decision parameters and the neglect of the explicit consideration that educational decisions are embedded in social contexts, a new literature has emerged that adopts the basic rational choice axioms of utility-maximizing

4.2 Rational choice theories of educational attainment

and rational decision makers who derive utility from education but departs from the conventional economic approach by modeling the utility individuals seek to maximize to have an economic as well as an explicit social dimension (Davies et al. 2002; Jæger 2007). Also, this new sociological rational choice literature assumes students to make decisions based on expected rather than on actual benefits and costs, and in consideration of the subjective probability of success that is associated with a given educational alternative (Jæger 2007; Stocké 2012).

An early but particularly influential expansion of the economic model was presented by Boudon (1974), who described the emergence of educational disparities as a two-component process that involves primary and secondary effects of stratification. Primary effects refer to a systematically different distribution of students from different social strata with respect to dimensions that affect their probability of educational success, such as educational achievement. Due to their poorer cultural background, students from families of lower social status have a systematically lower probability of success than their peers from families in more favorable positions from the beginning on. Secondary effects result from systematically different educational decisions according to the position in the stratification system even when students do not differ with respect to primary effects.

As regards the explanation for the existence of secondary effects, Boudon explicitly dispensed with assumptions about inter-class variations in the value people attach to education and elaborated on Keller and Zavalloni's (1964) social position theory, which assumes more ambitious educational choices in higher-class families to result from the higher social distance lower-class students have to overcome to attain high levels of education. When choosing between two educational alternatives, of which one is more prestigious in terms of being more likely to lead to a higher social status, the probability to choose the more prestigious option will be an increasing function of the family's social position due to the socially stratified structure of the costs and benefits that are associated with a given educational alternative. The more prestigious alternative is associated with higher benefits for families of higher social status as they face the risk of social demotion, whereas students from lower backgrounds may expect upward mobility from choosing exactly the same educational alternative. Also, not choosing the more prestigious alternative is associated with a high social cost for children from middle-class families if most of their friends have chosen it, whereas choosing the more prestigious alternative represents a high cost for children from lower classes if most of their friends have not. Similarly, choosing the more prestigious alternative may reinforce family solidarity in the middle class but weaken it in lower social classes. Assuming that the utility of choosing a given educational alternative is greater the lower the expected costs and the greater the expected benefits, and that the probability to choose a given educational option is an increasing function of the utility associated with this choice, both the utility and the probability of choosing the more prestigious alternative will be an increasing function of the family's social status.

In sum, Boudon's approach constitutes an extension of the economic model in that people are assumed to behave rationally in terms of making educational decisions that maximize utility on the one hand, but to behave within decisional fields that are structured by their position in the stratification system on the other hand (Morgan 2005). As regards the relative importance of primary and secondary effects, Boudon referred to the interpretation of cultural inequality as the major influence of educational disparities as a "cross sectional illusion" (Boudon 1974, p. 110) and maintained that "[…] the primary effects necessarily become attenuated over time, whereas the secondary effects are exponential" (Boudon 1974, p. 111). Although his framework neither offers a formalization of the decision situation nor associates quantitative measures to the decision parameters, it was pioneering with respect to the distinction of different levels at which educational differentials are generated and constitutes the basis of more formalized sociological rational choice models that emerged several years later (key theoretical contributions include Gambetta 1987; Erikson and Jonsson 1996; Breen and Goldthorpe 1997; Morgan 1998, 2002, 2005; cf. Maaz et al. 2010). All sociological rational choice models share the core theoretical arguments of rationally acting individuals who aim to maximize expected utility by investing in education, and that educational choices serve both economic and social goals. Yet, they differ along dimensions such as the degree of formalization and explication of behavioral assumptions and the assumed degree of rationality in human action. Also, they comprise a range of theoretical perspectives and differ rather widely with respect to the hypothesized mechanisms of how the decision parameters interact with social origin (Jæger 2007; Kristen 1999; Maaz et al. 2010; Stocké 2012).

For instance, as regards the hypothesis that families in higher social positions invest more in education than families from lower backgrounds due to the social returns they expect from intergenerational status preservation, the preservation of existing social networks and conformity to dominant peer group behavior (Boudon 1974; Keller and Zavalloni 1964), Erikson and Jonsson (1996) argued that lower-class families may as well expect higher returns from ambitious educational choices as they lack alternative resources for economic advancement, such as the inheritance of capital or business. Gambetta (1987) argued that precisely due to initial social distances the benefits associated with ambitious educational choices may not be lower but higher for students from lower strata because the same income increase leads to a greater positive mobility jump for them. Assumptions such as weaker social sanctions for leaving school in the working class and that individuals maximize utility on the basis of 'psychic costs' may "simply provide greater scope for ex-post rationalization of what nonetheless remains a non-desirable outcome" (Gambetta 1987, p. 183; cf. also R. Becker and Lauterbach 2007).

Similarly, it is most commonly assumed that cultural constraints affect students' educational outcomes at the level of primary effects due to differences in the family's educationally-relevant resources, the opportunity to acquire school-relevant skills and parents' capacity to navigate their children through the educational system (e.g., Boudon 1974; Breen and Goldthorpe 1997; Erikson and Jonsson 1996). In contrast, Gambetta (1987) argued that cultural constraints generate disparities primarily at the level of secondary effects. Opposed to the human capital theoretical assumption that it is the objective possibility of achieving significant returns once on the labor market that mostly matters to students' educational choices, Gambetta maintained that what essentially counts are students' life plans: Students who plan to pursue future careers that do not require high educational qualifications will invest lower amounts in education because they expect lower returns to education as their life plans will not allow them to take full advantage of high educational qualifications. Hence, a poor cultural background will affect educational choices through mechanisms such as a reduced capacity to construct ambitious life plans rather than by directly altering the opportunities for their fulfillment.

4.3   Empirical evidence: Socialization or individual choice?

Both status socialization theory and rational choice approaches have received considerable empirical attention and theoretical discussion in the last decades and are commonly drawn on to explain educational differentials across the population (Konczal and Haller 2008; Lloyd et al. 2008; Morgan 2005; Relikowski et al. 2012). Both research traditions share important key assumptions by emphasizing the role of different preconditions for educational success on the one hand, and of students' social environments on the other hand. Yet, they differ rather strongly with respect to the mechanisms they assume to mediate the effect from social origin on attainment. Rational choice theories start from the assumption that students form their own expectations after considering the same exogenous influences as their significant others (Boudon 1974; Jæger 2007; Lloyd et al. 2008). The Wisconsin researchers identified the influence of students' significant others, and most specifically adoption processes, as the central mechanism in the attainment process. Besides the controversial assumption of a causal effect from aspirations on attainment levels, the view of students as more or less passive respondents that do not evaluate outside influences themselves but primarily obtain their aspirations from their "definers" (Haller and Woelfel 1972, p. 594) clearly contrasts with the conception of students as active and rational decision makers (Lloyd et al. 2008).

Recalling the consideration that respondent-reported educational plans may not be understood as value orientations but reflect students' perceptions of the opportunity structure, Morgan (1998, 2002) made the case that a causal interpretation of the association between significant others' influence and student aspirations is not necessarily inconsistent with the assumption of rationally acting individuals. If educational plans are conceptualized as reality-based expectations, adoption and imitation processes must not be irrational responses to external coercion but can alternatively be specified as lower-order mechanisms by which students form their subjective probability of successfully completing a given educational alternative. As students cannot fully rely on level of past performance as accurate indicators for likely future success, for instance due to a lack of information about learning tasks they will encounter in college, they may consider the views and actions of their significant others to overcome this lack of knowledge: Their subjective probability of success may be influenced by the observation of the success or failure of similar others, supportive parents will be more able to convince their children that they will receive adequate financial support, and teachers may convince students that they will succeed in higher education (Manski 2004; Morgan 1998, 2002). Then, the extent to which students' expectations can be considered as rational will partly depend on the degree to which adoption and imitation mechanisms dominate rational self-reflection, and on the extent to which the expectations and actions of students' significant others are based on rational criteria. Following the observation that significant others' expectations are influenced by both student and family characteristics (Sewell et al. 1969; Sewell et al. 1970), Morgan (1998) argued that the latter assumption can be expected to be met at least to some extent.

Having established that the extent to which the hypothesized mechanisms of both research traditions can be conceived of as conflicting is a matter of the precise theoretical meaning which given to student aspirations, or in other words that the Wisconsin model can as well be explained from a rational choice perspective, the question remains to be addressed whether there is evidence to claim supremacy of one perspective over the other. The reconceptualization of educational plans as rational expectations does not validate the Wisconsin model as the possibility cannot be excluded that the association between the influence of significant others and students' college plans is the product of the joint perception and evaluation of the same exogenous influences by both parties (Jencks et al. 1983; Morgan 1998). Further, the validity of the model was challenged by the observation that it failed to fully mediate the effect from social origin on attainment levels on the one hand, and due to its limited power to explain the variation in the attainments of Blacks on the other hand. At first sight, rational choice theoretical approaches appear to be advantageous with respect to both considerations. They can explain lower investments in education by minority groups by their lower expected returns in the labor market, and they can theoretically fully explain the association between social origin and educational attainment with reference to secondary effects of stratification. Yet, the hypothesized mechanisms the sociological rational choice literature assumes to generate disparities were shown to be discussed controversially. While the formalization of theoretical models and the explication of behavioral assumptions is one of the major contributions of the sociological rational choice literature, direct empirical evidence that leaves no alternative interpretations is scarce (some exceptions are R. Becker 2003; R. Becker and Hecken 2009; Davies et al. 2002).

Partly, this situation results from the preference of many rational choice researchers to use actual transition and attainment data instead of subjective data in the form of respondent-reported aspirations and expectations (Jæger 2007; Morgan 1998, 2002, 2004, 2005). While the latter may be biased and endogenous, the inference of preference distributions from observed transitions not only rests on the strong assumption that what individuals are observed to do is precisely what they intended to do. Also, it was discussed that analyses of actual transition data provide empirical results that are typically consistent with alternative rational-choice theoretical perspectives and specifications of preferences and expectations (Jæger 2007; Manski 2004). For instance, peer effects are often interpreted as a product of socializing environmental factors, but results from existing studies are equally consistent with the rational choice theoretical explanation that students themselves choose to conform to the dominant behavior in their peer groups to maximize social utility (Hechter and Kanazawa 1997; Jæger 2007).

Following these considerations, Morgan (1996, 1998) argued that the question whether educational attainment is most usefully considered as the product of socialization mechanisms or of individual choices can be answered only when outside influences are explicitly considered that may simultaneously influence the cost-benefit analysis of students and their significant others. His analysis of the development of the educational expectations of Blacks and Whites in the United States provided some first insight by showing that student expectations are not only significantly associated with significant others' influence but that they also follow labor market trends (Morgan 1996). This observation has important implications insofar that it simultaneously suggests the potential value of the inclusion of exogenous variables to improve the explanatory power of status attainment models, and that respondent-reported expectations are beliefs that are based on reality considerations and may in fact matter to students' educational behavior. From these findings, Morgan (1996, 1998, 2002) concluded that rational choice theories provide a clear starting point for micro-models to explain the variation in educational attainment, but that there is no evidence that the Wisconsin model can be outperformed by a structural model that does not explicitly model students' own beliefs. Rather, a combined theory that explicitly models belief formation and its implications for everyday commitment may serve to provide additional insight into how students orient themselves toward the future (Morgan 1998, 2002, 2005).

In consideration that it is not the objective but the perceived costs and returns that affect the formation of educational expectations and decisions, and that revealed preference analysis may be overly pessimistic and rely on unrealistic (and untestable) assumptions about how aspirations are formed and affect educational choices, researchers from different disciplines have come to the conclusion that choice data alone does not provide an adequate empirical foundation for the econometric analysis of decision making with partial information (Jensen 2010; Manski 1993, 2004; Morgan 2002). For instance, observations such as a gap between respondent-reported aspirations and eventual attainment levels, and deviations from actual and perceived returns to education, do not prove that subjective beliefs are meaningless expressions that are not formed based on reality considerations. Instead, it may as well be the case that decisions are influenced by other factors that were unknown to students at the time aspirations or expected returns were reported, or that they were formed on the basis of incorrect information (Manski 1993, 2004; Morgan 2002). In this vein, Manski (2004, p. 1336) raised the legitimized question: "If experts disagree on the returns to schooling, is it plausible that youth have rational expectations? I think not." Acknowledging that the combination of choice data with subjective data will improve the ability to predict behavior by allowing to relax and validate assumptions about the explanatory potential and formation of student aspirations and expectations (Manski 2004), researchers from different disciplines, including economists, have turned to the investigation of subjective data to obtain more fine-grained insight into the micro-mechanisms that generate attainment differentials (Manski 1993, 2004; Morgan 1996, 1998, 2002, 2004, 2005; Schneider and Stevenson 1999).

References

Alexander, K. L., Cook, M., & McDill, E. L. (1978). Curriculum Tracking and Educational Stratification: Some Further Evidence. *American Sociological Review, 43*(1), 47-66.
Alexander, K. L., & Cook, M. A. (1979). The Motivational Relevance of Educational Plans: Questioning the Conventional Wisdom. *Social Psychology Quarterly, 42*(3), 202-213.
Alexander, K. L., & Eckland, B. K. (1975). Contextual Effects in the High School Attainment Process. *American Sociological Review, 40*(3), 402-416.
Alexander, K. L., Eckland, B. K., & Griffin, L. J. (1975). The Wisconsin Model of Socioeconomic Achievement: A Replication. *American Journal of Sociology, 81*(2), 324-342.
Becker, G. (1964). *Human Capital: A Theoretical and Empirical Analysis, with Special Reference to Education* (1st ed.). Chicago: University of Chicago Press.
Becker, G. (1993). *Human Capital: A Theoretical and Empirical Analysis, with Special Reference to Education* (3rd ed.). Chicago: University of Chicago Press.
Becker, R. (2003). Educational Expansion and Persistent Inequalities of Education: Utilizing Expected Utility Theory to Explain Increasing Participation Rates in Upper Secondary School in the Federal Republic of Germany. *European Sociological Review, 19*(1), 1-24.
Becker, R., & Hecken, A. E. (2009). Higher Education or Vocational Training? An Empirical Test of the Rational Action Model of Educational Choices Suggested by Breen and Goldthorpe and Esser. *Acta Sociologica, 52*(1), 25-45.
Becker, R., & Lauterbach, W. (2007). Bildung als Privileg – Ursachen, Mechanismen, Prozesse und Wirkungen. In R. Becker & W. Lauterbach (Eds.), *Bildung als Privileg? Erklärungen und Befunde zu den Ursachen der Bildungsungleichheit* (pp. 9-41). Wiesbaden: VS Verlag für Sozialwissenschaften.
Blau, P. M., & Duncan, O. D. (1967). *The American Occupational Structure*. New York: Wiley.
Boudon, R. (1974). *Education, Opportunity and Social Inequality: Changing Prospects in Western Society*. New York: Wiley.
Breen, R., & Goldthorpe, J. H. (1997). Explaining Educational Differentials: Towards a Formal Rational Action Theory. *Rationality and Society, 9*(3), 275-305.
Coleman, J. S., Campbell, E. Q., Hobson, J. C., McPartland, J., Mood, A. M., Weinfeld, F. D., & York, R. L. (1966). *Equality of Educational Opportunity*. Washington, D.C.: U.S. Government Printing Office.
Davies, R., Heinesen, E., & Holm, A. (2002). The Relative Risk Aversion Hypothesis of Educational Choice. *Journal of Population Economics, 15*, 683-713.
Erikson, R., & Jonsson, J. O. (1996). Explaining Class Inequality in Education: The Swedish Test Case. In R. Erikson & J. O. Jonsson (Eds.), *Can Education Be Equalized? The Swedish Case* (pp. 1-63). Stockholm: Westview Press.
Gambetta, D. (1987). *Were They Pushed Or Did They Jump? Individual Decision Mechanisms in Education*. Cambridge: Cambridge University Press.
Haller, A. O. (1982). Reflections on the Social Psychology of Status Attainment. In R. M. Hauser, A. O. Haller, D. Mechanic & T. S. Hauser (Eds.), *Social Structure and Behavior: Essays in Honor of William Hamilton Sewell* (pp. 3-28). New York: Academic Press.
Haller, A. O., & Portes, A. (1973). Status Attainment Processes. *Sociology of Education, 46*(1), 51-91.

Haller, A. O., & Woelfel, J. (1972). Significant Others and Their Expectations: Concepts and Instruments to Measure Interpersonal Influence on Status Aspirations. *Rural Sociology, 87*(4), 591-622.

Hechter, M., & Kanazawa, S. (1997). Sociological Rational Choice Theory. *Annual Review of Sociology, 23*, 191-214.

Jæger, M. M. (2007). Economic and Social Returns to Educational Choices: Extending the Utility Function. *Rationality and Society, 19*(4), 451-483.

Jencks, C., Crouse, J., & Mueser, P. (1983). The Wisconsin Model of Status Attainment: A National Replication with Improved Measures of Ability and Aspiration. *Sociology of Education, 56*(1), 3-19.

Jensen, R. (2010). The (Perceived) Returns to Education and Demand for Schooling. *The Quarterly Journal of Economics, 125*(2), 515-548.

Keller, S., & Zavalloni, M. (1964). Ambition and Social Class: A Respecification. *Social Forces, 43*(1), 58-70.

Kerckhoff, A. C. (1976). The Status Attainment Process: Socialization or Allocation? *Social Forces, 55*(2), 368-381.

Kerckhoff, A. C. (1977). The Realism of Educational Ambitions in England and the United States. *American Sociological Review, 42*(4), 563-571.

Kerckhoff, A. C., & Campbell, R. T. (1977). Social Status Differences in the Explanation of Educational Ambition. *Social Forces, 5*(3), 701-714.

Kerckhoff, A. C., & Huff, J. L. (1974). Parental Influence on Educational Goals. *Sociometry, 37*(3), 307-327.

Konczal, L., & Haller, W. (2008). Fit to Miss, but Matched to Hatch: Success Factors Among the Second Generation's Disadvantaged in South Florida. *The ANNALS of the American Academy of Political and Social Science, 620*, 161-176.

Kristen, C. (1999). *Bildungsentscheidungen und Bildungsungleichheit: Ein Überblick über den Forschungsstand* (MZES Working Paper No. 5). Retrieved August 7, 2012, from http://www.mzes.unimannheim.de/publications/wp/wp-5.pdf

Lloyd, K. M., Leicht, K. T., & Sullivan, T. A. (2008). Minority College Aspirations, Expectations and Applications under the Texas Top 10% Law. *Social Forces, 86*(3), 1105-1137.

Maaz, K., Baumert, J., & Trautwein, U. (2010). Genese sozialer Ungleichheit im institutionellen Kontext der Schule: Wo entsteht und vergrößert sich soziale Ungleichheit? In H.-H. Krüger, U. Rabe-Kleberg, R.-T. Kramer & J. Budde (Eds.), *Bildungsungleichheit Revisited: Bildung und soziale Ungleichheit vom Kindergarten bis zur Hochschule* (pp. 69-102). Wiesbaden: VS Verlag für Sozialwissenschaften.

Manski, C. F. (1993). Adolescent Econometricians: How Do Youth Infer the Returns to Education? In C. T. Clotfelter & M. Rothschild (Eds.), *Studies of Supply and Demand in Higher Education* (pp. 43-57). Chicago: University of Chicago Press.

Manski, C. F. (2004). Measuring Expectations. *Econometrica, 72*(5), 1329-1376.

Mickelson, R. A. (1990). The Attitude-Achievement Paradox Among Black Adolescents. *Sociology of Education, 63*(1), 44-61.

Morgan, S. L. (1996). Trends in Black-White Differences in Educational Expectations: 1980-1992. *Sociology of Education, 69*(4), 308-319.

Morgan, S. L. (1998). Adolescent Educational Expectations: Rationalized, Fantasized, or Both? *Rationality and Society, 10*(2), 131-162.

References

Morgan, S. L. (2002). Modeling Preparatory Commitment and Non-Repeatable Decisions: Information-Processing, Preference Formation and Educational Attainment. *Rationality and Society, 14*(4), 387-429.

Morgan, S. L. (2004). Methodologist as Arbitrator: Five Models for Black-White Differences in the Causal Effect of Expectations on Attainment *Sociological Methods & Research, 33*(1), 3-53.

Morgan, S. L. (2005). *On the Edge of Commitment: Educational Attainment and Race in the United States.* Stanford, CA: Stanford University Press.

Paulus, W., & Blossfeld, H.-P. (2007). Schichtspezifische Präferenzen oder sozioökonomisches Entscheidungskalkül? Zur Rolle elterlicher Bildungsaspirationen im Entscheidungsprozess beim Übergang von der Grundschule in die Sekundarstufe. *Zeitschrift für Pädagogik, 53*(4), 491-508.

Portes, A., & Wilson, K. L. (1976). Black-White Differences in Educational Attainment. *American Sociological Review, 41*(3), 414-431.

Reder, M. W. (1967). Gary Becker's Human Capital: A Review Article. *The Journal of Human Resources, 2*(1), 97-104.

Relikowski, I., Yilmaz, E., & Blossfeld, H.-P. (2012). Wie lassen sich die hohen Bildungsaspirationen von Migranten erklären? Eine Mixed-Methods-Studie zur Rolle von strukturellen Aufstiegschancen und individueller Bildungserfahrung [Special issue]. *Kölner Zeitschrift für Soziologie und Sozialpsychologie,* 111-136.

Schneider, B. L., & Stevenson, D. (1999). *The Ambitious Generation: America's Teenagers, Motivated but Directionless.* New Haven: Yale University Press.

Sewell, W. H., Haller, A. O., & Ohlendorf, G. W. (1970). The Educational and Early Occupational Status Attainment Process: Replication and Revision. *American Sociological Review, 35*(6), 1014-1027.

Sewell, W. H., Haller, A. O., & Portes, A. (1969). The Educational and Early Occupational Attainment Process. *American Sociological Review, 34*(1), 82-92.

Stocké, V. (2012). Das Rational-Choice Paradigma in der Bildungssoziologie. In U. Bauer, U. H. Bittlingmayer & A. Scherr (Eds.), *Handbuch Bildungs- und Erziehungssoziologie* (pp. 423-436). Wiesbaden: VS Verlag für Sozialwissenschaften.

Xiao, J. (2002). Determinants of Salary Growth in Shenzhen, China: An Analysis of Formal Education, On-the-job Training, and Adult Education with a Three-level Model. *Economics of Education Review, 21*(6), 557-577.

Educational aspirations, expectations and choices of migrants

5

The models presented above were originally developed to explain inter-class variations in educational attainment. In the context of an increased awareness of the existence and persistence of wide disparities in the educational outcomes of natives and migrants in many western countries, features and frameworks from both research traditions have been increasingly employed to address questions of ethnic attainment differentials. In view of the negative selection of many first-generation migrants in terms of social origin and (country-specific) human capital compared to natives, traditional explanations that focus on a systematically different distribution of economic, cultural and social resources across families certainly appear promising as potential explanations for the lower attainment levels of migrants (R. Becker and Schubert 2011; Gresch et al. 2012; Heath and Brinbaum 2007; Kalter 2006; Kalter and Granato 2002; Kristen and Dollmann 2010). Indeed, measures of the family's socioeconomic position explain a significant proportion of the performance and attainment gap between natives and migrants (Heath and Brinbaum 2007; Stanat and Christensen 2006a). Also, empirical studies consistently point to significantly higher background-adjusted educational aspirations, and often expectations, in migrant families (Heath and Brinbaum 2007; Stanat and Christensen 2006a).

Yet, empirical evidence points to a relatively stable pattern of mixed evidence for the background-adjusted attainment levels and transition probabilities of different groups of immigrants in western OECD countries. While the attainment gap converges and certain immigrant groups even outperform the native population when background characteristics are taken into account, the gap does not completely vanish in the case of others (for overview over different countries see Heath and Brinbaum 2007). For instance, based on census data from 1991 to 2004,

Kristen and Granato (2007) found second-generation Turks, (Ex-)Yugoslavs, Italians, Spaniards and Portuguese in Germany to have a lower initial probability to attain the highest level of general education, or to be in preparation for the completion of this qualification if they were still in education, while Greeks have a chance to obtain this qualification similar to that of natives. When background characteristics are taken into account, these differences completely disappear for Turks and Yugoslavs. Greeks and Iberians outperform their German peers, but the attainment gap does not fully close in the case of Italians.

In view of the comparatively low correlation between the family's socioeconomic position and the children's attainment levels in the migrant population, the question has been raised whether traditional models and conventional measures can be used exactly as they are to account for the less advantageous transition patterns of migrants, or whether they have to be broadened to better understand the emergence of ethnic disparities (Diefenbach 2010; Heath and Brinbaum 2007; Lehmann et al. 2002; Nauck et al. 1998; Stanat and Christensen 2006a). The following sections consider the suitability of traditional approaches to explain social disparities in educational attainment to investigate the emergence of ethnic differentials in education in some detail. Section 5.1 provides an overview over methodological and human capital theoretical considerations that are discussed in the current literature to explain the observation of background-adjusted attainment differentials between natives and migrants. Section 5.2 discusses the mechanisms that are assumed to generate background-adjusted ethnic disparities in education with respect to empirical results. In this context, the question is addressed to what extent available evidence leaves conclusions about the role of educational aspirations in the explanation of the ethnic attainment gap.

5.1 Explaining background-adjusted ethnic differentials in education

A first consideration in the attempt to explain the significantly lower educational outcomes of migrants when background characteristics are controlled for is that conventional measures of the family's socioeconomic position, which are commonly based on level of parental education and occupation and assumed to reflect material and educationally-relevant resources, may capture the preconditions for students' educational success in migrant families to a lesser extent than in native families. For instance, highly educated immigrant parents may be forced to take on lower-level positions in the labor market than members of the majority group with a comparable educational background due to conditions such as a lack of demand for origin-specific human capital, the non-accreditation of educational qualifications or because of cross-country differences in the quality of education (Diefenbach 2010; Heath and Brinbaum 2007). Then, measures of the family's socioeconomic position may adequately reflect the financial situation in migrant families but not necessarily the availability of educationally-relevant resources in the form of cultural and social capital, which are considered particularly crucial for students' educational success in view of the moderate importance ascribed to economic resources due to the low cost of education in most western countries (Nauck 2011).

Following the consideration that measurement difficulties may contribute to but not fully explain the observation of background-adjusted educational differentials, the current literature explicitly takes into consideration the existence of migration-specific conditions that influence the educational outcomes of migrants *net* of social origin. A framework which has received increased attention in this attempt is Boudon's (1974) distinction between primary and secondary effects of stratification, which has been extended to effects of ethnic origin. Primary effects of ethnic origin relate to conditions that specifically affect the attainment levels of migrants by influencing their probability of success. Secondary effects of ethnic origin are the product of differential evaluations of the costs and benefits that are associated with a given educational alternative in native and migrant families net of their probability of success (R. Becker and Schubert 2011; Boudon 1974; Heath and Brinbaum 2007; Relikowski et al. 2010). In empirical studies, the term secondary effects of ethnic origin is often used to refer to significantly different transition probabilities of natives and migrants when level of educational performance and stratification effects are taken into account (Heath and Brinbaum 2007; Kristen and Dollmann 2010).

At the level of primary effects, a central explanation for the observation of background-adjusted educational disparities between natives and migrants relates to the limited transferability of origin-specific human capital as a direct influence of students' educational performance. For instance, the educational resources that are required for the development of school-relevant skills are to some extent specific to the particular educational setting. If immigrant parents who grew up and attended school in a different context have not acquired them through their own educational careers, their resources may not prove as useful in the educational system in the receiving country: Parents who are less familiar with the educational system will be less able to support their children in the acquisition of educationally-relevant skills, to give strategic advice such as what to study most intensively and to interfere when difficulties occur (Kristen and Granato 2007; Kristen et al. 2011; Schuchart and Maaz 2007).

Another prime example for country-specific cultural capital are language skills. While majority language skills not only predict the educational outcomes of migrants but also those of their native peers, the former face specific conditions insofar as their heritage language(s) often differ(s) from the language of instruction in school, and that they may have poorer opportunities for language acquisition due to the use of (a) language(s) other than the majority language in the family (Esser 2006; Klieme et al. 2010; Kristen and Dollmann 2010; Relikowski et al. 2010). Besides the direct effect of low levels of majority language skills in students themselves, lacking fluency in the majority language in parents may affect students' educational outcomes due to a lower capacity to provide support with school work and the learning of school-relevant skills. Also, language barriers may limit the access to important information about the educational system and reinforce the negative effects of lacking knowledge about the educational setting in the receiving country (Diefenbach 2010).

Variations in the social capital of migrant and native students are discussed as a further source of educational differentials (Kao and Thompson 2003; Nauck 2011; Roth et al. 2010). The term 'social capital' is discussed along several dimensions, including broader conceptions and approaches that assume the social network to influence students' educational outcomes by promoting or discouraging motivation and achievement by communicating expectations or by influencing students' perceptions of the value of education for future socioeconomic mobility (Caplan et al. 1991; Fuligni 1997, 1998; Kao and Thompson 2003). Human capital theoretical approaches often use the term to refer to the actual and potential resources individuals have at their disposal not only within the family but also in the wider social network. As regards the situation of migrants, the negative effects of the systematically unequal distribution of educationally-relevant resources across families may be reinforced if migrants primarily entertain relationships in a relatively homogenous network in terms of economic and country-specific human capital that cannot provide access to additional resources such as information, help with school work and financial support (Bourdieu 1983; Kao and Thompson 2003; Lin 2001; Nauck 2011; Roth et al. 2010; Beck et al. 2010).

Besides the existence of conditions that lower migrants' actual and perceived probabilities of success, the literature discusses the possibility that attainment differentials between natives and migrants are generated at the level of secondary effects. As migrants may face conditions that influence their evaluation of the costs and benefits that are associated with a given educational alternative and are not related to their position in the stratification system, they may make systematically different investment decisions than native families (Diefenbach 2010). For instance, high educational qualifications may be perceived as less instrumental for economic advancement if migrants plan to live in their country of origin, or fear to be forced to move to their country of origin in the case of an uncertain resident status. If the educational qualifications obtained in the receiving country are formally valueless in the event of remigration, they may be perceived as constituting unnecessary cost in terms of the money, time and effort associated with an additional educational investment (Diefenbach 2010; Nauck 2011). The human capital paradigm assumes conditions that lower students' expected returns to education, such as anticipated labor market discrimination, to lead to less ambitious educational decisions in migrant families (G. Becker 1993). A further consideration is that migrant parents may identify career options for their children that allow them to become economically successful in the ethnic economy and do not necessarily require high levels of education. While prestigious positions in the ethnic network may be continuous with existing social bonds and can be attained comparatively easily, in-group career options generally have a relatively low ceiling and may lead to an underinvestment in education that, in the longer run, limits the opportunities for upward mobility in the larger society (Diefenbach and Nauck 1997; Wiley 1967, 1970).

The direction in which migration-specific conditions will influence the attainment outcomes of migrants at the level of secondary effects is less clear compared to the mechanisms that are assumed to lead to their lower performance outcomes. For example, opposed to the notion that migrants may perceive high educational qualifications as less instrumental than natives, it has been suggested that migrants assign comparatively high instrumental value to education to achieve upward mobility in the receiving country. As many first-generation migrants find themselves in comparatively unfavorable labor-market positions, high educational qualifications of their children may be perceived as the main path to upward mobility (Kao and Tienda 1995; Relikowski et al. 2012; Vallet 2007). Similarly, anticipated labor market discrimination must not necessarily lead to lower investments in education but may as well encourage students to make ambitious educational choices to compensate for this disadvantage and due to the lower opportunity cost of additional education (Sue and Okazaki 1990).

5.2 Empirical evidence and discussion

Despite the growing endeavor to obtain more fine-grained insight into the processes that shape ethnic disparities in education, direct evidence remains scarce (Beck et al. 2010; R. Becker and Hecken 2009; Relikowski et al. 2012; Van der Werfhorst and van Tubergen 2007). Existing studies often provide data on the distribution of the educational aspirations, expectations or decisions in native and migrant families. Yet, they provide little data on individual belief-formation and decision-making processes (Kristen and Dollmann 2010). With few exceptions (e.g., Kristen et al. 2008), empirical studies provide indirect evidence by estimating background-adjusted coefficients for migrants in models to explain educational aspirations, expectations or transition probabilities, and present a variety of hypotheses to explain the existence of significant coefficients of which all or at least several are in line with empirical results. As regards evidence for Germany, empirical applications of models to explain the attainment gap have almost exclusively been confined to the analysis of subjective data in the form of respondent-reported educational aspirations and expectations.

Also, the empirical investigation of the mechanisms that generate ethnic effects is related to several methodological difficulties. First, biased estimates will result from the use of conventional measures of the family's socioeconomic position due to conditions such as the limited transferability of origin-specific human capital in migrant families. Second, it is difficult to identify and disentangle the precise mechanisms that generate educational differentials in view that the same conditions may simultaneously influence students' achievements at the level of primary and secondary effects, and that different mechanisms may mutually reinforce, decrease or offset one another (B. Becker 2010). For example, anticipated discrimination is most commonly assumed to primarily influence attainment outcomes at the level of secondary effects by means of altering students' expected returns to education. Yet, directly or indirectly experienced discrimination may as well affect students' beliefs in the value of education for getting ahead and thereby directly influence level of achievement motivation and performance (Fordham and Ogbu 1991; Heath and Brinbaum 2007; Ogbu 1991). Homogenous networks of migrants that do not provide access to additional educationally-relevant resources were discussed to potentially reinforce the negative effects of the unequal distribution of cultural and economic capital across native and migrant families. Alternatively, it has been argued that comparatively high levels of ambition in migrant networks may reduce these effects (cf. B. Becker 2010; Vallet 2007; Zhou 1997).

Further, available data sets do typically not allow for complex subgroup analyses, if at all. However, the considerations above suggest that the mechanisms the literature assumes to potentially lead to a systematically different investment behavior in native and migrant families do not universally apply to the 'whole migrant population' but vary in extent and direction depending on the precise migration circumstances (Diefenbach 2010; Relikowski et al. 2010). For example, there is evidence that migrant networks are less advantageous for students' educational advancement in terms of the lower-prestige positions mi-

5.2 Empirical evidence and discussion

grants occupy in the labor market, and that certain immigrant groups tend to primarily maintain relationships with persons from their own ethnic group (for Germany, e.g., Roth et al. 2010). Yet, an orientation toward an inner-ethnic career requires a sufficient size of the ethnic network, and more specifically the existence of an ethnic economy (Diefenbach 2010; Wallace 2007). Similarly, it is plausible to assume that the option to remigrate to the country of origin may negatively influence migrants' expected returns to education only if high qualifications are indeed perceived as less instrumental in the case of remigration. As a counterexample, Kristen et al. (2008) showed adolescents of Turkish origin in Germany to be more likely to enter higher education than their native peers provided they had obtained the entrance qualification, and could partly ascribe this pattern to the fact that vocational education and training is much less valued in Turkey compared to the competitive VET system in Germany. On the one hand, these considerations may, at least partly, account for the observed variation in the background-adjusted educational success across different groups of immigrants in Germany. On the other hand, they suggest that cross-country variations in the extent to which the attainment gap closes when background characteristics are taken into account can – apart from the use of different data and measurement techniques – be explained by contextual differences and the focus on different immigrant groups (Heath and Brinbaum 2007; Kristen and Dollmann 2010).

Despite the lack of knowledge about the precise mechanisms that are theoretically assumed to generate primary and secondary effects of ethnic origin, available evidence gives rise to several implications with respect to the applicability of traditional models to explain social disparities in educational attainment to the explanation of ethnic disparities in education. The findings that the family's socioeconomic position explains a large part of the attainment gap between natives and migrants, and that migrants have significantly higher background-adjusted educational aspirations, and often expectations, than natives, support the notion that educational attainment is a function of social origin not only in native but also in migrant families (R. Becker and Schubert 2011; Heath and Brinbaum 2007). However, the literature also points to a clear pattern of comparatively high educational aspirations in migrant families even when the family's social position is not taken into account (for overview over different countries see Stanat and Christensen 2006a; Kristen and Dollmann 2010; Stubbe et al. 2012). Empirical studies on the transition from primary into secondary education further provide evidence that secondary effects of social origin play a less important role in shaping the educational decisions of migrants compared to their native counterparts (R. Becker and Schubert 2011; Relikowski et al. 2012).

The latter findings indicate that the educational behavior of migrants from lower social backgrounds does not conform to the orientations in native families in a comparable social position (Schuchart and Maaz 2007) and challenge the interpretation of ethnic disparities in educational attainment as a result of a socially stratified structure of costs and benefits along the lines discussed by Boudon (1974) and Keller and Zavalloni (1964). Rather, available evidence is supportive of the hypothesis that lower-class families may expect higher benefits from ambitious educational choices due to the greater mobility jump they expect from high educational qualifications (Gambetta 1987) and the lack of alternative resources for economic advancement (Erikson and Jonsson 1996). These notions, in turn, are in line with the hypothesis of migrants' desire to achieve upward mobility in the receiving country as a central explanation for their comparatively high educational aspirations and expectations (Kao and Tienda 1995).

Empirical studies often explain significantly higher (background-adjusted) aspirations and expectations in migrant families with reference to rational choice theoretical considerations. Yet, as discussed in the previous chapter, available results can typically as well be explained from a socialization perspective. Although often not made explicit by researchers, the current literature can be shown to be based on the socialization mechanisms as identified and interpreted by the Wisconsin researchers (Sewell et al. 1969; Sewell et al. 1970): The interpretation of higher background-adjusted aspirations in the migrant population as indicating the existence of secondary effects of ethnic origin implies the assumption of a causal effect from aspirations on later attainment levels. The crucial role ascribed to students' significant others is not least reflected by the fact that empirical surveys typically investigate parental instead of students' own aspirations. While this approach can be partly explained by the strong focus on the investigation of the transition from primary into secondary education, when students are still fairly young and parents are conceived of as the primary decision makers, it is common practice to assess parental instead of students' own aspirations also at later stages of the educational career (e.g., Roth et al. 2010; Schuchart and Maaz 2007). As concerns the perhaps most popular explanation for the observation of higher educational aspirations in migrant families, the desire for upward mobility that is perceived as accessible by means of high educational qualifications obtained by the next generation, Heath and Brinbaum (2007) pointed out that "it is important to recognize that a crucial element of the positive selection argument when applied to the education of the children of immigrants is that parental aspirations are transmitted to the children" (Heath and Brinbaum 2007, p. 300). Apparently, such commonly used arguments exclude the interpretation of the association between students' and their parents' aspirations as the product of the simultaneous consideration and evaluation of the same exogenous influences by both parties, but imply the assumption of a causal effect from parents' on their children's aspirations.

As mentioned above, several researchers have interpreted the observation of higher (background-adjusted) educational aspirations, expectations and decisions in migrant families as indicating that it is not lower levels of ambition but primarily features of the opportunity structure that hinder migrants to translate their high motivational potential into attainment and matter most to the emergence and persistence of the attainment gap (e.g., Gresch et al. 2012; Klieme et al. 2010; Relikowski et al. 2010). Yet other researchers have interpreted the high aspirations in migrant families to mean that migrants are positively selected for their educational ambition due to the existence of conditions that are specific to the migration context (cf. Heath and Brinbaum 2007). The considerations above, along with the observation of comparatively high aspirations in migrant families when background characteristics are not taken into account, certainly appear to support this notion. However, the interpretation of available evidence requires considerable caution.

First, several theoretical arguments and empirical observations were discussed in chapter 3 to not only seriously challenge the predictive value of respondent-reported aspirations but also the notion of their causal effect on attainment levels. Also, the question was raised to what extent respondent-reported educational aspirations have the same meaning across students (B. Becker 2010; Goyette 2008). As regards the migrant population specifically, the concern has been voiced that migrants may be particularly likely to report unrealistically high aspirations due to the limited transferability of origin-specific human capital to the educational setting in the receiving country (R. Becker 2013b; Gresch et al. 2012; Relikowski et al. 2012). The finding that the aspirations of migrant parents often exceed teacher recommendations, and of comparatively large gaps between expressed aspirations and expectations and later attainment levels of migrant students, appear to support this notion (Ditton et al. 2005; Gresch et al. 2012; Harazd 2007). Also, there is tentative evidence to support the hypothesis of lesser knowledge about and awareness of the existence of barriers in the educational system in migrant families (Relikowski et al. 2012). These conditions may certainly affect the predictive value of the aspirations and expectations expressed by migrants. However, the possibility remains that students commit to their aspirations but fail to deal effectively with the barriers they experience in their implementation (cf. B. Becker 2010). Hence, existing evidence is neither in conflict with the hypothesis that migrants are positively selected for their educational ambition, nor with the claim that it is primarily features of the opportunity structure that matter to the emergence and persistence of ethnic differentials in educational attainment. Yet, it was also discussed that aspirations may not only reflect level of motivation but also students' subjective probabilities of success (Alexander and Cook 1979; Bourdieu 1973; Jencks et al. 1983; Kerckhoff 1976). As such, the possibility cannot be excluded either that the aspirations and expectations expressed by natives are adapted to their probabilities of success to a stronger extent compared to their peers with a migration background (cf. B. Becker 2010). Thus, it appears that the question of the extent to which the aspirations and expectations reported by natives and migrants are directly comparable, and hence whether the higher aspirations expressed by migrants can be interpreted as indicating lower levels of ambition among their native peers, remain to be empirically addressed.

Second, the great majority of empirical studies investigate the transitions from primary into secondary education (Beck et al. 2010; Maaz et al. 2010) and assess parents' but not students' own aspirations or expectations. This focus is, at least partly, attributable to the significance of this transition in determining students' future career opportunities and the particularly strong association between social and ethnic background and track selection at this early point in the German educational system (Maaz and Nagy 2009; Stubbe 2009; Stubbe et al. 2012). The respective studies not only point to significantly higher aspirations of migrant parents, but also to more favorable background-adjusted educational decisions and transitions into secondary education in migrant families (R. Becker and Schubert 2011; Relikowski et al. 2010). However, empirical data also shows that the type of secondary education attended is a rough indicator for students' eventual attainment levels only, and that track changes mostly occur in the direction of lower types of schools (Stubbe et al. 2012). Further, even though parents are conceived of as the primary decision makers when children are still fairly young, it has been widely acknowledged that students' own motivation becomes more important with increasing age, and that educational decisions will be taken more and more personally by students themselves in the course of their educational careers (B. Becker 2013a, p. 435; Henz and Maas 1995, p. 610; Erikson and Jonsson 1996, p. 54).

Against the background of these considerations, the question can certainly be raised to what extent available results provide conclusive evidence on the role of educational aspirations in the explanation of the emergence and persistence of ethnic differentials in education.

References

Alexander, K. L., & Cook, M. A. (1979). The Motivational Relevance of Educational Plans: Questioning the Conventional Wisdom. *Social Psychology Quarterly, 42*(3), 202-213.

Beck, M., Jäpel, F., & Becker, R. (2010). Determinanten des Bildungserfolgs von Migranten. In G. Quenzel & K. Hurrelmann (Eds.), *Bildungsverlierer: Neue Ungleichheiten* (Vol. 1, pp. 313-337). Wiesbaden: VS Verlag für Sozialwissenschaften.

Becker, B. (2010). *Bildungsaspirationen von Migranten: Determinanten und Umsetzung in Bildungsergebnisse* (MZES Working Paper No. 137). Retrieved Febuary 5, 2012, from http://www.mzes.unimannheim.de/publications/wp/wp-137.pdf

Becker, B. (2013a). Eltern von Vorschulkindern und ihre Bildungsaspirationen. In M. Stamm & D. Edelmann (Eds.), *Handbuch frühkindliche Bildungsforschung* (pp. 435-446). Wiesbaden: Springer.

Becker, G. (1993). *Human Capital: A Theoretical and Empirical Analysis, with Special Reference to Education* (3rd ed.). Chicago: University of Chicago Press.

Becker, R. (2013b). PISA und die Möglichkeiten der Analyse von Kontexteffekten. In R. Becker & A. Schulze (Eds.), *Bildungskontexte: Strukturelle Voraussetzungen und Ursachen ungleicher Bildungschancen* (pp. 85-116). Wiesbaden: Springer.

Becker, R., & Hecken, A. E. (2009). Higher Education or Vocational Training? An Empirical Test of the Rational Action Model of Educational Choices Suggested by Breen and Goldthorpe and Esser. *Acta Sociologica, 52*(1), 25-45.

Becker, R., & Schubert, F. (2011). Die Rolle von primären und sekundären Herkunftseffekten für Bildungschancen von Migranten im deutschen Schulsystem. In R. Becker (Ed.), *Integration durch Bildung: Bildungserwerb von jungen Migranten in Deutschland* (pp. 161-194). Wiesbaden: VS Verlag für Sozialwissenschaften.

Boudon, R. (1974). *Education, Opportunity and Social Inequality: Changing Prospects in Western Society*. New York: Wiley.

Bourdieu, P. (1973). Cultural Reproduction and Social Reproduction. In R. K. Brown (Ed.), *Knowledge, Education, and Cultural Change: Papers in the Sociology of Education* (pp. 71-112). London: Tavistock.

Bourdieu, P. (1983). Ökonomisches Kapital, kulturelles Kapital, soziales Kapital. In R. Kreckl (Ed.), *Soziale Ungleichheiten* (pp. 183-198). Göttingen: Schwartz.

Caplan, N. S., Choy, M. H., & Whitmore, J. K. (1991). *Children of the Boat People: A Study of Educational Success*. Ann Arbor: University of Michigan Press.

Diefenbach, H. (2010). *Kinder und Jugendliche aus Migrantenfamilien im deutschen Bildungssystem: Erklärungen und empirische Befunde* (3rd ed.). Wiesbaden: VS Verlag für Sozialwissenschaften.

Diefenbach, H., & Nauck, B. (1997). Bildungsverhalten als „strategische Praxis": Ein Modell zur Erklärung der Reproduktion von Humankapital in Migrantenfamilien. In J. Pries (Ed.), *Transnationale Migration* (pp. 277-291). Baden-Baden: Nomos.

Ditton, H., Krüsken, J., & Schauenberg, M. (2005). Bildungsungleichheit – der Beitrag von Familie und Schule. *Zeitschrift für Erziehungswissenschaft, 8*(2), 285-304.

Erikson, R., & Jonsson, J. O. (1996). Explaining Class Inequality in Education: The Swedish Test Case. In R. Erikson & J. O. Jonsson (Eds.), *Can Education Be Equalized? The Swedish Case* (pp. 1-63). Stockholm: Westview Press.

Esser, H. (2006). *Sprache und Integration*. Frankfurt: Campus.

Fordham, S., & Ogbu, J. (1991). Black Students' School Success: Coping with the 'Burden of Acting White'. *Urban Review, 18*(3), 176-206.

Fuligni, A. J. (1997). The Academic Achievement of Adolescents from Immigrant Families: The Roles of Family Background, Attitudes, and Behavior. *Child Developmental Psychology, 68*(2), 351-363.

Fuligni, A. J. (1998). Adolescents from Immigrant Families. In V. C. McLoyd & L. Steinberg (Eds.), *Studying Minority Adolescents: Conceptual, Methodological, and Theoretical Issues* (pp. 127-143). Mahwah, NJ: Earlbaum.

Gambetta, D. (1987). *Were They Pushed Or Did They Jump? Individual Decision Mechanisms in Education.* Cambridge: Cambridge University Press.

Goyette, K. A. (2008). College for Some to College for All: Social Background, Occupational Expectations, and Educational Expectations over Time. *Social Science Research, 37*(2), 461-484.

Gresch, C., Maaz, K., Becker, M., & McElvany, N. (2012). Zur hohen Bildungsaspiration von Migranten beim Übergang von der Grundschule in die Sekundarstufe: Fakt oder Artefakt? In P. Pielage, L. Pries & G. Schultze (Eds.), *Soziale Ungleichheit in der Einwanderungsgesellschaft: Kategorien, Konzepte, Einflussfaktoren* (pp. 56-67). Bonn: Friedrich-Ebert-Stiftung.

Harazd, B. (2007). *Die Bildungsentscheidung: Zur Ablehnung der Schulformempfehlung am Ende der Grundschulzeit.* Münster: Waxmann.

Heath, A. F., & Brinbaum, Y. (2007). Guest Editorial: Explaining Ethnic Inequalities in Educational Attainment. *Ethnicities, 7*(3), 291-304.

Henz, U., & Maas, I. (1995). Chancengleichheit durch die Bildungsexpansion? *Kölner Zeitschrift für Soziologie und Sozialpsychologie, 47*(4), 605-633.

Jencks, C., Crouse, J., & Mueser, P. (1983). The Wisconsin Model of Status Attainment: A National Replication with Improved Measures of Ability and Aspiration. *Sociology of Education, 56*(1), 3-19.

Kalter, F. (2006). Auf der Suche nach einer Erklärung für die spezifischen Arbeitsmarktnachteile von Jugendlichen türkischer Herkunft. Zugleich eine Replik auf den Beitrag von Holger Seibert und Heike Solga: „Gleiche Chancen dank einer abgeschlossenen Ausbildung? (ZfS 5/2005)". *Zeitschrift für Soziologie, 35*(2), 144-160.

Kalter, F., & Granato, N. (2002). Demographic Change, Educational Expansion, and Structural Assimilation of Immigrants: The Case of Germany. *European Sociological Review, 18*(2), 199-216.

Kao, G., & Thompson, J. S. (2003). Racial and Ethnic Stratification in Educational Achievement and Attainment. *Annual Review of Sociology, 29*, 417-442.

Kao, G., & Tienda, M. (1995). Optimism and Achievement: The Educational Performance of Immigrant Youth. *Social Science Quarterly, 76*(1), 1-19.

Keller, S., & Zavalloni, M. (1964). Ambition and Social Class: A Respecification. *Social Forces, 43*(1), 58-70.

Kerckhoff, A. C. (1976). The Status Attainment Process: Socialization or Allocation? *Social Forces, 55*(2), 368-381.

Klieme, E., Artelt, C., Hartig, J., Jude, N., Köller, O., Prenzel, M., Schneider, W., & Stanat, P. (2010). *PISA 2009: Bilanz nach einem Jahrzehnt.* Münster: Waxmann.

Kristen, C., & Dollmann, J. (2010). Sekundäre Effekte der ethnischen Herkunft: Kinder aus türkischen Familien am ersten Bildungsübergang. In B. Becker & D. Reimer (Eds.), *Vom Kindergarten bis zur Hochschule: Die Generierung von ethnischen und sozialen Dis-*

paritäten in der Bildungsbiographie (pp. 117-144). Wiesbaden: VS Verlag für Sozialwissenschaften.

Kristen, C., Edele, A., Kalter, F., Kogan, I., Schulz, B., Stanat, P., & Will, G. (2011). The Education of Migrants and their Children Across the Life Course. *Zeitschrift für Erziehungswissenschaft, 14*(2), 121-137.

Kristen, C., & Granato, N. (2007). The Educational Attainment of the Second Generation in Germany: Social Origins and Ethnic Inequality. *Ethnicities, 7*(3), 343-366.

Kristen, C., Reimer, D., & Kogan, I. (2008). Higher Education Entry of Turkish Immigrant Youth in Germany. *International Journal of Comparative Sociology of Education, 49*(2-3), 127-151.

Lehmann, R. H., Peek, R., Gänsfuß, R., & Husfeldt, V. (2002). *LAU 9 – Aspekte der Lernausgangslage und der Lernentwicklung – Klassenstufe 9: Ergebnisse einer längsschnittlichen Untersuchung in Hamburg.* Hamburg: Behörde für Schule, Jugend und Berufsbildung/ Behörde für Bildung und Sport.

Lin, N. (2001). *Social Capital. A Theory of Social Structure and Action.* Cambridge: Cambridge University Press.

Maaz, K., Baumert, J., & Trautwein, U. (2010). Genese sozialer Ungleichheit im institutionellen Kontext der Schule: Wo entsteht und vergrößert sich soziale Ungleichheit? In H.-H. Krüger, U. Rabe-Kleberg, R.-T. Kramer & J. Budde (Eds.), *Bildungsungleichheit Revisited: Bildung und soziale Ungleichheit vom Kindergarten bis zur Hochschule* (pp. 69-102). Wiesbaden: VS Verlag für Sozialwissenschaften.

Maaz, K., & Nagy, G. (2009). Der Übergang von der Grundschule in die weiterführenden Schulen des Sekundarschulsystems: Definition, Spezifikation und Quantifizierung primärer und sekundärer Herkunftseffekte [Special issue]. *Zeitschrif für Erziehungswissenschaft,* 153-182.

Nauck, B. (2011). Kulturelles und soziales Kapital als Determinante des Bildungserfolgs bei Migranten? In R. Becker (Ed.), *Integration durch Bildung: Bildungserwerb von jungen Migranten in Deutschland* (pp. 71-93). Wiesbaden: VS Verlag für Sozialwissenschaften.

Nauck, B., Diefenbach, H., & Petri, K. (1998). Intergenerationale Transmission von kulturellem Kapital unter Migrationsbedingungen: Zum Bildungserfolg von Kindern und Jugendlichen aus Migrantenfamilien in Deutschland. *Zeitschrift für Pädagogik, 44*(5), 701-722.

Ogbu, J. (1991). Minority Coping Responses and School Experiences. *Journal of Psychohistory, 18*(4), 433-456.

Relikowski, I., Schneider, T., & Blossfeld, H.-P. (2010). Primäre und sekundäre Herkunftseffekte beim Übergang in das gegliederte Schulsystem: Welche Rolle spielen soziale Klasse und Bildungsstatus in Familien mit Migrationshintergrund? In T. Beckers, K. Birkelbach, J. Hagenah & U. Rosar (Eds.), *Komparative empirische Sozialforschung* (pp. 143-167). Wiesbaden: VS Verlag für Sozialwissenschaften.

Relikowski, I., Yilmaz, E., & Blossfeld, H.-P. (2012). Wie lassen sich die hohen Bildungsaspirationen von Migranten erklären? Eine Mixed-Methods-Studie zur Rolle von strukturellen Aufstiegschancen und individueller Bildungserfahrung [Special issue]. *Kölner Zeitschrift für Soziologie und Sozialpsychologie,* 111-136.

Roth, T., Salikutluk, Z., & Kogan, I. (2010). Auf die „richtigen Kontakte" kommt es an! Soziale Ressourcen und die Bildungsaspirationen der Mütter von Haupt-, Real- und Gesamtschülern in Deutschland. In B. Becker & D. Reimer (Eds.), *Vom Kindergarten* bis zur Hochschule: Die Generierung von ethnischen und sozialen Disparitäten in der Bildungsbiographie (pp. 179-212). Wiesbaden: VS Verlag für Sozialwissenschaften.

Schuchart, C., & Maaz, K. (2007). Bildungsverhalten in institutionellen Kontexten: Schulbesuch und elterliche Bildungsaspiration am Ende der Sekundarstufe I. *Kölner Zeitschrift für Soziologie und Sozialpsychologie, 59*(4), 640-666.

Sewell, W. H., Haller, A. O., & Ohlendorf, G. W. (1970). The Educational and Early Occupational Status Attainment Process: Replication and Revision. *American Sociological Review, 35*(6), 1014-1027.

Sewell, W. H., Haller, A. O., & Portes, A. (1969). The Educational and Early Occupational Attainment Process. *American Sociological Review, 34*(1), 82-92.

Stanat, P., & Christensen, G. (2006a). *Schulerfolg von Jugendlichen mit Migrationshintergrund im internationalen Vergleich: Eine Analyse von Voraussetzungen und Erträgen schulischen Lernens im Rahmen von PISA 2003*. Berlin: Bundesministerium für Bildung und Forschung.

Stubbe, T. C. (2009). *Bildungsentscheidungen und sekundäre Herkunftseffekte: Soziale Disparitäten bei Hamburger Schülerinnen und Schülern der Sekundarstufe I*. Münster: Waxmann.

Stubbe, T. C., Bos, W., & Euen, B. (2012). Der Übergang von der Primar- in die Sekundarstufe. In W. Bos, I. Tarelli, A. Bremerich-Vos & K. Schwippert (Eds.), *IGLU 2011: Lesekompetenzen von Grundschulkindern in Deutschland im Internationalen Vergleich* (pp. 210-226). Münster: Waxmann.

Sue, S., & Okazaki, S. (1990). Asian-American Educational Achievements: A Phenomenon in Search of an Explanation. *American Psychologist, 45*(8), 913-920.

Vallet, L.-A. (2007). What Can We Do to Improve the Education of Children from Disadvantaged Backgrounds? In M. S. Sorondo, E. Malinvaud & P. Léna (Eds.), *Globalization and Education: Proceedings of the Joint Working Group. The Pontifical Academy of Sciences* (pp. 127-155). Berlin: De Gruyter.

van der Werfhorst, H. G., & van Tubergen, F. (2007). Ethnicity, Schooling, and Merit in the Netherlands. *Ethnicities, 7*(3), 416-444.

Wallace, C. (2007). *Jugendliche MigrantInnen in Bildung und Arbeit: Auswirkungen von Sozialkapital und kulturellem Kapital auf Bildungsentscheidungen und Arbeitsmarktbeteiligung*. Wien: Österreichisches Institut für Jugendforschung.

Wiley, N. F. (1967). The Ethnic Mobility Trap and Stratification Theory. *Social Problems, 15*(1), 147-159.

Wiley, N. F. (1970). The Ethnic Mobility Trap and Stratification Theory. In P. I. Rose (Ed.), *The Study of Society: An Integrated Anthology* (pp. 397-408). New York: Harper & Brothers.

Zhou, M. (1997). Segmented Assimilation: Issues, Controversies, and Recent Research on the New Second Generation. *International Migration Review, 31*(4), 975-1008.

Research objective and contribution to the field   6

The present study attempts to add a further dimension to the understanding of how students orient themselves toward the future by providing insight into their educational and future career aspirations, expectations and belief-formation processes at the end of lower secondary education. This point of transition, when students are approximately 15 to 17 years old in the German educational system, is a critical stage in students' educational careers due to several aspects, some of which are related to the peculiarities of the German educational system. After 9 or 10 years of general education (depending on the federal state and the type of school attended) students reach the end of compulsory full-time education and can leave the general educational system with the lowest or intermediate qualification and enter the vocational education and training (VET) system. Provided that students display sufficient levels of educational performance, they can alternatively remain in the general educational system and obtain qualifications that provide access to higher education after the completion of 12 or 13 years of full-time education.

As outlined above, the completion of the highest level of general education not only provides access to an academic career but also significantly increases students' chances of a successful transition into the VET system, regarding the overall probability and the time needed to find a position as well as the chance to enter higher-prestige positions that are associated with more favorable labor market prospects (Autorengruppe Bildungsberichterstattung 2014; Bundesministerium für Bildung und Forschung 2013). In view of the significance of high levels of general education in determining students' continued educational and professional careers, a primary concern at this stage of the educational career is that students unnecessarily or overly restrict their future opportunities due to a lack of motivation to obtain higher general educational qualifications on the one hand, and due to aspects such as the misperception of the opportunity structure, lacking or incorrect information about the full spectrum of career opportunities and the failure to deal effectively with anticipated or experienced barriers on the other hand (Gottfredson 1981, 1996; Morgan 2005).

Building on the conditions the literature discusses as potential influences of students' educational aspirations and attainment decisions, the study aims to identify the dimensions along which students construct their educational and future career aspirations as well as the barriers they encounter and/or perceive in implementing their aspirations. A first focus is to identify differences in the way native and migrant students construct their career aspirations and expectations. A second focus is to provide insight into the association between students' future career aspirations and their aspirations and expectations in general education. While the impact of educational qualifications on later labor market prospects is without controversy, researchers from different disciplines have brought forward theoretical considerations and empirical evidence to suggest that students' future career aspirations should be conceived of as a cause rather than the consequence of their educational aspirations and expectations (e.g., Goyette 2008; Looker and McNutt 1989; Xie and Goyette 2003). Following the consideration that it may not be objective possibilities of achieving significant returns once on the labor market but the extent to which students' future career aspirations will allow them to take full advantage of high educational qualifications that matter most to the construction of their educational aspirations (G. Becker 1993; Gambetta 1987), and that the extent to which aspirations motivate constructive educational behavior depends on dimensions like the strength of preference for a specific career alternative and the extent to which aspirations are clear and specific (Gambetta 1987; Gottfredson 1981, 2005; Haller and Miller 1963; Lent et al. 1994), the study investigates whether there is evidence that students construct their aspirations and expectations in general education in consideration of the educational requirements for their future career aspirations, or whether the latter can be conceived of as the mere result of their expectations in general education.

A second research objective is to shed light on the meaning of respondent-reported career aspirations. The theoretical part of the study discussed several arguments against a causal interpretation of the association between aspirations and later attainment levels. Among these are the concern that expressed aspirations may reflect students' perceptions and evaluations of the opportunity structure rather than index level of motivation (Alexander and Cook 1979; Bourdieu 1973; Jencks et al. 1983; Kerckhoff 1976), that aspirations and expectations may be the product of lacking or inaccurate information and unrealistic self-appraisals (Coleman et al. 1966; Kerckhoff 1977; Kerckhoff and Campbell 1977; Rosenbaum 1976, 1978, 1980) or constitute vague preferences or interests that have no meaning to students' everyday behavior (Alexander and Cook 1979; Coleman et al. 1966). Also, the question has been raised to what extent expressed aspirations have the same meaning and are directly comparable across students (B. Becker 2010; Goyette 2008). In view of existing evidence that shows students of the age group under consideration to tend to be insecure about their interests, abilities and values, to often lack knowledge about the educational requirements for different types of careers and to make opportunistic rather than rational career decisions (Gottfredson 1981, 1996; Schneider and Stevenson 1999; Simon 1955, 1957), these considerations may be particularly important to arrive at a reasonable interpretation of the results obtained from the present study. Following the approach adopted by the Wisconsin researchers, the study specifically addresses the question of the meaning of respondent-reported educational *plans*.

References

Alexander, K. L., & Cook, M. A. (1979). The Motivational Relevance of Educational Plans: Questioning the Conventional Wisdom. *Social Psychology Quarterly, 42*(3), 202-213.

Autorengruppe Bildungsberichterstattung (2014). *Bildung in Deutschland 2014. Ein indikatorengestützter Bericht mit einer Analyse zur Bildung von Menschen mit Behinderungen*. Bielefeld: Bertelsmann.

Becker, B. (2010). *Bildungsaspirationen von Migranten: Determinanten und Umsetzung in Bildungsergebnisse* (MZES Working Paper No. 137). Retrieved Febuary 5, 2012, from http://www.mzes.unimannheim.de/publications/wp/wp-137.pdf

Becker, G. (1993). *Human Capital: A Theoretical and Empirical Analysis, with Special Reference to Education* (3rd ed.). Chicago: University of Chicago Press.

Bourdieu, P. (1973). Cultural Reproduction and Social Reproduction. In R. K. Brown (Ed.), *Knowledge, Education, and Cultural Change: Papers in the Sociology of Education* (pp. 71-112). London: Tavistock.

Bundesministerium für Bildung und Forschung (2013). *Berufsbildungsbericht 2013*. Retrieved October 30, 2013, from http://www.bmbf.de/pub/bbb_2013.pdf

Coleman, J. S., Campbell, E. Q., Hobson, J. C., McPartland, J., Mood, A. M., Weinfeld, F. D., & York, R. L. (1966). *Equality of Educational Opportunity*. Washington, D.C.: U.S. Government Printing Office.

Gambetta, D. (1987). *Were They Pushed Or Did They Jump? Individual Decision Mechanisms in Education*. Cambridge: Cambridge University Press.

Gottfredson, L. S. (1981). Circumscription and Compromise: A Developmental Theory of Occupational Aspirations. *Journal of Counseling Psychology Monograph, 28*(6), 545-579.

Gottfredson, L. S. (1996). Gottfredson's Theory of Circumscription and Compromise. In D. Brown & L. Brooks (Eds.), *Career Choice and Development* (3 ed., pp. 179-232). San Francisco: Jossey–Bass.

Gottfredson, L. S. (2005). Applying Gottfredson's Theory of Circumscription and Compromise in Career Guidance and Counseling. In S. D. Brown & R. W. Lent (Eds.), *Career Development and Counseling: Putting Theory and Research to Work* (pp. 71-100). New Jersey: Wiley.

Goyette, K. A. (2008). College for Some to College for All: Social Background, Occupational Expectations, and Educational Expectations over Time. *Social Science Research, 37*(2), 461-484.

Haller, A. O., & Miller, I. W. (1963). *The Occupational Aspiration Scale: Theory, Structure and Correlates* (AES-TB No. 288). Retrieved September 9, 2011, from http://files.eric.ed.gov/fulltext/ED016712.pdf

Jencks, C., Crouse, J., & Mueser, P. (1983). The Wisconsin Model of Status Attainment: A National Replication with Improved Measures of Ability and Aspiration. *Sociology of Education, 56*(1), 3-19.

Kerckhoff, A. C. (1976). The Status Attainment Process: Socialization or Allocation? *Social Forces, 55*(2), 368-381.

Kerckhoff, A. C. (1977). The Realism of Educational Ambitions in England and the United States. *American Sociological Review, 42*(4), 563-571.

Kerckhoff, A. C., & Campbell, R. T. (1977). Social Status Differences in the Explanation of Educational Ambition. *Social Forces, 5*(3), 701-714.

Lent, R. W., Brown, S. D., & Hackett, G. (1994). Monograph: Toward a Unifying Social Cognitive Theory of Career and Academic Interest, Choice, and Performance. *Journal of Vocational Behavior, 45*, 79-122.

Looker, D. E., & McNutt, K. L. (1989). The Effect of Occupational Expectations on the Educational Attainments of Males and Females. *Canadian Journal of Education, 14*(3), 352-367.

Morgan, S. L. (2005). *On the Edge of Commitment: Educational Attainment and Race in the United States*. Stanford, CA: Stanford University Press.

Rosenbaum, J. E. (1976). *Making Inequality: The Hidden Curriculum of High School Tracking*. New York: Wiley.

Rosenbaum, J. E. (1978). The Structure of Opportunity in School. *Social Forces, 57*(1), 236-256.

Rosenbaum, J. E. (1980). Track Misperceptions and Frustrated College Plans: An Analysis of the Effects of Tracks and Track Perceptions in the National Longitudinal Survey. *Sociology of Education, 53*(2), 74-88.

Schneider, B. L., & Stevenson, D. (1999). *The Ambitious Generation: America's Teenagers, Motivated but Directionless*. New Haven: Yale University Press.

Simon, H. A. (1955). A Behavioral Model of Rational Choice. *The Quarterly Journal of Economics, 69*(1), 99-118.

Simon, H. A. (1957). *Models of Man: Social and Rational – Mathematical Essays on Rational Human Behavior in a Social Setting*. New York: Wiley.

Xie, Y., & Goyette, K. A. (2003). Social Mobility and the Educational Choices of Asian Americans. *Social Science Research, 32*(3), 467–498.

7 Study design

To empirically address the research questions outlined above, data was collected from ten classes of 9th-graders and ten classes of 10th-graders in three *Stadtteilschulen*[18] in Hamburg in the form of a questionnaire, a language assessment task and a test for cognitive abilities. The schools were selected by the social index KESS 7, which describes the composition of the student body in general schools in Hamburg in terms of the students' social situation.[19] The index ranges from 1 (strongly disadvantaged social situation of students) to 6 (privileged social situation of students). Apart from very few exceptions, schools with the highest indexes 5 or 6 were exclusively *Gymnasien* (i.e., the most demanding type of secondary education). Schools with the lowest index exclusively offered the lowest and/or intermediate track of secondary education and were very rare in number. To sample students from diverse social backgrounds, and to avoid a systematic overrepresentation of particularly high- or low-performing students, the final data was collected in schools with the indexes 2, 3 and 4.

Two pilot studies were carried out prior to the main survey (based on a sample of two classes of students each) to test the data collection procedure, to identify and adapt questions that cause comprehension difficulties and to identify relevant response categories. The final data collection in each class took 90 minutes (two teaching units). Students were asked to fill out a questionnaire in the first teaching

---

18 This type of secondary school does not offer (a) particular course(s) but allows students to obtain any general educational qualification (http://www.hamburg.de/contentblob/2372648/data/lb-gesellschaftswissenschaften-sts.pdf (accessed Oct. 19, 2013)).

19 The index used for the present study (http://carola-veit.de/wp-content/uploads/2009/03/sozialindizes-an-schulen-berechnungsgrundlagen.pdf (accessed Oct. 19, 2013)) was replaced by a new index in 2013 (http://cdu-hh.tmphost.de/fileadmin/content/pdf/SKA/20-07094.pdf (accessed Oct. 19, 2013)).

unit (45 minutes). After a short break, they took a non-verbal test for cognitive abilities (8 minutes) and a language assessment test in German (20 minutes).

The questionnaire consisted of two parts. The first part covered a variety of aspects related to students' and their families' communication practices, patterns of language use and language skills. The second part included detailed questions on students' educational and future career aspirations, expectations and belief-formation processes. Further, information was collected on students' migration and educational biographies as well as on several background variables, such as level of parental education and occupational status. Students' language skills were assessed using the standardized instrument 'Fast Catch Bumerang' (Reich et al. 2009), which was developed to assess the written (academic) language skills of natives and migrants at the end of lower secondary education. The task is to write an article for a youth magazine based on a sequence of pictures that illustrate the different steps of constructing a boomerang. The evaluation is based on several criteria that comprise different linguistic and non-linguistic dimensions, such as task accomplishment and vocabulary (Gogolin et al. 2011; Ilić 2012, 2013).[20] A nonverbal test was used to assess students' cognitive abilities.[21] In total, 349 students participated in all three tasks.

To obtain detailed information on students' belief-formation processes, the survey was carried out in the very end of the school year (2010/2011), when students faced the decision to remain in general education to obtain higher qualifications or to leave and enter the VET system. The analysis of cross-sectional data does not allow to assess the extent to which students' aspirations and expectation are associated with their eventual attainment outcomes. In view of the lack of knowledge about the mechanisms that shape students' educational aspirations and expectations, the present approach was preferred to obtain deeper insight into the *expected* costs and benefits of education and on students' *perceived* probabilities to successfully realize their educational plans.

---

20 The original version of the instrument further includes the task to write an application for an internship in the editorial office of the magazine. In the present analysis the Förmig scale was used to develop an overall index of students' productive language skills ($\alpha = 0.8$), cf. Gogolin et al. 2011, pp. 127; 163, note 30.

21 KFT4-12+R, subtest N2: figure analogies (Heller and Perleth 2000).

References

Gogolin, I., Dirim, I., Klinger, T., Lange, I., Lengyel, D., Michel, U., Neumann, U., Reich, H. H., Roth, H.-J., & Schwippert, K. (2011). *Förderung von Kindern und Jugendlichen mit Migrationshintergrund FörMig: Bilanz und Perspektiven eines Modellprogramms* (Vol. 7). Münster: Waxmann.

Heller, K., & Perleth, C. (2000). *Kognitiver Fähigkeitstest für 4. bis 12. Klassen, Revision: KFT 4-12+ R. Manual.* Göttingen: Beltz Test.

Ilić, V. (2012). Home-Literacy Practices and Academic Language Skills of Migrant Pupils. In J. Duarte & I. Gogolin (Eds.), *Tertium Comparationis* (Vol. 18, pp. 190-208). Münster: Waxmann.

Ilić, V. (2013). Sprachstandserhebungen unter der Bedingung von Mehrsprachigkeit in der Sekundarstufe I und II. In F. Hellmich & K. Siekmann (Eds.), *Sprechen, Lesen und Schreiben lernen - Erfolgreiche Konzepte der Sprachförderung* (pp. 29-53). Berlin: DGLS.

Reich, H. H., Roth, H.-J., & Döll, M. (2009). Fast Catch Bumerang – Auswertungshinweise, Schreibimpuls und Auswertungsbogen. In D. Lengyel, H. H. Reich, H.-J. Roth & M. Döll (Eds.), *Von der Sprachdiagnose zur Sprachförderung* (pp. 209–241). Münster: Waxmann.

Sample description 8

The following sections describe the sample in some detail. Starting off with a description of the sociodemographic composition of the sample, the analysis continues with a description of students' language skills and the patterns of language use in migrant families. Then, the analysis moves on to investigate students' educational and future career aspirations and expectations, the dimensions along which they construct their aspirations and expectations, and the barriers they perceive in implementing their aspirations.

8.1 Sociodemographic composition

Table 8.1 provides a description of the sociodemographic characteristics of the sample. 40% of students are 9th-graders and 60% are 10th-graders. The youngest participant is almost 15 and the oldest student almost 19 years of age. Slightly more than half of the students are females (55%). 46% come from families with at least one parent born abroad. Among the latter, 29% come from families with one parent born abroad and 71% from families with both parents born abroad. Unless indicated otherwise, the terms 'migration background' and 'migrant' are used to refer to students with either one or both parents born abroad in the remainder of the study.[22] 70% of migrants were born in Germany, and 30% were born in a foreign country and migrated to Germany themselves. The data clearly confirms

---

22 Third generation students, referring to students who themselves and whose parents were born in Germany but whose grandparents were born abroad, were classified as natives in the present study (26 students). 19 out of these students have one grandparent and seven students have two grandparents who were born abroad. Only in the case of one student all four grandparents were born abroad, and in this case all grandparents migrated to Germany from different countries. Only three third-generation students

that the identification of migrants based on their citizenship leads to a severe underestimation of the migration population. While almost half of the students have a migration background as defined in the present study, only 11% have a foreign citizenship and 6% have both German and a foreign citizenship.[23]

Table 8.1 Sociodemographic composition

	N	Mean	SD	Min.	Max.
Sex (1 = male)	349	0.44	0.5	0	1
Grade	349	9.4	0.49	9	10
Age	344	16.17	0.79	14.83	18.83
Migration background					
Natives	188	0.54	0.5	0	1
Migrants	161	0.46	0.5	0	1
One parent born abroad	46	0.13	0.34	0	1
Both parents born abroad	113	0.33	0.47	0	1
1st generation	48	0.14	0.35	0	1
2nd generation	111	0.32	0.47	0	1
Nationality: German	282	0.83	0.38	0	1
Nationality: German and other	19	0.06	0.23	0	1
Nationality: foreign only	39	0.11	0.32	0	1
Socioeconomic position (HISEI)		49.15	19.6	11.74	88.7
Natives (reference group)	157	55.2	17.23	19.66	86.72
Migrants	132	41.96 ***	19.88	11.74	88.7
One parent born abroad	38	47.56 *	20.17	14.21	86.72
Both parents born abroad	92	39.37 ***	19.49	11.74	88.7

NOTE: N = 349; * p < 0.05; ** p < 0.01; *** p < 0.001; reference group: natives

A remarkable observation is the high level of heterogeneity with regard to students' countries of origin. The sample includes students from as many as 44 countries. In line with the actual distribution in Germany, the largest proportion of migrants is of Turkish origin, followed by students with a Polish and Russian background (Statistisches Bundesamt 2013a, p. 8).[24] Both students from families with one and both parents born abroad are characterized by significantly lower socioeconomic positions compared to natives, but particularly large discrepancies

---

have (a) language(s) other than German as their first language(s), and only nine students use (a) language(s) other than German in the family.

23 In 2011, about 44% of students aged 6 to under 18 in Hamburg had a migration background according to the definition of the Federal Statistical Office, and about 13% had a foreign citizenship (Source: Statistische Ämter des Bundes und der Länder 2013, own calc.).

24 See Appendix A on http://www.ew.uni-hamburg.de/de/ueber-die-fakultaet/personen/trebbels.html for the composition of the sample by countries/regions of origin.

can be observed between natives and students from families with both parents born abroad.[25]

8.2   Language use and test scores

As outlined in the theoretical part of the study, majority language skills are considered an important prerequisite for the educational success of both natives and migrants. As the latter often grow up learning (a) language(s) other than the majority language or use (a) language(s) other than the majority language in the family, majority language skills are often discussed with reference to primary effects of ethnic origin (Heath and Brinbaum 2007; Kristen et al. 2011). Table 8.2 provides information on students' productive language skills as assessed by the text production task. In line with other empirical studies that assess students' receptive or productive majority language skills, migrants achieved significantly lower test scores than their peers without a migration background (Göbel et al. 2011; Klieme et al. 2010). A further differentiation of the migrant sample reveals that students from families with one parent born abroad did not perform significantly worse than natives. Conversely, significant discrepancies can be observed between the test scores achieved by natives and migrants with both parents born abroad. A differentiation of the migrant sample by the migration generation shows that both first- and second-generation students scored significantly lower than their native peers. The gap is particularly large between natives and first-generation students, which is in line with the high share among the latter who come from families where both parents were born abroad.

---

25 The family's socioeconomic position was measured by the highest ISEI-08 (International Socio-Economic Index of Occupational Status) score in the household, which scales occupations by the average level of education and the average earnings of job holders (Ganzeboom 2010).

Table 8.2 Language test scores

	N	Mean	SD	Med.	Min.	Max.
Migration background						
Natives	182	33.14	8.64	33.01	8.87	52.7
Migrants	149	29.77 ***	9.53	28.95	8.24	57.02
One parent born abroad	44	32.11	10.86	31.12	9.99	57.02
Both parents born abroad	103	28.92 ***	8.76	28.55	8.24	55.82
Migration generation						
1st generation	44	28.3 **	8.63	27.58	10.78	47.74
2nd generation	103	30.55 *	9.83	29.86	8.24	57.02

NOTE: * $p < 0.05$; ** $p < 0.01$; *** $p < 0.001$, reference group: natives.

Figure 8.1 provides information on the patterns of language acquisition and language use in migrant families. The smallest share of migrants grew up learning German only (20%), and about one third reported that German was not among their first languages. Accordingly, the great majority have both German *and* (an)other language(s) as their first languages. Among these students, the great majority have two first languages, and only 4% have three or more first languages (not shown in figure 8.1). The share of students who exclusively use German or (a) language(s) other than German is even smaller than the share who exclusively have German or (a) foreign language(s) as their first language(s). Only 9% of students exclusively use German in the family, and as little as 4% exclusively use (a) language(s) other than German. The remainder of students use both German *and* (an)other language(s) in the family (87%). Among these students, the great majority use two languages, and 16% use more than two languages (not shown in figure 8.1). Also, the data shows that the language use between parents does not conform to the language use of students. More than half of the parents use (a) language(s) other than German most often when talking to each other, and the smallest share exclusively use German most often.

8.2 Language use and test scores

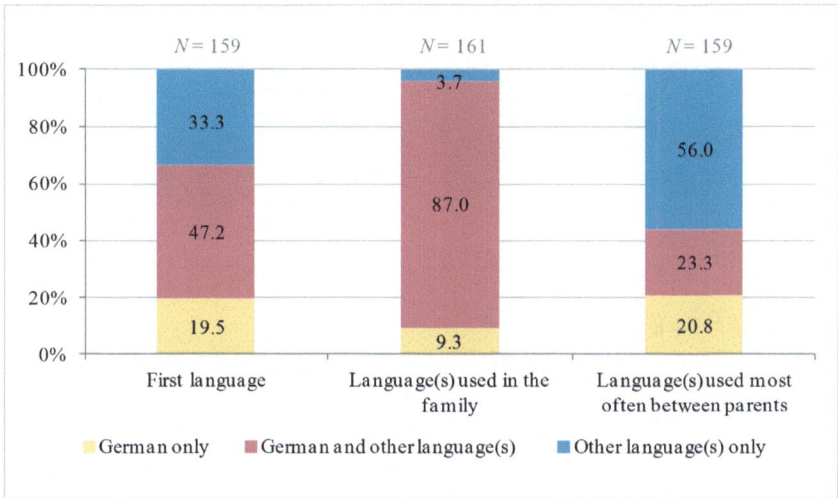

Figure 8.1 Language acquisition and use in migrant families

Figure 8.2 contains information on the language(s) used most often between students and their parents when talking to each other. The majority of migrant students use both German *and* (an)other language(s) most often when talking to their parents. The share who use German most often is slightly smaller, and the smallest share of students use (a) language(s) other than German most often. Conversely, the majority of parents use (a) language(s) other than German most often when talking to their children, followed by those who use German *and* (an)other language(s) most often. A comparatively small share of about one quarter of parents use German most often when talking to their children.[26]

---

26 The wording of the questions was "What language(s) do you and your mother/father use most often when talking to each other?"; Response categories (multiple answers allowed): German, other language(s) (free response); Students were explicitly asked to list all languages they use most often. The question was answered separately for the language use of the student, mother and father.

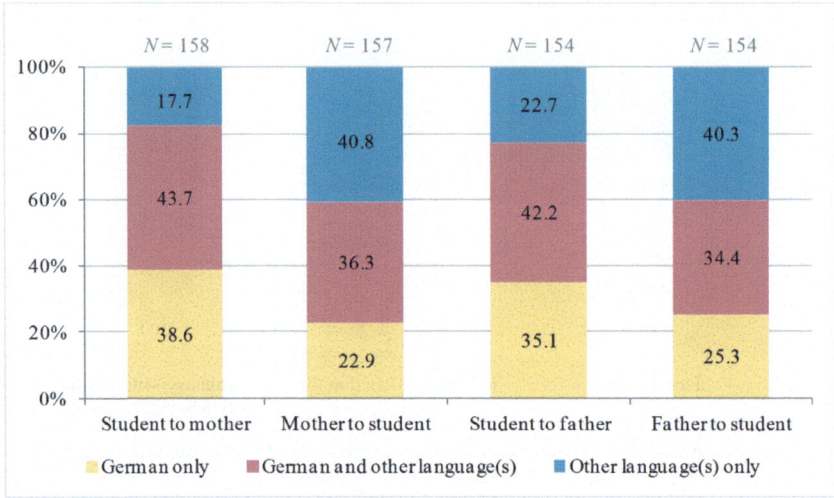

Figure 8.2 Language use between students and parents

In sum, the data clearly confirms the notion that the use of multiple languages is standard practice in migrant families (Gogolin 1994). As regards the discussion of communication practices in migrant families with reference to primary effects of ethnic origin, at first sight the present data appears to support the notion of a negative influence of the use of (a) language(s) other than German on the acquisition of majority language skills. However, it needs to be kept in mind that migrant students were shown to come from families of comparatively low social origin, and that the present data is not background-adjusted. Also, other migration-specific conditions that may contribute to the explanation of the lower majority language skills in migrants, such as the age of migration, are not taken into account at this point of the analysis. At any rate, though, the small selection of data on the patterns of language use and acquisition presented above clearly indicates that it may not be appropriate to capture the complex communication practices in migrant families by a dummy variable that merely differentiates students by whether German is used only or most often in the family or not, as is common practice in empirical studies (e.g., Klieme et al. 2010; Tarelli et al. 2012; c.f. Chlosta and Ostermann 2007).

8.3 Aspirations in general education

In line with the Wisconsin research tradition, students' educational aspirations were measured by the highest level of general education they *plan* to complete. Figure 8.3 shows the distribution of the educational plans of natives and migrants. As attested by the literature, students with a migration background have comparatively high educational aspirations even when family background characteristics are not taken into account (Heath and Brinbaum 2007; Kristen and Dollmann 2010; Stubbe et al. 2012). The share of students who plan to attain the highest level of general education is as high as 69% in the migrant subsample and exceeds the corresponding share among natives by six percentage points. Also, the share of migrants who plan to obtain the restricted higher education entrance qualification is higher than the share of natives who plan to obtain this qualification (11% and 7%, respectively). Accordingly, the share who plan to obtain the intermediate qualification is much higher in the subsample of natives (28% vs. 18% among migrants). The negligibly small share of students who plan to obtain the lowest degree can be partly explained by the fact that 10th-graders can be expected to be positively selected for level of educational performance and ambition as particularly poor performing or unambitious students may have left the general educational system after grade 9 already (cf. Morgan 1998). The data further shows that the educational plans of students with one parent born abroad are comparable to those of their native peers, whereas the share of students who plan to obtain high general educational qualifications is particularly high among migrants with both parents born abroad. However, students from the latter group also plan to attain the lowest level of general education more often compared to the other two groups.

Broken down by sex, the data reveals that the share of females who plan to attain the highest level of general education exceeds the corresponding share among their male peers in the group of natives and migrants with both parents born abroad but not in the group of migrants with one parent born abroad (not shown in figure 8.3). The smallest share who plan to complete the highest level of general education can be found in the group of male natives, and the highest share among females from families with both parents born abroad.

Parental aspirations for their children's educational careers exceed the educational plans of their children in all three groups (not shown in figure 8.3).[27] In

---

[27] Parental aspirations for their children's educational careers in the general educational system were assessed by the question "What is the highest level of general education your parents would like you to attain?"; Response categories: lowest degree, intermediate degree, restricted or full access to higher education.

line with the literature, parental aspirations are comparatively high in migrant families (e.g., Becker 2010; Ditton et al. 2005). As much as 92% of migrant parents compared to 78% of native parents would like their children to obtain the full or restricted higher education entrance qualification. No parents in either group would like their children to leave the general educational system after the completion of the lowest qualification.

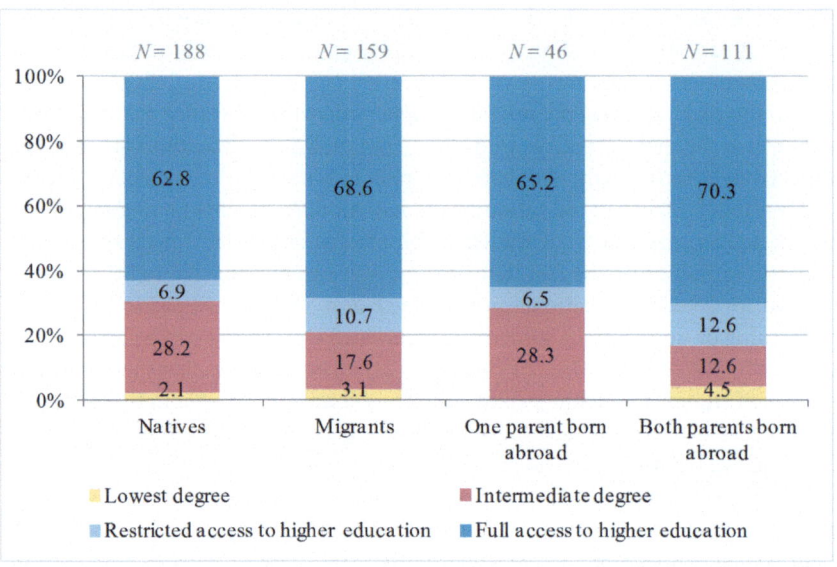

Figure 8.3 Aspirations in general education

To obtain insight into how students orient themselves toward the future, information was collected on the criteria based on which they have constructed their aspirations for their general educational qualifications. Specifically, students were asked to indicate the *most* important reason for their educational plans among the following labor market-related and social-psychological criteria:

- The jobs I am interested in do not require any higher qualification [*low job requirement*]
- I would prefer to obtain a higher degree but my grades are not high enough [*low grades*]

8.3 Aspirations in general education

- I need this particular degree to be able to pursue my future career aspirations [*future career*]
- To have a broad range of career opportunities [*opportunities*]
- Good Chances to find a job [*security*]
- My parents expect me to attain this level of education [*parents*]
- I want to attain the same level of education as my friends/ acquaintances [*friends*]
- I don't feel confident enough to go for a higher degree [*confidence*]
- I don't feel like staying in school any longer [*motivation*]
- I want to make my own living as soon as possible [*own living*]
- Open answer [*Other*]

Figure 8.4 provides information on the criteria based on which natives and migrants with one and both parents born abroad have primarily constructed their educational plans. In all three groups, the most important reason are labor market opportunities in general. As much as 40% of natives, 35% of students with both parents born abroad and 31% of migrants with one parent born abroad reported this aspect to be most important to the construction of their educational plans. The second most important reason for natives and both migrant groups is their need for a particular educational qualification to be able to pursue their future career aspirations. For native students, the next most important reason is the consideration that the realization of their future career aspirations does not require any higher general educational qualifications. This consideration is comparatively less important to migrants, for whom good chances to find a job are the third most important reason. A comparatively small share of 5% of natives, 7% of migrants with one parent born abroad and 9% of migrants with both parents born abroad would prefer to obtain a higher qualification if their grades were better. Other reasons were chosen by less than 5% of students in each group.[28]

In sum, the data clearly indicates that career-related aspects play the most important role in the construction of students' general educational plans. Yet, it needs to be kept in mind that students were explicitly asked to indicate the *one* reason that is *most* important to them. This approach was adopted in order to as-

---

28 *Parents*: natives 0.6%, one parent born abroad 0%, both parents born abroad 4.2%; *Friends, own living*: natives 0.6%, one parent born abroad 0%, both parents born abroad 1%; *Confidence*: natives 1.2%, one parent born abroad 0%, both parents born abroad 0%; *Motivation*: natives 2.3%, one parent born abroad 2.4%, both parents born abroad 1%; *Other*: natives 2.9%, one parent born abroad 2.4%, both parents born abroad 1%. Students who reported 'other' reasons exclusively referred to a need for more time to figure out what they want to do after leaving the general educational system.

sess the *relative* importance students attribute to different criteria in constructing their aspirations, to identify students for whom low levels of educational performance constitute a binding constraint in realizing their most preferred educational options, and to exclude the possibility that students choose all or several response categories. Hence, the present findings do not necessarily imply that aspects such as the expectations and actions of students' significant others do not play an important role in the construction of their educational plans.

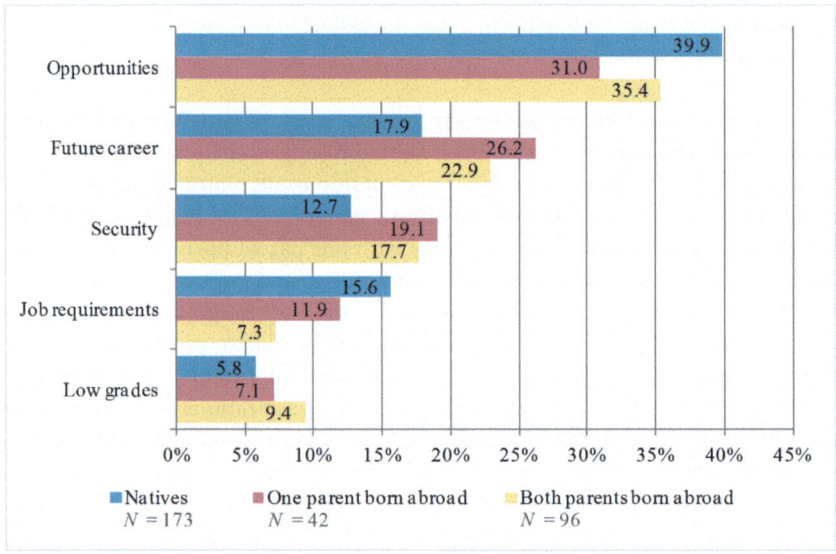

Figure 8.4 Motives for aspirations in general education

8.4   Expectations in general education

In consideration that students' educational plans may not necessarily reflect the level of education they realistically expect to complete, they were asked to indicate how certain they are to realize their expressed educational plans in a follow-up question (figure 8.5).[29] A first observation is that students indeed reported com-

---

29 Based on a 4-point scale with the outcomes very uncertain, rather uncertain, rather certain, very certain.

8.4 Expectations in general education

paratively high levels of uncertainty to realize their educational plans. About one quarter of students in the group who plan to obtain full or restricted access to higher education and about one third of students who plan to obtain the intermediate qualification are very certain to accomplish their educational plans. In both groups, about half of the students reported to be rather certain to realize their plans. Very few students reported to be very uncertain to attain the planned level of education. Yet, the share who are rather uncertain to realize their educational plans is considerably high in all three groups. Due to the very small share of only nine students who plan to attain the lowest level of general education, this group is not considered in more detail.

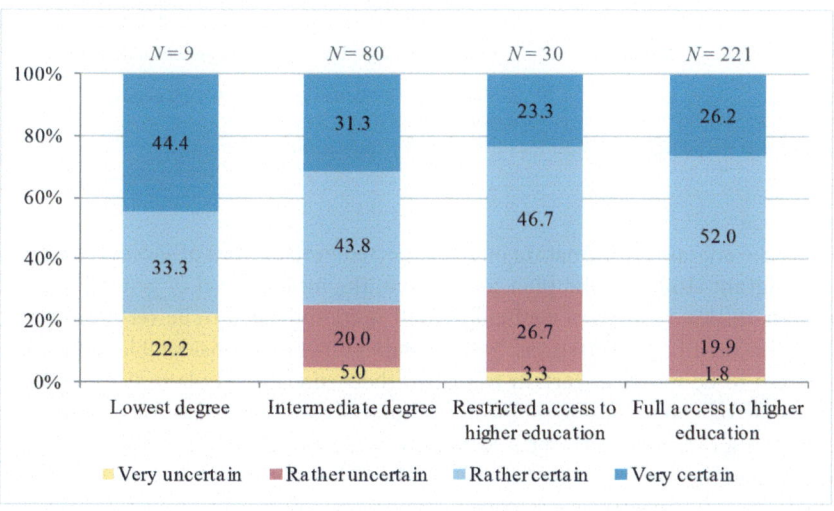

Figure 8.5 Expected probabilities of success, by educational aspiration

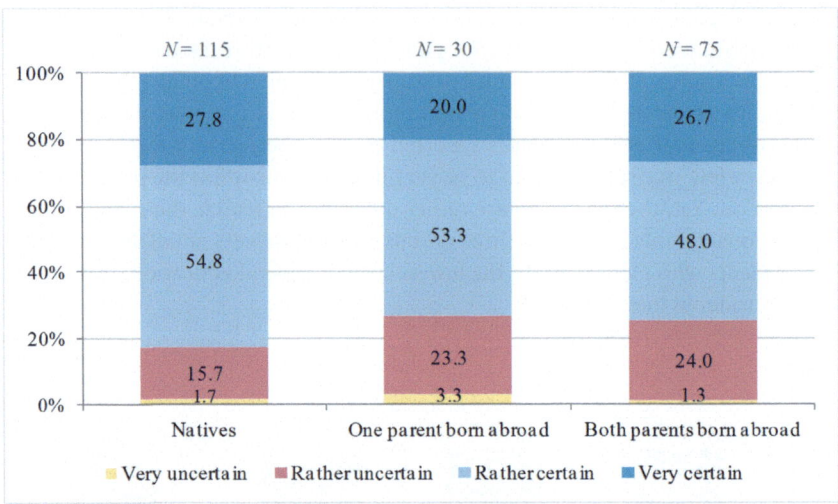

Figure 8.6 Expected probabilities of success, by migration background

Figure 8.6 contains information on the expected probabilities of success of native and migrant students who plan to complete the highest level of general education. In all three groups, a negligibly small share indicated to be very uncertain to realize their high aspirations. Yet, the data points to a considerable share who reported to be rather uncertain to realize their educational plans. This share is comparatively large among migrants and makes as much as almost one quarter of both migrant groups (compared to only 16% among natives). Also, the figure reveals that the share who are very certain to complete the highest level of general education is smaller among students with one parent born abroad compared to the other two groups, who differ slightly only in the shares who are very certain to accomplish their educational plans.

Broken down by sex, females can be found to be less certain to accomplish their educational plans than their male peers (not shown in figure 8.6). The share who are very certain to obtain the highest qualification is as small as 17% among females from both migrant groups and thus as much as seven percentage points smaller than the corresponding share in the group of female natives. The share who are very certain to complete the highest general qualification is highest among male migrants from families with both parents born abroad (44%), followed by male natives (33%) and males from families with one parent born abroad (25%).

Those students who did not report to be very certain to realize their educational plans were further asked to report the reasons for their uncertainty.[30] Low levels of past performance and the concern about future levels of educational performance are clearly the most important reason for the uncertainty on the part of natives and both migrant groups to realize their educational plans (about three quarters in each group). This finding, along with the observation that students tend to report ambitious educational plans even when they are uncertain to be able to realize these aspirations, suggests that it is students' expectations for success rather than their educational plans themselves that are conditioned by their perceptions of the opportunity structure. Yet, the data also points to a considerable share of about 11% both among native and migrant students who did not report to face any such barriers but who referred to a lack of motivation to stay in school much longer as the *only* reason for their uncertainty. This observation is illuminating insofar as it suggests that a gap between students' educational aspirations and expectations cannot necessarily be conceived of as the product of features of the opportunity structure.

8.5 Future educational aspirations

As regards students' future career aspirations, a pattern can be observed similar to the distribution of students' plans for their general educational qualifications (figure 8.7).[31] While the future educational aspirations of migrants from families with one parent born abroad are comparable to those of their native peers, migrants with both parents born abroad can be found to have career plans that strongly exceed those of the other two groups. More than half of the latter group plan to enter higher education after leaving the general educational system. This applies to a much smaller share in the other two groups where the majority of

---

30 The question was an immediate follow-up to the question how certain students are to eventually accomplish their educational plans. The wording was: "If you are not very certain, what is your reason?"; Response categories (multiple answers allowed): My grades are/ may not be high enough, I am not sure whether I really want to continue in general education that much longer, open answer. $N = 106$ for natives; $N = 24$ for migrants with one parent born abroad; $N = 74$ for migrants with both parents born abroad.

31 The wording of the question was "What educational qualification do you plan to obtain after leaving school?"; Response categories: qualification from VET, master craftsman certificate/ vocational college, higher education degree, no further qualification, other (open answer).

students plan to enter the VET system. A remarkable observation is the very small share of students in all three groups who reported to be undecided what type of education to pursue after leaving the general educational system. The data further suggests that this finding is not merely attributable to students who plan to leave the general educational system in the near future and already know that they will pursue a career in the VET system: The share who are undecided what type of future education to pursue is comparably high among students who plan to obtain full or restricted access to higher education (not shown in figure 8.7).

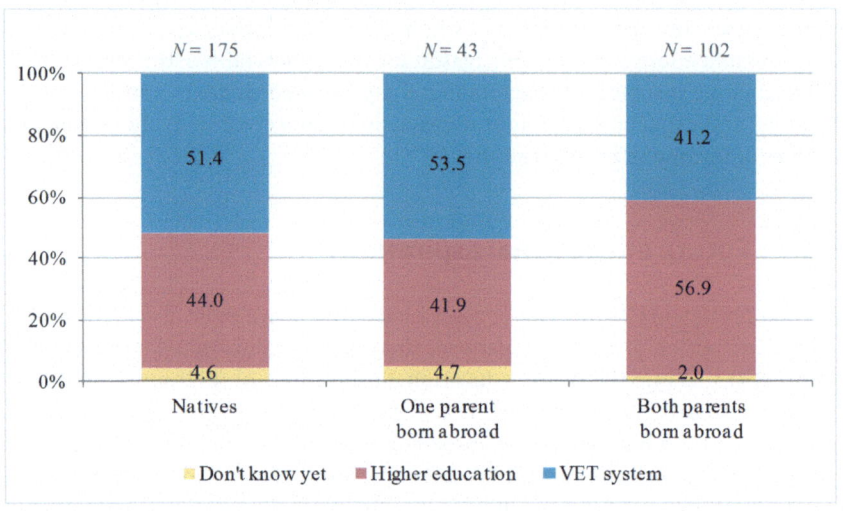

Figure 8.7 Future educational aspirations

Broken down by sex, the data shows that the share who plan to enter higher education is much higher among females than among males, and particularly high among females from families with both parents born abroad (not shown in figure 8.7). Among the latter, as much as 63% plan to enter higher education compared to less than half of their female peers from native families and families with one parent born abroad. The share of males who plan to enter higher education ranges from 31% among students with one parent born abroad to 39% among natives, and to as much as 48% among migrants with both parents born abroad. This pattern appears quite remarkable in view of the comparatively high levels of uncer-

8.5 Future educational aspirations

tainty to meet the entry requirements for higher education expressed by females, and in particular by female migrants.

Parents' aspirations for their children to complete higher education exceed students' own future educational plans in both migrant groups (not shown in figure 8.7).[32] Conversely, parental aspirations can be found to fall short of students' own future educational plans in native families. 37% of native parents would like their children to enter higher education. This applies to 57% in families with one parent born abroad and to as much as 65% of families with both parents born abroad.

Figure 8.8 contains information on the criteria students consider as *most* important in the construction of their future educational plans. With the exception of two minor changes, the same response categories were provided as in the analysis of students' reasons for their general educational plans. Above, students could indicate their need for the planned qualification to be able to pursue their future career aspirations [*future career*]. This response option was replaced by a category that refers to students' need for a particular vocational or post-secondary educational qualification to be able to attain their dream jobs [*dream job*]. Further, the concern that students' grades may not be high enough [*low grades*] was replaced by a category that refers to students' preference for a higher qualification which they perceive as inaccessible as they do not expect to meet the formal entry requirements [*entry barrier*].

---

[32] The wording of the question was: "What type of future career would your parents like you to pursue?" Response categories: career in VET, craftsman certificate, higher education, my parents have no preference, I don't know as we don't talk about this topic at home.

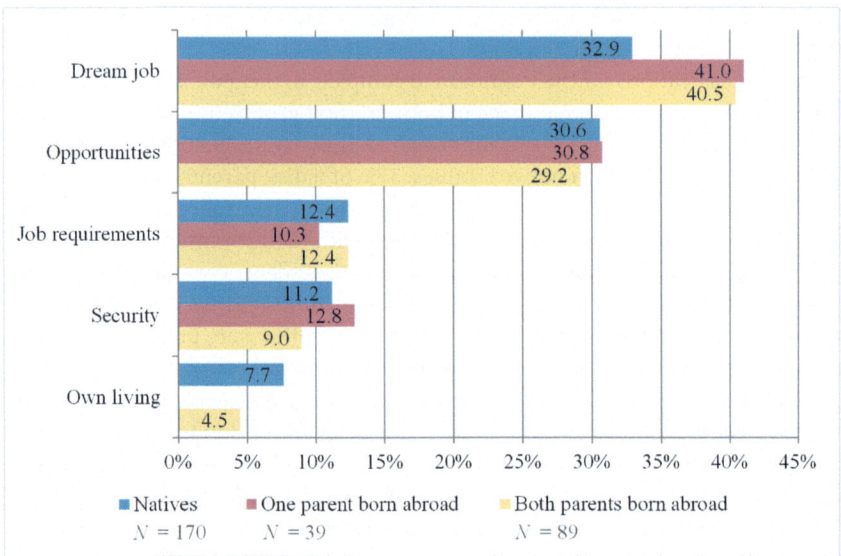

Figure 8.8 Motives for future educational aspirations

A first observation is the very high share of students in all three groups who have constructed their future educational plans primarily based on the consideration that they will need the respective qualification to be able to attain their dream jobs. Also, the data indicates that this reason is comparatively important to migrants (about 41% vs. 33% among natives). Almost one third of students from all three groups reported labor market opportunities in general to matter most to the construction of their future educational plans, followed by students who reported that the jobs they are interested in do not require any higher qualifications than the ones they plan to obtain and good chances to find a job as their most important reason for their career plans. Opposed to the construction of students' general educational plans, several students in the group of natives and migrants with both parents born abroad reported their desire to make their own living as soon as possible as their most important reason for their future educational plans. Other reasons were chosen rarely, if at all.[33]

---

33 *Parents*: natives 1.2%, one parent 0%, both parents 1.1%; *Friends*: all 0%; *Confidence*: natives 1.2%, one parent 0%, both parents 1.1%; *Entry barriers*: natives 1.8%; one parent 0%, both parents 1.1%; *Other*: natives 1.2%, one parent 2.6%, both parents 1.1%.

8.5 Future educational aspirations

The finding that a considerable share of students have constructed their future educational plans based on the consideration that they need a specific qualification to be able to attain their dream jobs, or do not plan to obtain any higher degrees because the careers they aspire to do not require any higher qualifications, suggests that students tend to have a relatively clear picture of their future career plans. Figure 8.9 contains information on the certainty with which students indicated to know what specific career to pursue after leaving the general educational system and gives rise to a different interpretation. In consideration that students who plan to leave the educational system after grade 9 or 10 will be much more certain what precise career to pursue than students who plan to continue in school (as much as 42% of the former group had already applied for a position in the VET system and as much as 53% out of these students had already found a position when the data was collected), the figure contains information on students who plan to obtain the full or restricted entrance qualification for higher education only.

A first observation is the comparatively small share who are very or rather certain what precise career to apply for after leaving the general educational system.[34] The great majority reported to have ideas but to be still uncertain, and more than one third to not have any idea yet what career to pursue. The middle and the right bar show that students who reported to pursue a particular future educational career to be able to attain their dream jobs are comparatively more certain what precise career to pursue than the remainder of students who have constructed their future educational plans primarily based on other criteria. Yet, the observation of comparatively high levels of uncertainty what precise career to pursue even among this group indicates that students may have a clear picture of the level of career they pursue in terms of the associated entry requirements, but that they have not necessarily decided on any specific career alternatives (cf. Gottfredson 1981, 1996). At any rate, the data strongly suggests that labor market-related criteria, and the perceived instrumentality of educational qualifications to be able to realize future career aspirations specifically, play a significant role in the construction of both students' general and future educational plans.

---

34 The wording of the question was: "How certain do you know what precise career you will apply for after leaving the general educational system?"; Response categories: very certain, rather certain, I have ideas but I am not sure yet, still open.

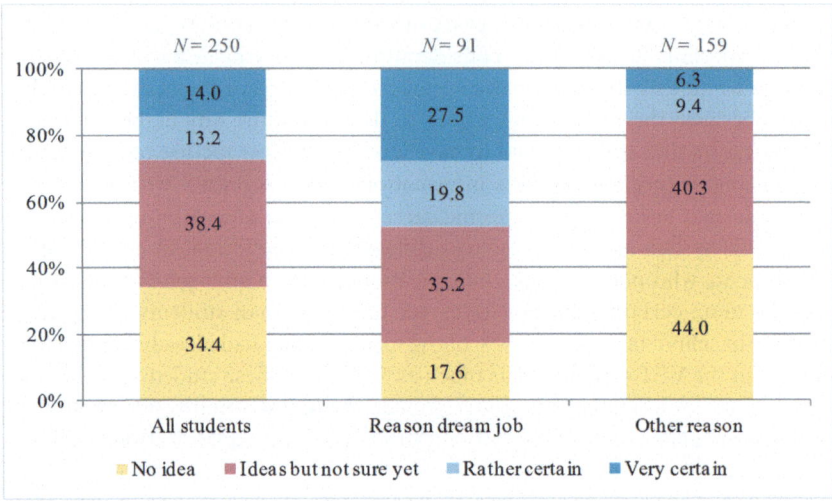

Figure 8.9 Certainty of career aspirations, by choice motive

8.6 Occupational aspirations

This section provides information on students' idealistic and realistic occupational aspirations. To assess students' idealistic aspirations, they were asked to list their dream occupation(s). To assess their realistic aspirations, they were asked what job or career they plan to apply for after leaving the general educational system. In order to obtain information on the career levels students realistically expect to attain in terms of the associated formal entry requirements also in the case of those students who did not have any precise career plans when the survey was carried out, students were asked to list the type of career(s) they can realistically imagine to pursue if they did not have any precise plans yet what specific career to pursue. Altogether, 291 dream jobs and 422 careers were listed that students realistically expect to pursue after leaving the general educational system.

Figure 8.10 shows that the majority of students from all three groups reported idealistic and realistic occupational aspirations. Also, the data shows that the majority of students from all three groups listed one single dream job only but several realistic occupational aspirations. This observation appears to be in line with the literature, which has shown students to compromise their most preferred career aspirations in terms of considering alternatives that they perceive as more realistically accessible as they anticipate or encounter barriers in the course of their educational careers (Gottfredson 1981; Heckhausen and Tomasik 2002). The share who did not report any occupational aspirations is comparatively high among migrants. Also, almost half of the group of native students reported at least two realistic occupational aspirations. This applies to a much smaller share in both migrant groups.

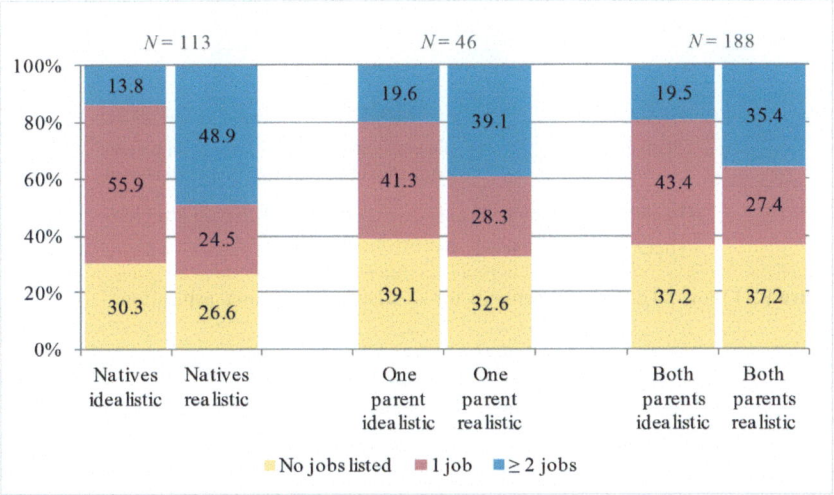

Figure 8.10 Number of occupational aspirations

To obtain further insight into whether students' realistic occupational aspirations are indeed associated with lower formal entry barriers than their idealistic aspirations, figures 8.11 and 8.12 provide information on the formal entry requirements for both types of occupational aspirations (given students expressed the respective type of aspiration). Each occupation was coded by whether it formally requires the highest level of general education (job type *highest level*), whether it does not formally require the highest level of general education (job type *lowest level*), or whether the occupation can be attained either through a career in VET or higher education (job type *ambiguous*; e.g., "game designer").

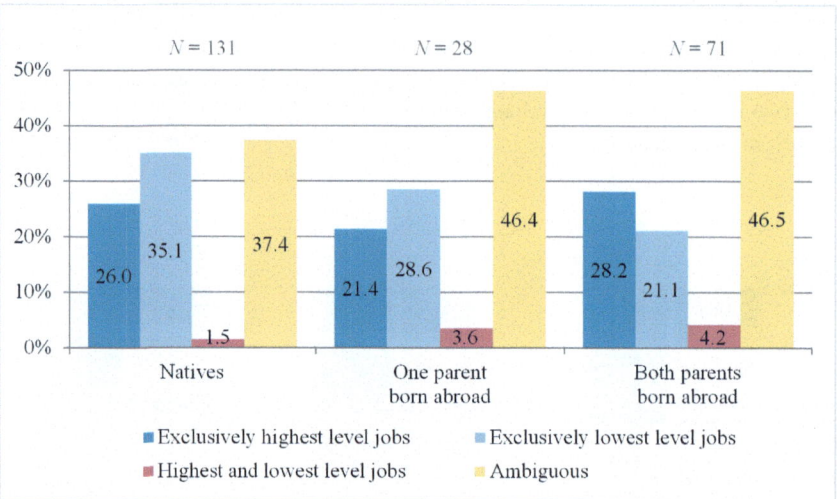

Figure 8.11 Formal entry requirements for idealistic occupational aspirations

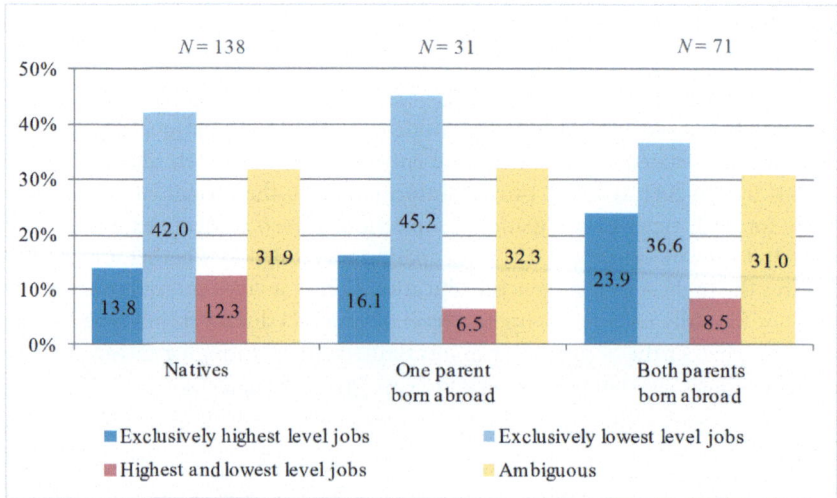

Figure 8.12 Formal entry requirements for realistic occupational aspirations

8.6 Occupational aspirations

As regards students' idealistic occupational aspirations, a first observation is the considerable share of students in all three groups who exclusively listed occupations that formally require the completion of the highest level of general education (*highest level*). This share is smallest among students with one parent born abroad and largest among students with both parents born abroad. The data further shows that the share who exclusively reported dream jobs that do not formally require the highest general educational qualification (*lowest level*) exceeds the share of students who exclusively listed jobs that formally require this qualification in the groups of natives and students with one parent born abroad, but points to a reverse pattern in the group of migrants from families with both parents born abroad. In line with the comparatively small share in all groups who reported more than one idealistic occupational aspiration, few students listed idealistic occupational aspirations of which some do but others do not formally require the completion of the highest level of general education (*highest and lowest level*). The largest share in all three groups listed careers of which all or some can either be attained through a career in VET or higher education (*ambiguous*).

Figure 8.12 contains information on the formal educational requirements for students' realistic occupational aspirations. As expected, the share of students who exclusively expressed realistic occupational aspirations that formally require the highest general educational qualification is much smaller than the share who exclusively reported idealistic occupational aspirations that require this level of education in all three groups. Also, the share who exclusively expressed realistic occupational aspirations that do not formally require this qualification is much higher compared to the share who exclusively reported idealistic occupational aspirations that do not require the completion of the highest level of general education. Also, a considerable share of students in all three groups listed occupations of which some do but others do not formally require the highest level of general education. This share is comparatively high among natives. On the one hand, these observations support the notion that both natives and migrants compromise their idealistic aspirations in terms of considering to pursue careers that are associated with lower formal entry barriers. On the other hand, they support the notion that students tend to entertain a range of future career aspirations that may vary in their formal educational requirements (cf. Gottfredson 1996; Haller and Miller 1963).

Yet, the interpretation of the present data requires considerable caution. As several students listed jobs that can be attained either through a career in VET or higher education and/or reported either one type of occupational aspiration only, the figures are not directly comparable. Among students who expressed at least one type of occupational aspiration, only 61% expressed both idealistic and realistic aspirations. Also, it needs to be kept in mind that students cannot necessarily be expected to realistically consider to pursue their idealistic occupational aspirations that are associated with comparatively low formal entry barriers (for example, "soccer player"). Further, even though the formal entry barriers for a given career certainly correlate with the associated level of prestige, more complex positions in the VET system may be associated with similar levels of prestige and income prospects as positions that formally require the completion of higher education (Bundesinstitut für Berufsbildung 2013). Finally, the observation that several students expressed career aspirations that are associated with different formal entry barriers points to the possibility that the occupations students listed in the questionnaire may not necessarily reflect the full spectrum of the careers they would prefer to or realistically consider to pursue but constitute a sample of the range of their aspirations only (Gottfredson 1981, 1996; Haller and Miller 1963).

To obtain insight into how students orient themselves toward their occupational futures, they were asked to indicate how important the following labor market-related and social-psychological criteria are to them in making their occupational choices:[35]

- The family's opinion and suggestions (adoption)
- Someone in the family or social network has the same or a similar job (imitation)
- Societal valuation of the job in Germany
- High income prospects
- Prospects for job promotion
- Demand for a given job in the heritage country

Figure 8.13 contains information on the importance students attribute to the family's opinion and suggestions. A very small share of 5% of natives consider this aspect as very important and almost one third as rather important to their career choices. The share of migrants with one parent born abroad who attribute very high importance to the family's opinion and suggestions is similarly small (7%). The share who consider the family's opinion to be rather important is as small as 20%. A quite different pattern can be observed for migrants from families where both parents were born abroad. The share who consider the family's opinion and suggestions as very important is as high as 21%, and an additional 42% of students from this group reported this criterion to be rather important to them in making

---

35 A 5-point scale was used with the response categories: not important at all, rather unimportant, not sure, rather important, very important".

8.6 Occupational aspirations

their occupational choices. Also, the share of students who do not attribute any importance to the family's opinion is very small in the group of migrants with both parents born abroad compared to the other two groups.

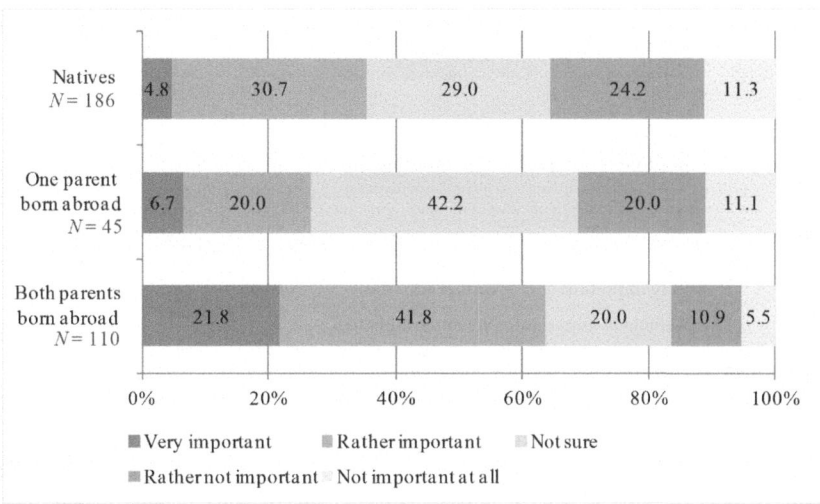

Figure 8.13 Importance of adoption mechanisms

As regards the importance students attribute to whether someone in the family or social network has the same or a similar job, figure 8.14 indicates that imitation processes are much less important than adoption mechanisms. No native student rated this criterion as very important and only 4% as rather important. A slightly larger share of 9% consider similar jobs in the family or social network as very or rather important among students with one parent born abroad. Among students with both parents born abroad, the share who consider this criterion as very important is also very small (2%). However, a comparatively large share of 13% rated this aspect as rather important (13%).

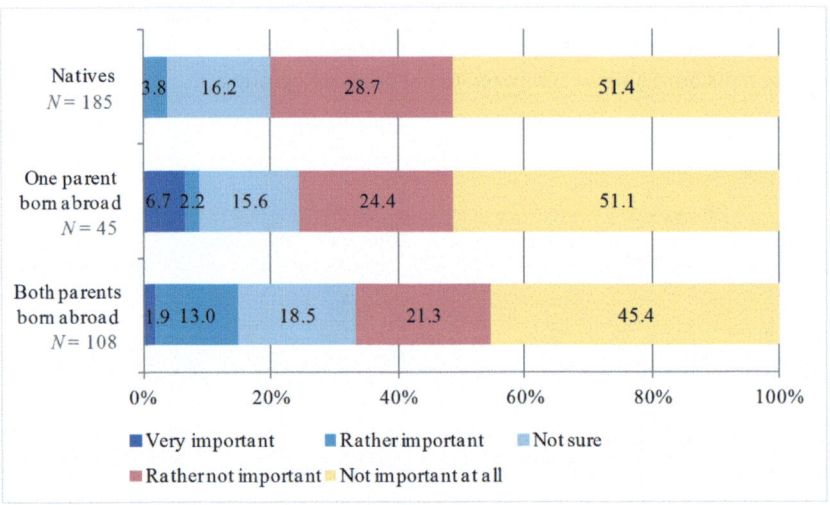

Figure 8.14 Importance of imitation mechanisms

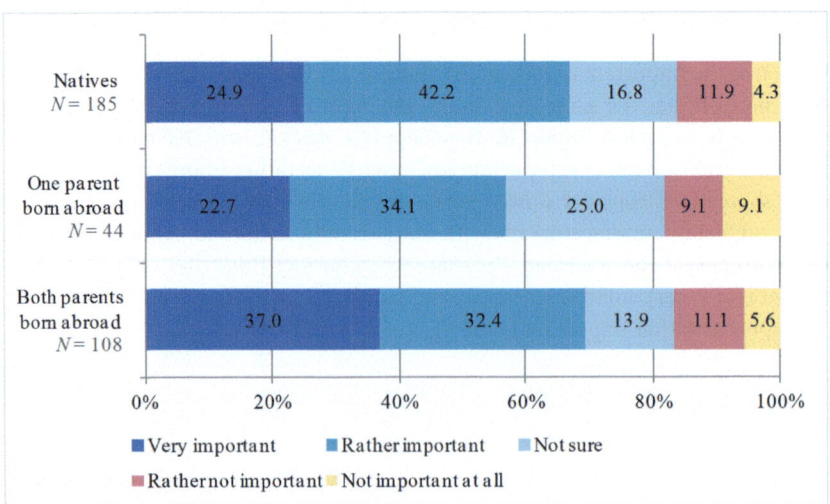

Figure 8.15 Importance of societal valuation

8.6 Occupational aspirations

A quite different pattern can be observed with respect to the importance students attribute to the societal valuation of a given occupation in Germany, which was rated as very important by a high share of students from all three groups (figure 8.15). As much as one quarter of natives attribute very high importance to this aspect, and an additional 42% consider this aspect as rather important. While the corresponding shares among migrants with one parent born abroad are slightly smaller, the societal valuation associated with a given occupation appears to be particularly important to students with both parents born abroad. In this group, more than one third consider this aspect as very important and another third as rather important in making their occupational choices.

High income prospects are perceived as very important by an even larger share of students from both migrants groups, and especially by students from families with both parents born abroad (figure 8.16). Conversely, the share of natives who attribute very high importance to this criterion is smaller than the share who consider societal valuation as very important. The data further points to a clear pattern of a very small share in all three groups who attribute little or no importance to income prospects.

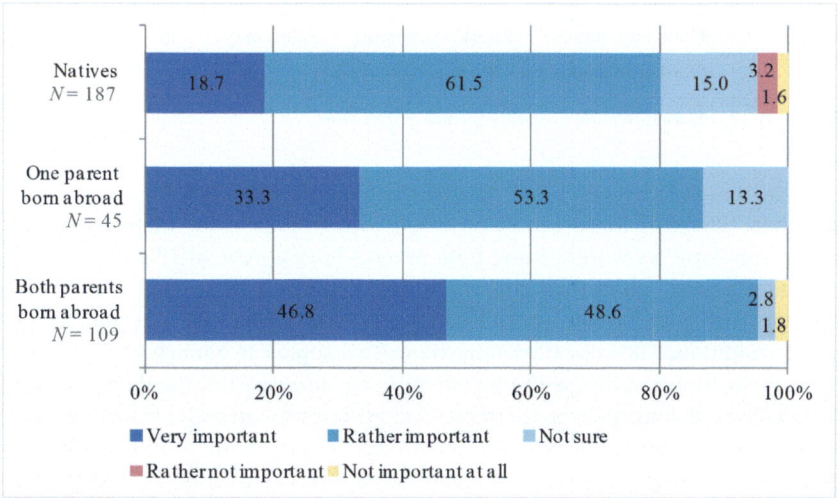

Figure 8.16 Importance of income prospects

Finally, prospects for job promotion appear to be the most important criterion based on which students make their occupational choices (figure 8.17). In all three groups, this criterion was rated as very important more often than any of the other criteria. Also, the share who consider this criterion as not or rather not important to their career choices is negligibly small in all three groups. Again, the share who consider prospects for job promotion as very important is comparatively large among migrants, and in particular among migrants with both parents born abroad.

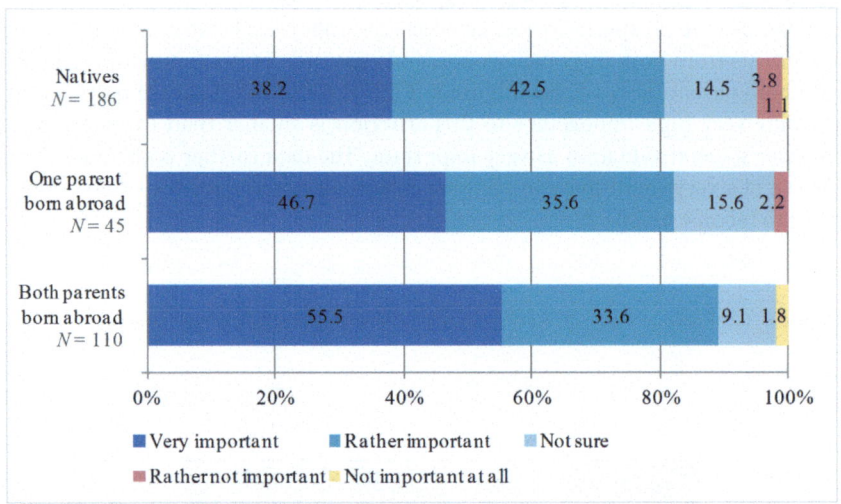

Figure 8.17 Importance of prospects for job promotion

A rather different pattern can be observed with respect to the importance students from families with one and both parents born abroad attribute to the demand for a given job in their country of origin (figure 8.18). As much as 19% of students with both parents born abroad perceive this criterion as very important and an additional 18% as rather important. This applies to a much smaller share of students from families with one parent born abroad. Also, the data points to a high share of students from both migrant groups who attribute little or no importance to the demand for a given job in their heritage country. In line with the comparatively high importance students from families with both parents born abroad attribute to the demand for a given job in the country of origin, the share who consider this criterion as (rather) not important is comparatively small in this group.

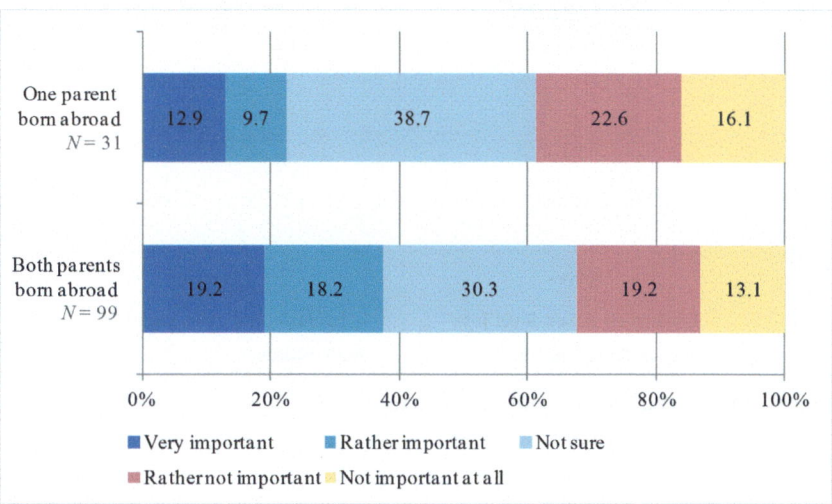

Figure 8.18 Importance of labor market demand in country of origin

8.7 Comparing future educational and occupational aspirations

The analysis above showed that the majority of students reported their plans to enter the VET system or higher education after leaving the general educational system, while very few students reported to be undecided what type of future education to pursue. This observation appears quite remarkable in view of the considerable share of students who expressed realistic occupational aspirations that are associated with different formal entry requirements. To obtain further insight into this matter, figures 8.19 and 8.20 provide information the formal educational requirements for the realistic occupational aspirations of students who plan to enter the VET system (figure 8.19) and who plan to pursue a career in higher education (figure 8.20) after leaving the general educational system (provided information is available both on their future educational plans and their realistic occupational aspirations). To avoid small case numbers, migrants with one and both parents born abroad are treated as one group.

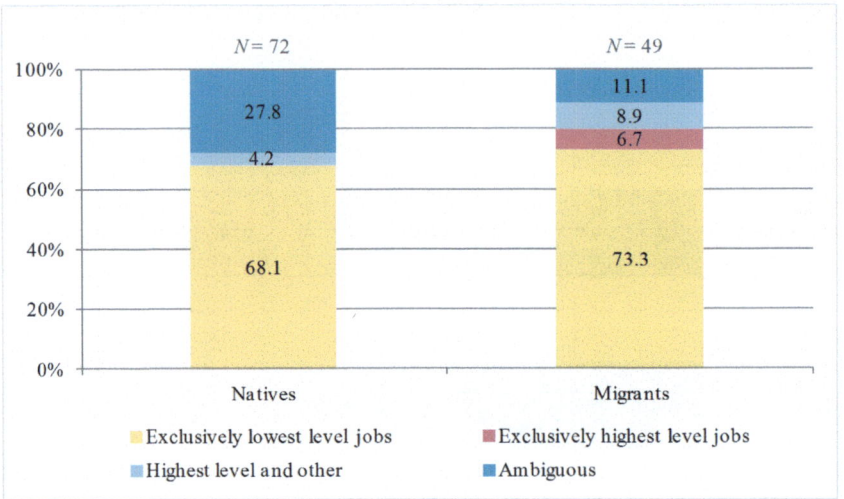

Figure 8.19 Realistic occupational aspirations and VET

As regards students who plan to pursue a career in the VET system, the great majority expressed realistic occupational aspirations with formal entry barriers that correspond to their future educational aspirations. More than two thirds in both groups exclusively listed jobs that can be realized through a career in the VET system and do not formally require the completion of higher education (*lowest level*). A comparatively small share in both groups listed occupations of which some only formally require the highest general educational qualification, while others do not formally require this level of education or can be entered either through a career in VET or higher education (*highest level and other*). The latter share is about twice as high in the group of migrants. Also, almost 7% of migrants but no native student exclusively reported realistic occupations that formally require the completion of the highest level of general education (*highest level*). The remainder of students exclusively listed occupations that can be attained either through a career in VET or through higher education, or both jobs that can be attained through VET or through different career paths (*ambiguous*). While no further information is available on the precise career plans of the latter group, on the whole the data does not point to any major deviations of students' future educational aspirations from the formal educational requirements for their realistic occupational aspirations.

An entirely different pattern can be observed for the group of students who reported to plan to enter higher education after leaving the general educational system. Only about one third of students in both groups exclusively expressed realistic occupational aspirations that formally require the highest level of general education. Even, a considerable share in both groups exclusively reported occupational aspirations that do not formally require this qualification. Further, as much as one quarter of the subsample of natives and 14% among migrants listed realistic occupational aspirations of which some do but others do not formally require the highest level of general education. The remainder of students listed jobs that require the completion of higher education as well as careers that can be attained either through a career in VET or higher education, or exclusively occupational aspirations that can be realized through different career paths (*ambiguous*). Even though no conclusions can be drawn with respect to the precise realistic occupational aspirations of the latter group, the data clearly points to a rather strong mismatch between the future educational aspirations and the formal entry requirements for students' realistic occupational aspirations in the group of students who plan to enter higher education.

As regards differences in the congruence between the future educational and realistic occupational aspirations expressed by natives and migrants, it needs to be kept in mind that the figures above are not directly comparable. On the one hand, no information is available on the precise career plans of several students. On the other hand, the possibility was discussed that the occupational aspirations students reported in the questionnaire may constitute a sample but not the full range of careers they realistically consider to pursue (Gottfredson 1981, 1996; Haller and Miller 1963).

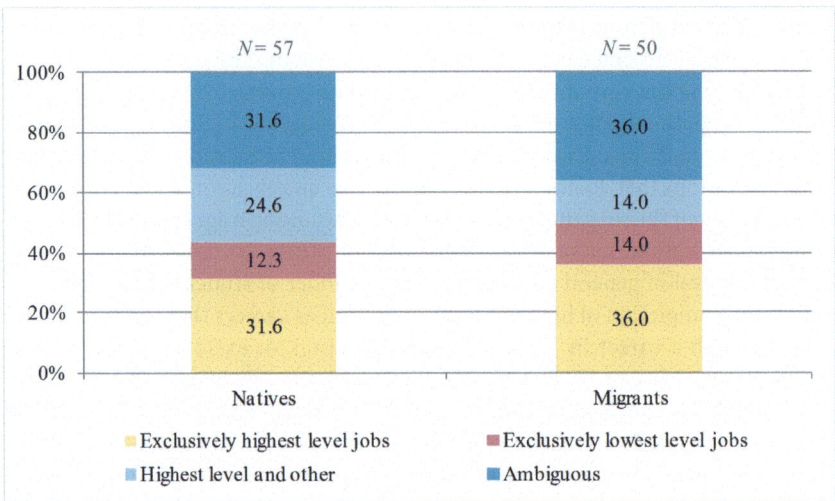

Figure 8.20 Realistic occupational aspirations and higher education

References

Becker, B. (2010). *Bildungsaspirationen von Migranten: Determinanten und Umsetzung in Bildungsergebnisse* (MZES Working Paper No. 137). Retrieved Febuary 5, 2012, from http://www.mzes.unimannheim.de/publications/wp/wp-137.pdf

Bundesinstitut für Berufsbildung (2013). *Datenreport zum Berufsbildungsbericht 2013: Informationen und Analysen zur Entwicklung der beruflichen Bildung.* Retrieved October 30, 2013, from http://datenreport.bibb.de/media2013/BIBB_Datenreport_2013.pdf

Chlosta, C., & Ostermann, T. (2007). Warum fragt man nach der Herkunft, wenn man die Sprache meint? Ein Plädoyer für eine Aufnahme sprachbezogener Fragen in demographische Untersuchungen. In Bundesministerium für Bildung und Forschung (Ed.), *Migrationshintergrund von Kindern und Jugendlichen: Wege zur Weiterentwicklung der amtlichen Statistik* (pp. 55-65). Berlin.

Ditton, H., Krüsken, J., & Schauenberg, M. (2005). Bildungsungleichheit – der Beitrag von Familie und Schule. *Zeitschrift für Erziehungswissenschaft, 8*(2), 285-304.

Ganzeboom, H. B. G. (2010). *A New International Socio-Economic Index [ISEI] of Occupational Status for the International Standard Classification of Occupation 2008 [ISCO-08] Constructed with Data from The ISSP 2002-2007.With an Analysis of Quality of Occupational Measurement in ISSP.* Paper presented at the Annual Conference of International Social Survey Programme, Lisbon. Retrieved August 29, 2013, from http://home.fsw.vu.nl/hbg.ganzeboom/isco08/qa-isei-08.htm

Göbel, K., Rauch, D., & Vieluf, S. (2011). Leistungsbedingungen und Leistungsergebnisse von Schülerinnen und Schülern türkischer, russischer und polnischer Herkunftssprachen. *Zeitschrift für Interkulturellen Fremdsprachenunterricht, 16*(2), 50-65.
Gogolin, I. (1994). Lebensweltliche Mehrsprachigkeit. In K.-R. Bausch, F. G. Königs & H.-J. Krumm (Eds.), *Mehrsprachigkeit im Fokus. Arbeitspapiere der 24. Frühjahrskonferenz zur Erforschung des Fremdsprachenunterrichts* (pp. 55-61). Tübingen: Narr.
Gottfredson, L. S. (1981). Circumscription and Compromise: A Developmental Theory of Occupational Aspirations. *Journal of Counseling Psychology Monograph, 28*(6), 545-579.
Gottfredson, L. S. (1996). Gottfredson's Theory of Circumscription and Compromise. In D. Brown & L. Brooks (Eds.), *Career Choice and Development* (3 ed., pp. 179-232). San Francisco: Jossey–Bass.
Haller, A. O., & Miller, I. W. (1963). *The Occupational Aspiration Scale: Theory, Structure and Correlates* (AES-TB No. 288). Retrieved September 9, 2011, from http://files.eric.ed.gov/fulltext/ED016712.pdf
Heath, A. F., & Brinbaum, Y. (2007). Guest Editorial: Explaining Ethnic Inequalities in Educational Attainment. *Ethnicities, 7*(3), 291-304.
Heckhausen, J., & Tomasik, M. J. (2002). Get an Apprenticeship Before School is Out: How German Adolescents Adjust Vocational Aspirations When Getting Close to a Developmental Deadline. *Journal of Vocational Behavior, 60*, 199-219.
Klieme, E., Artelt, C., Hartig, J., Jude, N., Köller, O., Prenzel, M., Schneider, W., & Stanat, P. (2010). *PISA 2009: Bilanz nach einem Jahrzehnt*. Münster: Waxmann.
Kristen, C., & Dollmann, J. (2010). Sekundäre Effekte der ethnischen Herkunft: Kinder aus türkischen Familien am ersten Bildungsübergang. In B. Becker & D. Reimer (Eds.), *Vom Kindergarten bis zur Hochschule: Die Generierung von ethnischen und sozialen Disparitäten in der Bildungsbiographie* (pp. 117-144). Wiesbaden: VS Verlag für Sozialwissenschaften.
Kristen, C., Edele, A., Kalter, F., Kogan, I., Schulz, B., Stanat, P., & Will, G. (2011). The Education of Migrants and their Children Across the Life Course. *Zeitschrift für Erziehungswissenschaft, 14*(2), 121-137.
Morgan, S. L. (1998). Adolescent Educational Expectations: Rationalized, Fantasized, or Both? *Rationality and Society, 10*(2), 131-162.
Statistische Ämter des Bundes und der Länder. (2013). Bevölkerung nach Migrationsstatus regional: Ergebnisse des Mikrozensus 2011. Wiesbaden.
Statistisches Bundesamt (2013a). *Bevölkerung und Erwerbstätigkeit: Bevölkerung mit Migrationshintergrund: Ergebnisse des Mikrozensus 2011* (Series 1, 2.2). Wiesbaden. Retrieved June 6, 2013, from https://www.destatis.de/DE/Publikationen/Thematisch/Bevoelkerung/AlteAusgaben/MigrationshintergrundAlt.html
Stubbe, T. C., Bos, W., & Euen, B. (2012). Der Übergang von der Primar- in die Sekundarstufe. In W. Bos, I. Tarelli, A. Bremerich-Vos & K. Schwippert (Eds.), *IGLU 2011: Lesekompetenzen von Grundschulkindern in Deutschland im Internationalen Vergleich* (pp. 210-226). Münster: Waxmann.
Tarelli, I., Valtin, R., Bos, W., Bremerich-Vos, A., & Schwippert, K. (2012). IGLU 2011: Wichtige Ergebnisse im Überblick. In W. Bos, I. Tarelli, A. Bremerich-Vos & K. Schwippert (Eds.), *IGLU 2011: Lesekompetenzen von Grundschulkindern in Deutschland im Internationalen Vergleich* (pp. 11-25). Münster: Waxmann.

Explaining students' educational aspirations   9

The analysis above provided insight into the educational and future career aspirations and expectations of natives and migrants but did not take into account background characteristics. The following sections develop a model to investigate the conditions and mechanisms that shape students' educational aspirations and to identify differences in the background-adjusted probability to plan to complete the highest level of general education between natives and migrants. In line with common specifications of models of educational aspirations, expectations and choice, the analysis proceeds in a stepwise manner. In a first step, a base model that contains exogenous variables only is successively extended by variables that are assumed to capture effects of social and ethnic origin. In a second step, variables are introduced that reflect the formal educational requirements for students' future career aspirations to investigate the extent to which they can predict students' aspirations in general education. Even though the data does not allow for causal attribution, the analysis further investigates whether there is evidence to support the notion that students construct their educational aspirations in consideration of the educational requirements for their future career aspirations. In a last step, social-psychological variables are added to obtain a better understanding of how students construct their educational aspirations. The variables utilized in the analysis are summarized in table 9.1.

Table 9.1 Summary of variables, students' educational aspirations

	Mean	SD	Min.	Max.
Sex (1=male)	0.37	0.48	0	1
Grade 10	0.45	0.5	0	1
Individual and family characteristics				
One parent born abroad	0.12	0.33	0	1
Both parents born abroad	0.29	0.46	0	1
Nr. of books in household > 200	0.55	0.5	0	1
Socioeconomic position (HISEI)	49.88	19.22	14.21	88.7
Cognitive abilities test score	42.68	9.45	25	67
Language test score	33.49	8.7	9.99	55.82
Self-efficacy beliefs	3.02	0.42	1.2	4
Educational plans and aspirations				
Student aspiration: highest general qualification	0.68	0.47	0	1
Student aspiration: higher education	0.46	0.5	0	1
Student aspiration: VET	0.46	0.5	0	1
Parental aspiration: highest general qualification	0.84	0.37	0	1
Parental aspiration: higher education	0.48	0.5	0	1
Parental aspiration: VET	0.26	0.44	0	1
Occupational aspirations				
Realistic: all jobs require highest qualification	0.12	0.33	0	1
Realistic: no job requires highest qualification	0.27	0.44	0	1
Idealistic: all jobs require highest qualification	0.18	0.39	0	1
Idealistic: no job requires highest qualification	0.2	0.4	0	1

NOTE: $N = 208$.

In consideration of different patterns of missing data, only those students are included in the analysis who answered all relevant questions and who participated both in the language test and the test for cognitive abilities to keep the sample size consistent across models ($N = 208$). Following the primary interest in whether students plan to attain the highest level of general education or not, and to avoid estimation difficulties that may result from the comparatively small sample size, students' educational aspirations are collapsed into a binary variable that takes on the value 1 if a student plans to complete the highest level of general education and 0 otherwise. In line with this binary operationalization, logistic regression analyses are carried out to identify predictors of the probability that students plan to attain the highest level of general education. While the relatively small sample size makes it more difficult to identify statistical significance, the analysis may as well provide unstable estimates and reveal significant coefficients that have no real meaning as they reflect differences between groups that include very few observations only. To take these considerations into account, conservative bootstrap standard errors and test statistics were additionally estimated.

9.1 Primary effects of social and ethnic origin

Model 1a (table 9.2) contains the coefficients of the base model that includes information on students' sex, the grade attended and on their migration background, indicating whether at least one parent is born abroad or not.[36] Females and migrants, and in particular female migrants, were shown in the descriptive analysis to have comparatively high educational plans. The grade attended at the time of data collection was introduced in consideration of several mechanisms that may lead to a systematically different distribution of the educational plans of 9th- and 10th-graders. 10th-graders are likely to be positively selected for level of educational performance and motivation as particularly poor performing and unambitious students may have left the general educational system after grade 9 already. Also, 9th-graders may be comparatively uncertain with respect to their educational potential due to a lack of information about the learning tasks they will encounter in higher grades and be more cautious with respect to the expression of high educational plans (cf. Morgan 1996, 1998). Conversely, the majority of 10th-graders already knew whether their grades allowed them to continue in general education or not at the time of data collection. However, it was also discussed that students tend to compromise their aspirations in the course of their educational careers in terms of relinquishing their most preferred options for less compatible but more accessible ones as they experience or anticipate barriers in implementing their most preferred choices (Gottfredson 1981, 2005). Then, a more realistic appraisal of the educational potential on the part of 10th-graders may as well lead to the expression of less ambitious educational plans in this group. When considering the three variables simultaneously, none of the coefficients is significant at any common level and the model is not significant.

---

36 See Appendix B on http://www.ew.uni-hamburg.de/de/ueber-die-fakultaet/personen/trebbels.html for bootstrap results.

Table 9.2 Educational aspirations, primary effects (one migrant dummy)

Educational aspiration	Model 1a	Model 2a	Model 3a	Model 4a
Male	-0.133 (0.312)	-0.223 (0.321)	-0.328 (0.33)	0.097 (0.361)
10th grade	-0.02 (0.305)	0.064 (0.312)	0.082 (0.32)	0.184 (0.344)
Migrant	0.204 (0.306)	0.483 (0.329)	0.807 * (0.357)	1.345 ** (0.408)
Cultural capital		0.909 ** (0.325)	0.634 (0.338)	0.529 (0.355)
Socioeconomic status			0.032 ** (0.01)	0.034 ** (0.01)
Cognitive abilities				0.026 (0.019)
Language skills				0.08 ** (0.024)
Constant	0.743 ** (0.256)	0.157 (0.33)	-1.319 * (0.567)	-5.504 *** (1.336)
Model fit				
Pseudo R^2	0.00	0.03	0.08	0.14
LR χ^2	0.68	8.75	20.22	36.88
Prob > χ^2	0.8772	0.0677	0.0011	0.0000
Bootstrap replicates (est.)	1000	1000	1000	1000
LR test		(vs. 1a)	(vs. 2a)	(vs. 3a)
LR χ^2		8.06	11.48	16.66
Prob > χ^2		0.0045	0.0007	0.0002

NOTE: $N = 208$; * $p < 0.05$; ** $p < 0.01$; *** $p < 0.001$. Standard errors in parentheses. Bolt coefficients at least significant at the 5% level based on bootstrap standard errors, generated using STATA 11 to draw (with replacement) 1000 replicated samples of size N. Bootstrap replicates (est.) = number of replicates (out of 1000) where all parameters could be estimated.

Models 2a and 3a (table 9.2) include additional variables to take into account the family's cultural capital, measured by whether a family is in possession of more than 200 books or less than that, and its socioeconomic position, measured by the highest ISEI score in the household (*HISEI*).[37] As expected, the family's cultural capital is positively and significantly associated with the probability that students plan to attain the highest level of general education. While the variable significantly improved the fit of the model, it remains insignificant. The positive coefficient for migrants increased but also remains insignificant. The family's so-

---

[37] The number of books in the household was measured using the following response categories: 0-10 books, 11-25 books, 26-100 books, 101-200 books, more than 200 books. Due to the comparatively small sample size the data was collapsed into a binary variable in consideration that the threshold of 200 books is often used to compare family resources across the population (e.g., Bos et al. 2007, p. 228; Blömeke et al. 2010, p. 144).

cioeconomic position is also positively and significantly associated with the probability to plan to complete the highest general educational qualification. Also, the introduction of the variable significantly improved the fit of the model, which is now significant at the 1% level. In line with the literature, the coefficient for migrants increased considerably and is significant at the 5% level when the family's socioeconomic position is taken into account, indicating that students with a migration background have a significantly higher background-adjusted probability to plan to complete the highest level of general education than their native peers.

The fact that the family's cultural capital is not significant anymore when its socioeconomic position is taken into account can be explained by the relatively crude measure of the number of books in the household and the correlation between the two variables. First, the possession of books requires financial resources, which can be assumed to be higher in families where parents occupy more favorable labor market positions. Second, from a human capital theoretical perspective it can be argued that the family's cultural capital is causal for its socioeconomic position as it promotes the accumulation of human capital and thereby enhances labor market opportunities. Then, the imprecise operationalization of the family's cultural capital as a binary variable, which was used to arrive at a more parsimonious model specification but cannot be expected to adequately reflect the availability of educationally-relevant resources, may lead to the fact that the fine-grained measure of the family's socioeconomic position overrides the effect of the proxy for the family's cultural capital.

Model 4a includes two further variables that reflect students' cognitive abilities and the scores they achieved in the text production task. On the one hand, cognitive abilities and majority language skills are considered important prerequisites for students' educational success and can be assumed to capture some of the variation in level of educational potential. On the other hand, majority language skills are introduced to explicitly consider conditions that may particularly strongly affect the educational success of students with a migration background (Gogolin 2009; Gogolin and Lange 2011). Students' cognitive abilities are not systematically associated with the probability to plan to complete the highest level of general education (neither when introduced into the model separately), but the scores achieved in the language assessment test are positively and significantly associated with the probability to plan to obtain this qualification. As outlined above, majority language skills are not only conceived of as a prerequisite for the educational success of migrants but also of natives. Yet, the finding that the language coefficient is significant when the family's socioeconomic position is taken into account, and that the coefficient for the family's socioeconomic background remains stable when students' language skills are added to the model, suggests the interpretation of language skills in terms of primary effects of ethnic origin. In line with these considerations, the coefficient for migrants considerably increased and is significant at the 1% level. Also, the introduction of the additional variables significantly improved the model fit.

Table 9.3 Educational aspirations, primary effects (two migrant dummies)

Educational aspiration	Model 1b	Model 2b	Model 3b	Model 4b
Male	-0.117 (0.314)	-0.201 (0.323)	-0.306 (0.331)	0.133 (0.364)
10th grade	-0.031 (0.306)	0.049 (0.314)	0.051 (0.323)	0.145 (0.349)
One parent born abroad	-0.106 (0.459)	0.15 (0.479)	0.331 (0.503)	0.647 (0.553)
Both parents born abroad	0.344 (0.35)	0.635 (0.373)	**1.031** * (0.404)	**1.668** *** (0.458)
Cultural capital		**0.914** ** (0.325)	0.62 (0.339)	0.491 (0.359)
Socioeconomic status			**0.033** ** (0.01)	**0.036** ** (0.011)
Cognitive abilities				0.028 (0.019)
Language skills				**0.084** *** (0.024)
Constant	**0.742** ** (0.256)	0.152 (0.33)	**-1.38** * (0.569)	**-5.784** *** (1.352)
Model fit				
Pseudo R²	0.01	0.04	0.08	0.15
LR χ²	1.45	9.60	21.86	39.88
Prob > χ²	0.835	0.0874	0.0013	0.0000
Bootstrap replicates (est.)	1000	1000	1000	1000
LR test		(vs. 1b)	(vs. 2b)	(vs. 3b)
LR χ²		8.15	12.26	18.02
Prob > χ²		0.0043	0.0005	0.0001

NOTE: $N = 208$; * $p < 0.05$; ** $p < 0.01$; *** $p < 0.001$. Standard errors in parentheses. Bolt coefficients at least significant at the 5% level based on bootstrap standard errors, generated using STATA 11 to draw (with replacement) 1000 replicated samples of size N. Bootstrap replicates (est.) = number of replicates (out of 1000) where all parameters could be estimated.

To take into account the observation of rather strong variations in the educational plans and preconditions for educational success across the migrant sample, the models above were reestimated based on the more fine-grained differentiation of the sample by the number of parents born abroad (table 9.3).[38] As above, no signif-

---

38 See Appendix C on http://www.ew.uni-hamburg.de/de/ueber-die-fakultaet/personen/trebbels.html for bootstrap results.

icant differences can be observed between natives and students with either one or both parents born abroad in the base model (model 1b). While the coefficient for both migrant groups steadily increases with the successive introduction of variables that are assumed to capture different preconditions for educational success, the results indicate that the significance of the coefficient for the binary migrant variable in the previous models is largely attributable to the group of students from families with both parents born abroad. The coefficient for students with one parent born abroad remains insignificant, whereas students with both parents born abroad have a significantly higher probability than natives to plan to attain the highest level of general education when variables are considered that are assumed to capture effects of social and ethnic origin. These observations are in line with the descriptive finding that students from families with both parents born abroad have comparatively high educational plans even when background characteristics are not taken into account, and that they achieved significantly lower language test scores and come from families in significantly lower socioeconomic positions than natives. Contrarily, students with one parent born abroad were found to have educational aspirations that slightly exceed those of their native peers only, and to be less disadvantaged with respect to the family's socioeconomic position. Also, this group achieved language test scores that are not significantly lower than those of their native peers. In line with the additional information provided by the more fine-grained variable to capture students' migration background, the model fits the data slightly better than the model that included the binary migrant variable.

As outlined in the theoretical part of the study, significant coefficients for migrants and the family's socioeconomic position in models to explain educational decisions or transitions that control for primary effects are often discussed with reference to secondary effects of ethnic and social origin, respectively. The significance of the positive coefficient for the family's socioeconomic position supports the notion that educational aspirations are an increasing function of social origin (e.g., Boudon 1974; Breen and Goldthorpe 1997; Erikson and Jonsson 1996; Gambetta 1987). The positive and significant coefficient for migrants is in line with the hypothesis that migrants are positively selected for their educational ambition due to migration-specific mechanisms such as their desire for upward mobility (Heath and Brinbaum 2007; Kao and Tienda 1995; Vallet 2007) and supportive of the notion that it is features of the opportunity structure that matter most to the emergence of ethnic disparities in educational attainment (e.g., Gresch et al. 2012; Klieme et al. 2010; Relikowski et al. 2010).

However, the interpretation of the present data requires considerable caution. First, it is unlikely that the variables that are sought to capture primary effects fully capture the variation in the educational preconditions across students. Second, it was discussed that standard measures of the family's socioeconomic position may not reflect the educationally-relevant resources in migrant families to the same extent as in native families due to the restricted transferability of country-specific human capital in migrant parents. Hence, both the coefficient for ethnic and stratification effects may be over- or underestimated (cf. Maaz et al. 2010). In view of the comparatively low performance levels that are consistently attested for mixed migrant samples, an insufficient control for primary effects is most likely associated with an underestimation of the migrant coefficients. Also, the finding that language skills and social origin are not systematically related may, at least partly, be attributable to the lack of control for primary effects. Finally, the question remains open to what extent students' educational plans are associated with the actions they take for their enactment.

9.2   Future career aspirations

The following sections extend the models above to include information on the formal educational requirements for students' future career aspirations. As regards the potential existence of a causal effect from students' future career aspirations on their plans in general education, the underlying consideration is that students whose future career aspirations formally require the completion of the highest level of general education may be more likely to plan to obtain this qualification than their peers who pursue careers that are associated with lower formal entry requirements as the completion of this qualification constitutes a prerequisite for them to be able to realize their future career plans. Contrarily, in view of the absence of formal entry requirements in the dual VET system, and formal entry requirements for positions in full-time school-based vocational education that for the most part do not require the completion of the highest level of general education, additional general education may be perceived as constituting unnecessary cost in terms of effort, time and money by students who plan to pursue a career in the VET system. This reasoning rests on the relatively strong assumption that students are not aware of the instrumental value of high general educational qualifications to realize their future career aspirations in the absence of formal entry barriers for their future career aspirations. Yet, empirical studies have shown that students often construct their career plans and expectations based on insufficient or incorrect information about labor market requirements (Gottfredson 1981, 1996, 2005; Relikowski et al. 2012; Reynolds et al. 2006; Schneider and Stevenson 1999). Hence, this assumption can be expected to hold for at least several students.

In consideration of the descriptive finding of a considerable share of students who reported their plans to enter higher education but who also or even exclusively reported realistic occupational aspirations that do not require this type of education, the analysis considers both the educational requirements for students' future educational and occupational aspirations. In a first step of the analysis, binary variables are introduced that reflect whether students plan to enter the VET system (section 9.2.1) and whether students exclusively expressed realistic occupational aspirations that do not formally require the highest level of general education (section 9.2.2). As regards students' future educational aspirations, the reference group includes students who plan to enter higher education as well as students who are undecided what type of educational career to pursue after leaving the general educational system. Provided that students indeed seriously consider to pursue the career aspirations they reported in the questionnaire, the latter should perceive the completion of the highest level of general education just as instrumental to realize their future career aspirations as their peers who plan to enter higher education in order to not eliminate any of the career alternatives they will eventually decide to pursue. As regards students' realistic occupational aspirations, the reference group is much more heterogeneous. It not only includes all students who exclusively or also listed occupations that formally require the completion of the highest level of general education. Also, it comprises students who also or exclusively listed occupations that can be attained either through a career in VET or higher education as well as students who did not express any realistic occupational aspirations. Hence, the operationalization of the variable that captures students' realistic occupational aspirations additionally rests on the strong assumptions that students who listed occupations that can be attained through alternative career paths indeed consider to enter higher education, and that students who did not express any realistic occupational aspirations do in fact not have any occupational aspirations and will perceive the completion of the highest level of general education as instrumental to not limit their range of career opportunities.[39] Section 9.2.3 utilizes an alternative operationalization to capture students' future career aspirations that allows to relax these assumptions.

9.2.1 Future educational aspirations

Model 5b (table 9.4) includes a binary variable that reflects students' future educational aspirations and takes on the value 1 if students plan to enter the VET

---

39 This aspect is discussed in more detail below.

system and 0 otherwise. A first observation is the considerably strong and significant association between students' future educational aspirations and the dependent variable, indicating that students who plan to enter a career in the VET system have a significantly lower probability to plan to attain the highest level of general education than their peers who plan to enter higher education or who are undecided what type of education to pursue after leaving the general educational system.

Table 9.4 Educational aspirations, future career aspirations

Educational aspiration	Model 5b	Model 6b	Model 7b
Male	0.263	0.153	0.241
	(0.413)	(0.396)	(0.375)
10th grade	-0.155	0.267	0.118
	(0.401)	(0.381)	(0.361)
One parent born abroad	0.593	0.607	0.532
	(0.606)	(0.616)	(0.581)
Both parents born abroad	0.987 *	**1.312 ****	**1.554 ****
	(0.499)	(0.476)	(0.47)
Cultural capital	0.194	0.342	0.309
	(0.397)	(0.385)	(0.369)
Socioeconomic status	0.027 *	**0.032 ****	**0.036 ****
	(0.012)	(0.011)	(0.011)
Cognitive abilities	0.019	0.023	0.021
	(0.021)	(0.021)	(0.02)
Language skills	**0.071 ***	**0.078 ****	**0.092 *****
	(0.028)	(0.026)	(0.025)
Future career aspirations			
Vocational education and training	**-2.506 *****		
(Ref. other)	(0.429)		
Real.: no job requires highest degree		**-1.818 *****	
(Ref. other)		(0.379)	
Ideal.: no job requires highest degree			**-1.337 ****
(Ref. other)			(0.41)
Constant	-2.619	**-4.512 ****	**-5.359 *****
	(1.571)	(1.479)	(1.407)
Model fit			
Pseudo R²	0.32	0.25	0.2
LR χ²	82.87	63.99	50.82
Prob > χ²	0.0000	0.0000	0.0000
Bootstrap replicates (est.)	1000	1000	1000
LR test	(vs. 4b)	(vs. 4b)	(vs. 4b)
LR χ²	42.99	24.11	10.94
Prob > χ²	0.0000	0.0000	0.0009

NOTE: $N = 208$; * $p < 0.05$; ** $p < 0.01$; *** $p < 0.001$. Standard errors in parentheses. Bolt coefficients at least significant at the 5% level based on bootstrap standard errors, generated using STATA 11 to draw (with replacement) 1000 replicated samples of size N. Bootstrap replicates (est.) = number of replicates (out of 1000) where all parameters could be estimated.

9.2 Future career aspirations

The variable significantly increased the model fit, but a considerable proportion of the variation in students' general educational aspirations remains unexplained. Even if the assumption was true that students construct their aspirations in general education based on the entry requirements for their future career aspirations, this observation may have several explanations. For instance, the existence of informal entry barriers for VET positions that are associated with comparatively high levels of complexity and prestige (Bundesministerium für Bildung und Forschung 2013) may lead to a comparatively low correlation between the plan to enter the VET system and the probability to plan to attain the highest level of general education. If students aspire to attain any such positions and are aware of their informal educational requirements, they should perceive high levels of general education as instrumental to realize their career aspirations. Conversely, the association between the plan to enter the VET system and the plan to attain the highest level of general education can be expected to be comparatively strong if students are not aware of the existence of informal entry barriers in the VET system or plan to attain positions that largely employ graduates with low educational qualifications.

No direct information is available on the extent to which students are aware of the existence of informal entry requirements in the VET system, but information on the precise VET careers students plan to attain and data on the educational qualifications of graduates that were employed in the respective positions in 2011 was combined to obtain some additional insight into this matter.[40] This data indicates that students who plan to attain the highest level of general education indeed pursue careers in the VET system that employ comparatively high shares of graduates who obtained the full or restricted higher education entrance qualification. Among students who plan to complete the highest level of general education, 50% listed positions that employed 48% or more highly qualified graduates, and 25% of students from this group plan to enter positions which employed 58% or more highly qualified graduates (i.e., students who obtained either full or restricted access to higher education) in 2011. Among students who do not plan to complete the highest level of general education, 50% plan to attain positions that employed at least 15% of highly qualified graduates, and 25% of these students aspire to VET positions that employed at least 28% of students who had obtained the full or restricted entry qualification for higher education in 2011.[41] These observations

---

40 Data provided by the Federal Employment Agency: http://berufenet.arbeitsagentur.de/berufe/ (accessed Oct. 20, 2013).
41 This data is derived from the investigation of the jobs students listed that are associated with the highest employment shares of highly qualified graduates (if they listed multi-

appear to support the hypothesis that students are, to a certain extent, aware of the existence of informal entry barriers in the VET system. However, the interpretation of the present data requires caution. Information on the educational background of graduates that are employed in different VET positions is available for occupations in the dual system only, but 43 out of 96 students who plan to pursue a career in VET do not (exclusively) consider to start a career in the dual VET system but (also) to attain positions in full-time school-based vocational education. Besides, it was discussed that students' expressed occupational aspirations may constitute a sample only of the full spectrum of careers they realistically consider to pursue (Gottfredson 1981, 1996; Haller and Miller 1963).

While the results obtained so far are not counter to the hypothesis that at least several students construct their educational plans in consideration of the instrumental value of high educational qualifications to realize their future career plans, the possibility cannot be excluded that students who plan to pursue a career in the VET system would prefer to pursue careers that are associated with higher formal entry barriers but compromised their future aspirations due to constraints such as low levels of perceived or actual educational potential (Gottfredson 1981, 1996, 2005; Heckhausen and Tomasik 2002). The additional consideration of students' most important reasons for their educational plans, however, gives rise to the interpretation that constraints in the form of insufficient levels of educational performance and low educational expectations may not be the only explanation for the observed association between students' future educational aspirations and the probability to plan to complete the highest level of general education. Only 16% of students who pursue a career in the VET system and who do not plan to complete the highest level of general education would prefer to complete higher levels of general education if their grades were better. The majority of the respective students reported reasons for their low general educational plans that are not related to level of educational performance. In fact, as much as 34% of students in this group have constructed their educational plans primarily based on the consideration that the careers they are interested in do not require any higher general educational qualifications. This observation suggests that a universally non-causal interpretation of the significant coefficient estimated for students' future career aspirations may not apply either. However, the possibility remains that students

---

ple occupations). A similar picture can be obtained for the jobs with the lowest informal entry barriers. Students who plan to complete the highest level of general education: 50% (25%) listed jobs that employed at least 26% (54%) of highly qualified graduates; remainder of students: 50% (25%) listed jobs that employed at least 14% (27%) of highly qualified graduates.

9.2 Future career aspirations

had not only compromised their realistic but also their idealistic career aspirations when the survey was carried out (Armstrong and Crombie 2000; Gottfredson 1981, 2005; Heckhausen and Tomasik 2002).

As concerns changes in the remaining coefficients, a noteworthy observation is the strong decrease in the coefficients for migrants and the family's socioeconomic position. The coefficient for migrants with both parents born abroad decreased in size and is significant at the 5% level only, and not at all based on bootstrap confidence intervals. Similarly, the coefficient for the family's socioeconomic position decreased in size and is significant at a lower level. These observations give rise to several interpretations. Assuming that the formal entry requirements for students' future career aspirations are causal for the general educational aspirations of at least some students, the decrease in the large coefficients that were observed for the binary migrant variable and for migrants with both parents born abroad in the previous models is in line with the hypothesis that migrants have more ambitious future career aspirations than their native peers due to their desire for upward mobility, which is certainly more probable through the path of higher education (Kao and Tienda 1995; Vallet 2007). The decrease in the coefficient for the family's socioeconomic position is in line with the literature insofar as it not only suggests students' general educational plans but also their future career aspirations to be a function of social background, be it due to the risk of status demotion in higher classes, for reasons of family solidarity or due to the incapacity of students from lower social backgrounds to construct ambitious life plans (Boudon 1974; Breen and Goldthorpe 1997; Erikson and Jonsson 1996; Gambetta 1987). However, it was also discussed that the coefficient may be systematically overestimated due to an insufficient control for primary effects. Hence, the possibility remains that the decrease in the coefficient for the family's socioeconomic position cannot be fully attributed to the higher future educational plans of students from families from higher social origin. Assuming that students construct their future career plans in consideration of past experiences of success and failure (Lent et al. 1994; Sewell et al. 1970), it is likely that the coefficient also decreased because students' future career aspirations to some extent reflect level of (perceived) educational potential. Similarly, the change in the language coefficient, which decreased but remains significant when students' future career aspirations are taken into account, suggests that productive majority language skills to some extent capture the variation in (perceived) educational potential across the sample.

9.2.2 Occupational aspirations

The analysis below replaces the variable that reflects whether students plan to pursue a career in VET or not by a variable that reflects the formal educational requirements for their realistic occupational aspirations (model 6b, table 9.4). In correspondence with the operationalization of students' future educational aspirations, their realistic occupational aspirations are operationalized as a binary variable that takes on the value 1 if students exclusively listed occupations that do not formally require the highest level of general education and 0 otherwise. As expected due to the high share of students who plan to pursue a career in the VET system and who exclusively listed jobs that do not formally require the highest level of general education, the coefficient is highly significant and significantly improved the fit of the model. Yet, the coefficient is much smaller than the coefficient that was estimated for students' future educational aspirations in the previous model. Also, the present model is significant but does not fit the data as well as the previous model. These observations appear to indicate that students' future educational aspirations predict their general educational plans better than the formal educational requirements for their realistic occupational aspirations. Yet, the poorer fit of the present model may as well result from the comparatively heterogeneous reference group of the variable that reflects the formal entry requirements for students' realistic occupational aspirations. Several students did not list any realistic occupational aspirations or occupations that can be attained either through a career in VET or higher education. In fact, the latter groups constitute a considerable share of the reference group. As much as 35% of the reference group did not report any realistic occupational aspirations, and another 35% also or exclusively listed occupations that can be attained either through a career in VET or higher education. Based on the assumption that high levels of general education are perceived as instrumental to not restrict the range of future opportunities by students who are not sure what type of career to pursue after leaving the general educational system, both groups were assigned to the reference group. Yet, the possibility remains that the respective students exclusively consider to pursue careers that do not formally require the highest level of general education.

As concerns the remaining coefficients, similar changes can be observed as in the previous model. The coefficients for migrants with both parents born abroad, the family's socioeconomic position and students' language test scores decreased but remain significant when students' realistic occupational aspirations are added to the model. The observation that the coefficients decreased to a lesser extent compared to the previous model can, at least partly, be explained by the lower explanatory power of the variable that reflects the formal educational requirements for students' realistic occupational aspirations compared to the variable that contains information on students' plans to enter the VET system.

As regards the hypothesis of a possible causal effect from students' future career aspirations on their aspirations in general education, the introduction of a variable that reflects the formal educational requirements for students' realistic occupational aspirations is related to the same difficulties that were encountered in the previous model. To obtain further insight into the question whether low realistic occupational aspirations may be causal for the construction of low aspirations in general education, or whether they are the mere result of students' low general educational expectations, the model above was reestimated using information on the formal entry barriers for students' idealistic occupational aspirations (model 7b, table 9.4). The new variable can be expected to explain the variation in students' educational aspirations less well than their realistic occupational aspirations but may provide additional insight into the nature of the association between students' future career aspirations and their aspirations in general education: Above, it was discussed that students not only compromise their realistic aspirations but that they also tend to shift their idealistic aspirations in the direction of their realistic aspirations over time (Armstrong and Crombie 2000; Gottfredson 1981, 2005; Heckhausen and Tomasik 2002). However, the descriptive finding that the formal educational requirements for students' idealistic occupational aspirations exceed those of their realistic occupational aspirations at any rate indicates that students had adjusted their idealistic occupational aspirations to their educational expectations to a lesser extent than their realistic occupational aspirations when the survey was carried out.

As expected, the model fits the data less well than the model that contains information on the formal educational requirements for students' realistic occupational aspirations. Yet, students who exclusively expressed idealistic occupational aspirations that do not formally require the highest level of general education can be found to have a significantly lower probability to plan to attain the highest level of general education than the remainder of students. Also, whereas the coefficients for the family's socioeconomic position and students' language skills were strongly reduced through the introduction of the variables that captured students' future educational plans and their realistic occupational aspirations in the previous models, they remain stable in size and significance. The decrease of the coefficient for migrants with both parents born abroad is in line with the descriptive finding that a comparable share of students in this group and in the group of natives exclusively expressed idealistic aspirations that formally require the highest level of general education. The observation that the coefficient for the language test score remains highly significant in the present model further suggests that students' language skills are not systematically associated with their idealistic occupational aspirations. If the assumption was true that majority language skills capture the variation in (perceived) educational potential to some extent, this finding further supports the notion that students' idealistic occupational aspirations are compromised to a lesser extent than their realistic occupational aspirations, and is thus counter to the assumption of a universally non-causal effect from students' future career aspirations on their aspirations in general education.

As concerns the positive and significant coefficient for the family's socioeconomic position, two explanations were offered above to explain the strong decrease of the coefficient both in size and significance that was observed when information on students' future educational aspirations and their realistic occupational aspirations was taken into account. First, it was discussed that students from families in higher socioeconomic positions may have more ambitious future career aspirations due to considerations such as the risk of status demotion. Second, the possibility was discussed that students' future educational aspirations and their realistic occupational aspirations capture some of the variation in level of (perceived) educational potential that is not captured by the variables that are assumed to capture primary effects, which may have been partly captured by the family's socioeconomic position in the previous models. The finding that the coefficient for the family's socioeconomic position remains stable in size and significance in the present model is in favor of the latter hypothesis as it indicates that students' realistic but not their idealistic occupational aspirations are a function of social origin.

Yet, it needs to be kept in mind that the results of the present model are not directly comparable to those of the model that includes information on students' realistic occupational aspirations as several students either reported their idealistic or realistic occupational aspirations but not both: 59% of students listed both idealistic and realistic occupational aspirations, and about one third reported either one type of aspiration only. At any rate, though, the results are supportive of the notion that students' future career aspirations are causal for the general educational aspirations of at least several students.

9.2.3 Considerations of uncertainty

The binary variable operationalization used to capture students' future educational and occupational aspirations in the models above was based on the consideration that high educational qualifications are not only perceived as instrumental by students who plan to pursue future careers that formally require the

9.2 Future career aspirations

completion of higher education, but also by those who are undecided what type of future education to pursue or who expressed occupational aspirations that are associated with different formal educational requirements in order to not eliminate any career alternatives they may eventually decide to pursue. The operationalization of the variable that captures students' realistic occupational aspirations was discussed to additionally rest on the strong assumptions that students who listed occupations that can be attained through alternative career paths indeed consider to enter higher education, and that students who did not express any realistic occupational aspirations do in fact not have any occupational aspirations and will perceive the completion of the highest level of general education as instrumental to not limit their range of career opportunities. To relax these assumptions, the following models include variables that reflect the formal entry barriers that are associated with students' future career aspirations in a more fine-grained manner by treating students who are undecided whether to enter VET or higher education, or who expressed occupational aspirations that are associated with different formal entry barriers, as a separate outcome category.

In a first step, a variable is introduced that reflects students' future educational aspirations and has three outcomes: students who plan to enter the VET system (group 1), students who plan to enter higher education (group 2) and students who are undecided what type of future education to pursue (group 3) (table 9.5, model 8b). A first observation is the positive and highly significant coefficient for the group who plan to enter higher education, which is larger than the coefficient that was estimated for the binary variable used to reflect students' future educational plans in the model above. A smaller but positive coefficient can be observed for the group of students who are undecided what type of career to pursue after leaving the general educational system. Yet, the coefficient for the latter group is not significant at any common level, which indicates that students who are undecided whether to enter higher education or the VET system do not have a significantly higher probability to plan to attain the highest level of general education than students who plan to enter the VET system. Changing the reference group from students who plan to enter the VET system to their peers who plan to enter higher education further reveals the latter to have a probability to plan to complete the highest level of general education which significantly exceeds that of students who are undecided what type education to pursue after leaving the general educational system (table 9.6, model 8b). The model is highly significant, but the new variable operationalization did not significantly improve the model fit.

Table 9.5 Educational aspirations, considerations of uncertainty

Educational aspiration	Model 8b	Model 9b
Male	0.085 (0.421)	-0.019 (0.41)
10th grade	-0.116 (0.403)	0.404 (0.395)
One parent born abroad	0.647 (0.607)	0.619 (0.644)
Both parents born abroad	1.04 * (0.494)	1.213 * (0.486)
Cultural capital	0.287 (0.395)	0.343 (0.393)
Socioeconomic status	**0.027 *** (0.012)	**0.03 *** (0.012)
Cognitive abilities	0.015 (0.021)	0.023 (0.021)
Language skills	**0.073 ** ** (0.028)	**0.082 ** ** (0.026)
Future career aspirations		
Future education: undecided (Ref. VET)	1.033 (0.553)	
Future education: higher education (Ref. VET)	**2.799 ** *** (0.496)	
Some jobs require highest degree (Ref. no job requires highest degree)		**1.139 *** (0.457)
Other (Ref. no job requires highest degree)		**2.287 ** *** (0.442)
Constant	**-5.056 ** ** (1.524)	**-6.334 ** *** (1.529)
Model fit		
Pseudo R²	0.32	0.27
LR χ²	84.05	70.00
Prob > χ²	0.0000	0.0000
Bootstrap replicates (est.)	1000	1000
LR test	(vs. 5b)	(vs.6b)
LR χ²	1.18	6.01
Prob > χ²	0.2776	0.0142

NOTE: $N = 208$; * $p < 0.05$; ** $p < 0.01$; *** $p < 0.001$. Standard errors in parentheses. Bolt coefficients at least significant at the 5% level based on bootstrap standard errors, generated using STATA 11 to draw (with replacement) 1000 replicated samples of size N. Bootstrap replicates (est.) = number of replicates (out of 1000) where all parameters could be estimated.

The more fine-grained operationalization of the variable to capture the formal educational requirements for students' occupational aspirations turns out to be somewhat more complex. First, it is not clear how to classify students who did not list any occupational aspirations or aspirations that can be realized either through a career in VET or higher education. In the case of the binary variable, these students were assigned to the reference group based on the reasoning that high

9.2 Future career aspirations

general educational qualifications are not only required to be admitted to higher education but also to not unnecessarily restrict the range of future career opportunities if students have not decided what type of career to pursue. Yet, it was also discussed that the respective students may have been falsely assigned to the reference group as they may in fact exclusively consider to pursue careers that do not formally require the highest level of general education. Attempting to construct a variable that reflects the formal educational requirements for students' occupational aspirations in a more detailed manner, it is even less clear how to classify these students. Second, the extreme distribution of the general educational aspirations of students who exclusively listed jobs that formally require the highest level of general education is associated with estimation difficulties. The plan to enter higher education was shown to be strongly associated with the probability to plan to complete the highest level of general education. The data points to an even stronger association between the formal entry barriers for students' realistic occupational aspirations and their aspirations in general education: All students who exclusively expressed realistic occupational aspirations that formally require the highest general educational qualification plan to attain this level of education.

This observation alone gives rise to several implications. On the one hand, students who exclusively listed jobs that formally require the completion of the highest level of general education necessarily have general educational aspirations that exceed those of any other group. On the other hand, the better fit of the model that includes a binary variable to reflect students' future educational aspirations (section 9.2.1) compared to the variable that captures the formal educational requirements for students' realistic occupational aspirations (section 9.2.2) was interpreted as indicating that the former may predict students' aspirations in general education better than the formal educational requirements for their realistic occupational aspirations. Conversely, the present finding suggests that a variable which explicitly considers whether students exclusively reported occupational aspirations that formally require the highest level of general education or not may predict students' general educational aspirations even better than a variable that captures their plans to enter the VET system or higher education. However, it is not feasible to estimate a model that includes such a variable as it would perfectly predict the educational aspirations of students who exclusively expressed realistic occupational aspirations that formally require the highest level of general education. Hence, no further conclusions can be drawn with regard to this question.

To take into account at least some of the considerations above, a variable was constructed that has three outcomes: students who exclusively expressed realistic occupational aspirations that do not formally require the highest level of general education (group 1), students who listed at least one job that does not formally require the highest level of general education and at least one job that formally requires the highest level of general education or that can be attained either through a career in VET or higher education (group 2), and the remainder of students who did not explicitly report any realistic occupational aspirations that do not formally require the completion of the highest level of general education (group 3). The latter group includes all students who did not report any occupational aspirations and who exclusively listed jobs that formally require the highest level of general education and/or jobs that can be attained either through a career in VET or higher education. Even though several students in group 2 and 3 may be misclassified, group 2 is sought to represent students who have a range of career aspirations that differ in terms of their formal entry barriers, and group 3 to represent students with comparatively high realistic occupational aspirations.

The estimation results point to a much clearer pattern compared to the model that includes the variable to capture students' future educational aspirations in a more fine-grained manner (model 9b, table 9.5): Students who did not list any occupations that do not formally require the highest level of general education (group 3) can be found to have a significantly higher probability to plan to attain the highest level of general education than students who exclusively listed occupations that do not formally require this qualification (group 1). As in the previous model, the coefficient is much larger compared to the one estimated for the binary variable that differentiated between students whose realistic occupational aspirations do not formally require the highest level of general education and the remainder of students. Further, students who expressed realistic occupational aspirations that are associated with different educational requirements (group 2) can be found to have a significantly higher probability to plan to attain the highest level of general education than students who exclusively reported careers that do not formally require this qualification. The coefficient is smaller than the one estimated for the group who did not report any occupations that do not formally require the highest level of general education (group 3) but significant at the 5% level. Changing the reference group to students who did not report any occupations that do not formally require the highest level of general education (group 3) further shows that students from this group have a significantly higher probability to plan to complete the highest level of general education than students who not only but also expressed realistic occupational aspirations that do not formally require this qualification (group 2) (table 9.6, model 9b). Opposed to the model that includes information on students' future educational plans, the more detailed operationalization of the variable that reflects the educational requirements for students' realistic occupational aspirations significantly improved the fit of the model.

Table 9.6 Educational aspirations, considerations of uncertainty, changed reference group

Educational aspiration	Model 8b	Model 9b
Male	0.085	-0.019
	(0.421)	(0.41)
10th grade	-0.116	0.404
	(0.403)	(0.395)
One parent born abroad	0.647	0.619
	(0.607)	(0.644)
Both parents born abroad	**1.04** *	**1.213** *
	(0.494)	(0.486)
Cultural capital	0.287	0.343
	(0.395)	(0.393)
Socioeconomic status	**0.027** *	**0.03** *
	(0.012)	(0.012)
Cognitive abilities	0.015	0.023
	(0.021)	(0.021)
Language skills	**0.073** **	**0.082** **
	(0.028)	(0.026)
Future career aspirations		
Future education: undecided (Ref. higher education)	**-1.766** **	
	(0.654)	
Future education: VET (Ref. higher education)	**-2.799** ***	
	(0.496)	
Some jobs require highest degree (Ref. other)		**-1.148** *
		(0.519)
No job requires highest degree (Ref. other)		**-2.287** ***
		(0.442)
Constant	-2.257	**-4.047** **
	(1.598)	(1.512)
Model fit		
Pseudo R^2	0.32	0.27
LR χ^2	84.05	70.00
Prob > χ^2	0.0000	0.0000
Bootstrap replicates (est.)	995	1000

NOTE: $N = 208$; * $p < 0.05$; ** $p < 0.01$; *** $p < 0.001$. Standard errors in parentheses. Bolt coefficients at least significant at the 5% level based on bootstrap standard errors, generated using STATA 11 to draw (with replacement) 1000 replicated samples of size N. Bootstrap replicates (est.) = number of replicates (out of 1000) where all parameters could be estimated.

Above, it was discussed that several students may be falsely classified due to a lack of information about their precise realistic occupational aspirations. This possibility specifically concerns students who did not report any realistic occupational aspirations and those who listed careers that can either be attained through a career in the VET system or through higher education. According to the present variable operationalization, students who listed at least one job that does not formally require the highest level of general education and at least one career that can be attained either though a career in VET or higher education were assigned to group 2, which is sought to represent the group of students who have realistic occupational aspirations that are associated with different formal entry barriers. Yet, several of these students may in fact exclusively consider to realize their aspirations through a career in the VET system and should have been assigned to group 1. Similarly, both students who did not list any jobs and who exclusively expressed occupational aspirations that can be attained either through a career in VET or higher education were assigned to group 3, which is sought to represent students who have comparatively high realistic occupational aspirations. However, the latter may as well exclusively consider to enter the VET system (and should have been assigned to group 1) or have realistic occupational aspirations that are associated with different formal educational requirements (and should have been assigned to group 2).

Also, it was discussed that the occupations students listed in the questionnaire may constitute a sample but not the full range of the career alternatives they consider to pursue (Gottfredson 1981, 1996; Haller and Miller 1963). Then, students will be falsely assigned to group 1 if they exclusively listed jobs that do not formally require the highest general educational qualification but in fact also consider to pursue careers that are associated with higher formal entry barriers. Similarly, students who exclusively expressed occupational aspirations that formally require the highest level of general education will be falsely assigned to group 3 if they also consider to pursue but did not list careers that do not formally require this qualification.

Yet, the risk associated with this imprecise operationalization is the underestimation of the hypothesized differences in the probability to plan to complete the highest level of general education between the three groups. Thus, the identification of significant coefficients provides ample support for the actual existence of such differences. As such, the results support the notion that it may indeed not necessarily be the case that students seriously consider to pursue their expressed careers aspirations (Alexander and Cook 1979; Coleman et al. 1966; Jencks et al. 1983; Kerckhoff 1976; Rosenbaum 1976, 1980): Provided that students who expressed career aspirations of which some do and other do not formally require the highest level of general education indeed consider to pursue these career alternatives, they should not have a significantly lower probability to plan to meet the formal entry barriers for their most ambitious aspirations than their peers who did not list any occupations that do not formally require the completion of the highest level of general education. However, it was also discussed that these findings may, at least partly, be attributable to a lack of knowledge about the formal entry barriers that are associated with different types of careers.

9.3 Social-psychological correlates

Attempting to provide deeper insight into how students orient themselves toward the future, the models above are further extended to include variables that reflect parental aspirations for their children's educational careers and students' self-efficacy beliefs. The central role of parental aspirations for their children's educational careers is widely acknowledged and was discussed in detail in the theoretical part of the study. The Wisconsin model assumes parents to primarily indirectly influence their children's attainment levels by means of transmitting expectations and value orientations to them (Sewell et al. 1969; Sewell et al. 1970). Rational choice researchers assume parents to influence their children's evaluations of the costs and benefits as well as the probability of success associated with continuing education (e.g., Boudon 1974; Breen and Goldthorpe 1997; Erikson and Jonsson 1996; cf. also Lloyd et al. 2008). Students' self-efficacy beliefs, referring to "people's judgments of their capabilities to organize and execute courses of action required to attain designated types of performances" (Bandura 1986, p. 391), are conceived of as one of the most central and pervasive mechanism of personal agency. Self-efficacy beliefs are assumed to directly influence performance accomplishments by helping people to interpret, organize and apply their skills, and have been identified as a significant predictor of both educational and occupational choices (Bandura 1986, 1991; Caprara et al. 2008; Lent et al. 1994).

Besides the investigation of the direct association between parental aspirations, students' self-efficacy beliefs and their educational aspirations, the introduction of these variables may provide further insight into the association that was identified between the formal educational requirements for students' future career aspirations and their aspirations in general education. Assuming that parental aspirations for their children's educational careers are based on reasonable appraisals of students' abilities (cf. Morgan 1998), they can be conceived of as a further control for variations in students' educational potential. Similarly, self-efficacy beliefs have been shown to be strongly influenced by past experiences of success and failure and may serve as a further control at the level of primary effects (Bandura 1986; Caprara et al. 2008; Lent et al. 1994). Also, the introduction of the variable allows to take into account the consideration that individuals differentially recall, weight, and process past performance information, and that the effect from experiences of success and failure, as well as from other aspects of the opportunity structure, on educational aspirations may vary across students (Bandura 1991; Lent et al. 1994). Thus, the explicit consideration of students' self-efficacy beliefs will contribute to the understanding of the extent to which the association between students' future career aspirations and their aspirations in general education simply reflects variations in their efficacy beliefs.

Table 9.7 contains the regression results of the models above that are extended to include information on parental aspirations for their children's general and future educational careers. Parents' aspirations for their children's general educational careers take on the value 1 if parents would like their children to attain the full or restricted higher education entry qualification and 0 otherwise. In analogy to students' own future educational aspirations, parents' aspirations for their children's future educational careers take on the value 1 if parents would like their children to pursue a career in the VET system and 0 otherwise.

9.3 Social-psychological correlates

Table 9.7 Educational aspirations, parental aspirations

Educational aspiration	Model 10b	Model 11b	Model 12b
Male	0.184 (0.472)	0.15 (0.468)	0.201 (0.454)
10th grade	-0.236 (0.445)	-0.07 (0.442)	-0.237 (0.437)
One parent born abroad	0.099 (0.683)	0.061 (0.745)	-0.27 (0.708)
Both parents born abroad	0.495 (0.547)	0.592 (0.542)	0.662 (0.536)
Cultural capital	0.368 (0.441)	0.372 (0.449)	0.338 (0.436)
Socioeconomic status	0.017 (0.013)	0.021 (0.013)	0.024 (0.013)
Cognitive abilities	0 (0.024)	0.002 (0.025)	-0.005 (0.024)
Language skills	**0.095** ** (0.032)	**0.097** ** (0.031)	**0.107** *** (0.03)
Future career aspirations			
Vocational education and training (Ref. other)	**-1.777** *** (0.49)		
Real.: no job requires highest degree (Ref. other)		**-1.471** ** (0.437)	
Ideal.: no job requires highest degree (Ref. other)			**-1.335** ** (0.496)
Parental aspirations			
Highest general degree (Ref. lower qualification)	**2.185** ** (0.654)	**2.169** *** (0.618)	**2.347** *** (0.627)
Vocational education and training (Ref. other)	**-1.218** * (0.502)	**-1.785** *** (0.469)	**-1.91** *** (0.461)
Constant	**-3.814** * (1.849)	**-4.619** ** (1.774)	**-4.974** ** (1.741)
Model fit			
Pseudo R^2	0.42	0.41	0.4
LR χ^2	109.40	106.65	102.63
Prob > χ^2	0.0000	0.0000	0.0000
Bootstrap replicates (est.)	996	997	996
LR test	(vs. 5b)	(vs. 6b)	(vs. 7b)
LR χ^2	26.52	42.67	51.81
Prob > χ^2	0.0000	0.0000	0.0000

NOTE: $N = 208$; * $p < 0.05$; ** $p < 0.01$; *** $p < 0.001$. Standard errors in parentheses. Bolt coefficients at least significant at the 5% level based on bootstrap standard errors, generated using STATA 11 to draw (with replacement) 1000 replicated samples of size N. Bootstrap replicates (est.) = number of replicates (out of 1000) where all parameters could be estimated.

Parents' aspirations both for their children's general and future educational careers are significantly associated with the probability that students plan to complete the highest level of general education, and the introduction of the variables significantly improved the model fit. Students whose parents would like them to attain high levels of general education have a significantly higher probability to plan to complete the highest level of general education than their peers whose parents have any lower aspirations for them. Students whose parents would like them to pursue a career in the VET system have a significantly lower probability to plan to complete the highest level of general education than the remainder of students. In particular the latter finding is illuminating as it shows students' general educational aspirations to systematically vary with their parents' future career aspirations net of parents' aspirations for their children's general educational careers. Put differently, even if all parents held the same aspirations for their children's careers in general education, students whose parents would like them to pursue a career in VET after leaving the general educational system have a significantly lower probability to plan to complete the highest level of general education than the remainder of students. This observation may have several explanations. For instance, parents who communicate more ambitious future career aspirations to their children may be more persuasive and provide more support for their children to succeed in general education, or influence their children's beliefs in the efficacy of education for getting ahead.

The finding that the coefficient for parental aspirations for their children's general educational careers is larger than the one estimated for parents' aspirations for their children's future educational careers can, at least partly, be explained by the same reasons for which students' own future educational aspirations were discussed to have limited power to predict their aspirations in general education. As parents may be well aware of the value of high general educational qualifications to increase their children's chances of a successful transition into the VET system, the fact that they would like their children to pursue a career in the VET system does not necessarily imply that they would not like them to complete high levels of general education. Also, the more precise operationalization of parents' aspirations for their children's general educational qualifications may contribute to the comparatively large coefficient for this variable: Whereas all students reported their parents' aspirations for their general educational qualifications, more than a quarter indicated that their parents do not have any aspirations for their future educational careers or were not aware of their parents' aspirations.

As regards the strength of the association between parental aspirations and students' own educational aspirations, several aspects deserve consideration that may lead to a systematic over- or underestimation of the present coefficients. First, parental aspirations were assessed by asking what type of future education they *would like* their children to complete, whereas students' own aspirations were measured as their educational *plans*. Second, even though a comparatively small share of students only plan to obtain the restricted entrance qualification for higher education, the fact that the measure for parental aspirations does not differentiate between the preference for their children to obtain the full or restricted entry qualification for higher education may weaken the association between students' educational plans and their parents' aspirations. Third, the possibility was discussed that students may project their own aspirations onto their significant others (Kerckhoff and Huff 1974). If this interpretation applies, the association will be overestimated as parental aspirations were measured as perceived by students. Finally, in consideration of the existence of conditions that determine both students' and their parents' educational aspirations, the variables that reflect parental aspirations are likely to be endogenous.

The question whether and to what extent the association between parents' educational aspirations and their children's own educational aspirations can be given a causal interpretation, or whether it results from the simultaneous consideration of the opportunity structure by both parties, cannot be answered based on the present data. Yet, the results provide some tentative insight into this matter. First, the fact that the coefficients for parental aspirations are significant when students' own future career aspirations are taken into account indicates that students whose parents would like them to pursue a career in VET are less likely to plan to complete the highest level of general education than their peers whose parents have more ambitious aspirations even if all students held the same future career aspirations. Second, the coefficient for students' own future career aspirations decreased through the introduction of the variables that capture parental aspirations but remains significant. This observation further gives rise to the interpretation that students may comply with their parents' aspirations, or carry out the same cost-benefit calculations as their parents, in some but not in all cases. Put differently, given that all parents held the same aspirations for their children's educational careers, students who plan to pursue a career in the VET system, or who exclusively listed occupational aspirations that do not formally require the completion of the highest level of general education, still have a significantly lower probability to plan to obtain this qualification than their peers who expressed future career aspirations that are associated with higher formal entry barriers.

The introduction of the new variables further led to several noteworthy changes in the remaining coefficients. The coefficient for students' language skills remains highly significant. In contrast, the positive coefficient for the family's socioeconomic position decreased and is not significant anymore. This finding is in line with the hypothesized mechanisms of the Wisconsin model, which identified the influence of significant others as the primary mediating factor between social origin and students' own educational and occupational aspirations (Sewell et al.

1969; Sewell et al. 1970). If this interpretation applies, the finding that the coefficient for migrants with both parents born abroad is not significant anymore when parental aspirations are considered is in line with the hypothesis of the upward mobility argument, which assumes migrant parents to transmit their high aspirations to their children (cf. Heath and Brinbaum 2007).

However, as discussed above, it may as well be the case that the coefficient for the family's socioeconomic position was overestimated due to an insufficient control for primary effects in the previous models. Assuming that parents' aspirations for their children's educational careers are constructed based on students' past performance outcomes and on reasonable appraisals of their children's abilities, the decrease in the coefficient for the family's socioeconomic position must not necessarily imply higher aspirations in families from higher social backgrounds. Just as was argued to explain the decrease in the coefficient for the family's socioeconomic position when students' own future career aspirations were taken into account, this observation may as well be attributable to the fact that parental aspirations to some extent capture the variation in the preconditions for students' educational success that may have been captured by the coefficient for the family's socioeconomic position in the previous models.

Table 9.8 presents the estimates of the model that additionally contains information on students' self-efficacy beliefs (scale by Schwarzer and Jerusalem 1995, $\alpha = 0.9$). The variable is not significant in the model that includes information on students' future educational aspirations (model 13b) and significant at the 5% level in the model that includes information on the formal educational requirements for students' realistic occupational aspirations based on standard errors that are not bootstrapped (model 14b).

This observation may have several explanations. On the one hand, the insignificance of the variable is in line with the descriptive finding that it is students' expectations for success rather than their educational plans which appear to be strongly conditioned by the opportunity structure. On the other hand, the insignificance of the variable may, at least partly, be attributable to the fact that a general measure was used to assess students' self-efficacy beliefs. Treating self-efficacy beliefs as a generalized personality trait rather than as context-specific judgments may be related to problems of predictive relevance as students must make judgments about their capabilities without a clear activity or task in mind (Bandura 1986). Yet, the finding that the coefficient for students' future career aspirations remains stable and significant when students' self-efficacy beliefs are added to the model is at any rate counter to the notion that the strong association between the formal educational requirements for students' future career aspirations and their general educational aspirations merely results from a variation in students' self-efficacy beliefs. Rather, the present findings are supportive of the notion that a non-causal interpretation of the effect from students' future career aspirations on their general educational aspirations may not universally apply.

Table 9.8 Educational aspirations, self-efficacy beliefs

Educational aspiration	Model 13b	Model 14b	Model 15b
Male	0.036 (0.483)	0.021 (0.475)	0.049 (0.462)
10th grade	-0.364 (0.455)	-0.237 (0.452)	-0.413 (0.446)
One parent born abroad	0.113 (0.684)	0.049 (0.756)	-0.284 (0.711)
Both parents born abroad	0.533 (0.553)	0.573 (0.552)	0.688 (0.547)
Cultural capital	0.352 (0.445)	0.302 (0.455)	0.297 (0.442)
Socioeconomic status	0.02 (0.013)	0.024 (0.013)	0.027* (0.013)
Cognitive abilities	-0.005 (0.025)	-0.005 (0.025)	-0.012 (0.025)
Language skills	**0.101** ** (0.032)	**0.105** ** (0.032)	**0.115** *** (0.031)
Future career aspirations			
Vocational education and training (Ref. other)	**-1.772** *** (0.497)		
Real.: no job requires highest degree (Ref. other)		**-1.584** *** (0.451)	
Ideal.: no job requires highest degree (Ref. other)			**-1.479** ** (0.51)
Parental aspirations			
Highest general degree (Ref. lower qualification)	**2.033** ** (0.658)	**1.934** ** (0.626)	**2.15** ** (0.637)
Vocational education and training (Ref. other)	**-1.414** ** (0.528)	**-2.052** *** (0.497)	**-2.147** *** (0.489)
Self-efficacy beliefs	0.863 (0.542)	1.096 * (0.546)	1.092 * (0.537)
Constant	**-6.204** * (2.418)	**-7.523** ** (2.37)	**-7.934** ** (2.353)
Model fit			
Pseudo R^2	0.42	0.41	0.4
LR χ^2	112.01	110.96	107.03
Prob > χ^2	0.0000	0.0000	0.0000
Bootstrap replicates (est.)	996	995	998
LR test	(vs. 10b)	(vs. 11b)	(vs. 12b)
LR χ^2	2.61	4.3	4.4
Prob > χ^2	0.106	0.038	0.0359

NOTE: $N = 208$; * $p < 0.05$; ** $p < 0.01$; *** $p < 0.001$. Standard errors in parentheses. Bolt coefficients at least significant at the 5% level based on bootstrap standard errors, generated using STATA 11 to draw (with replacement) 1000 replicated samples of size N. Bootstrap replicates (est.) = number of replicates (out of 1000) where all parameters could be estimated.

9.3 Social-psychological correlates

This interpretation is further supported by the results of the reestimation of the models using information on students' idealistic instead of their realistic occupational aspirations, which reveal a stable and significant coefficient for the formal educational requirements for students' idealistic occupational aspirations when parental aspirations and students' self-efficacy beliefs are taken into account (model 15b, table 9.8). Assuming the existence of a causal effect from parental on their children's educational aspirations, this finding suggests that students' idealistic occupational aspirations are not conditioned by their parents' aspirations. If the alternative hypothesis applies that students and their parents carry out the same cost-benefit calculations, the present results suggest that these evaluations matter to the construction of students' realistic but not of their idealistic occupational aspirations.

A further noteworthy observation is the very large and significant coefficient for parental aspirations. While the fit of the model that includes a variable to capture students' realistic occupational aspirations was much better than that of the model that contains information on the educational requirements for their idealistic occupational aspirations when parental aspirations were not taken into account, the fit of the models is comparably high when parental aspirations are added to the model. This observation gives rise to several implications. Above, several observations were revealed to suggest that the variables that were introduced to reflect students' future educational and realistic occupational aspirations to some extent capture the variation in students' (perceived) educational potential. Following this consideration, the finding of the extreme improvement of the model fit through the introduction of parental aspirations gives rise to the assumption that parental aspirations reflect students' educational potential to a similar extent as students' own future educational and realistic occupational aspirations. On the one hand, this finding suggests that students' own future career plans are indeed conditioned by their expected probability to succeed in general education, and does not support the hypothesis of a causal influence from students' future career aspirations on their aspirations in general education. On the other hand, given that parental aspirations reflect their children's educational ability to a similar extent as students' own realistic future career aspirations, the observation that both students' idealistic and realistic future career aspirations remain significant when parental aspirations are taken into account renders a universally non-causal interpretation of the effect from students' future career aspirations on their aspirations in general education unlikely as well. In sum, even though the results do not constitute conclusive evidence, on the whole they strongly give rise to believe that the formal entry barriers for students' future career aspirations are neither universally causal nor universally non-causal for the construction of their aspirations in general education.

References

Alexander, K. L., & Cook, M. A. (1979). The Motivational Relevance of Educational Plans: Questioning the Conventional Wisdom. *Social Psychology Quarterly, 42*(3), 202-213.
Armstrong, P. I., & Crombie, G. (2000). Compromises in Adolescents' Occupational Aspirations and Expectations from Grades 8 to 10. *Journal of Vocational Behavior, 56*(1), 82-98.
Bandura, A. (1986). Human Agency in Social Cognitive Theory. *American Psychologist, 44*(9), 1175-1184.
Bandura, A. (1991). Social Cognitive Theory of Self-Regulation. *Organizational Behavior and Human Decision Processes, 50*(2), 248-287.
Blömeke, S., Buchholtz, C., & Hacke, S. (2010). Demographischer Hintergrund und Berufsmotivation angehender Primarstufenlehrkräfte im internationalen Vergleich. In S. Blömeke, G. Kaiser & R. Lehmann (Eds.), *TEDS-M 2008: Professionelle Kompetenz und Lerngelegenheiten angehender Primarstufenlehrkräfte im internationalen Vergleich* (pp. 131-169). Münster: Waxmann.
Bos, W., Schwippert, K., & Stubbe, T. C. (2007). Die Koppelung von sozialer Herkunft und Schülerleistung im internationalen Vergleich. In W. Bos, S. Hornberg, K.-H. Arnold, G. Faust, L. Fried, E.-M. Lankes, K. Schwippert & R. Valtin (Eds.), *IGLU 2006: Lesekompetenzen von Grundschulkindern in Deutschland im internationalen Vergleich* (pp. 225-247). Münster: Waxmann.
Boudon, R. (1974). *Education, Opportunity and Social Inequality: Changing Prospects in Western Society*. New York: Wiley.
Breen, R., & Goldthorpe, J. H. (1997). Explaining Educational Differentials: Towards a Formal Rational Action Theory. *Rationality and Society, 9*(3), 275-305.
Bundesministerium für Bildung und Forschung (2013). *Berufsbildungsbericht 2013*. Retrieved October 30, 2013, from http://www.bmbf.de/pub/bbb_2013.pdf
Caprara, G. V., Fida, R., Vecchione, M., Del Bove, G., Vecchio, G. M., Barbaranelli, C., & Bandura, A. (2008). Longitudinal Analysis of the Role of Perceived Self-efficacy for Self-regulated Learning in Academic Continuance and Achievement. *Journal of Educational Psychology, 100*(3), 525-534.
Coleman, J. S., Campbell, E. Q., Hobson, J. C., McPartland, J., Mood, A. M., Weinfeld, F. D., & York, R. L. (1966). *Equality of Educational Opportunity*. Washington, D.C.: U.S. Government Printing Office.
Erikson, R., & Jonsson, J. O. (1996). Explaining Class Inequality in Education: The Swedish Test Case. In R. Erikson & J. O. Jonsson (Eds.), *Can Education Be Equalized? The Swedish Case* (pp. 1-63). Stockholm: Westview Press.
Gambetta, D. (1987). *Were They Pushed Or Did They Jump? Individual Decision Mechanisms in Education*. Cambridge: Cambridge University Press.

References

Gogolin, I. (2009). Zweisprachigkeit und die Entwicklung bildungssprachlicher Fähigkeiten. In I. Gogolin & U. Neumann (Eds.), *Streitfall Zweisprachigkeit – The Bilingualism Controversy* (pp. 263-280). Wiesbaden: VS Verlag für Sozialwissenschaften.

Gogolin, I., & Lange, I. (2011). Bildungssprache und durchgängige Sprachbildung. In S. Fürstenau & M. Gomolla (Eds.), *Migration und schulischer Wandel: Mehrsprachigkeit* (pp. 107-127). Wiesbaden: VS Verlag für Sozialwissenschaften.

Gottfredson, L. S. (1981). Circumscription and Compromise: A Developmental Theory of Occupational Aspirations. *Journal of Counseling Psychology Monograph, 28*(6), 545-579.

Gottfredson, L. S. (1996). Gottfredson's Theory of Circumscription and Compromise. In D. Brown & L. Brooks (Eds.), *Career Choice and Development* (3 ed., pp. 179-232). San Francisco: Jossey-Bass.

Gottfredson, L. S. (2005). Applying Gottfredson's Theory of Circumscription and Compromise in Career Guidance and Counseling. In S. D. Brown & R. W. Lent (Eds.), *Career Development and Counseling: Putting Theory and Research to Work* (pp. 71-100). New Jersey: Wiley.

Gresch, C., Maaz, K., Becker, M., & McElvany, N. (2012). Zur hohen Bildungsaspiration von Migranten beim Übergang von der Grundschule in die Sekundarstufe: Fakt oder Artefakt? In P. Pielage, L. Pries & G. Schultze (Eds.), *Soziale Ungleichheit in der Einwanderungsgesellschaft: Kategorien, Konzepte, Einflussfaktoren* (pp. 56-67). Bonn: Friedrich-Ebert-Stiftung.

Haller, A. O., & Miller, I. W. (1963). *The Occupational Aspiration Scale: Theory, Structure and Correlates* (AES-TB No. 288). Retrieved September 9, 2011, from http://files.eric.ed.gov/fulltext/ED016712.pdf

Heath, A. F., & Brinbaum, Y. (2007). Guest Editorial: Explaining Ethnic Inequalities in Educational Attainment. *Ethnicities, 7*(3), 291-304.

Heckhausen, J., & Tomasik, M. J. (2002). Get an Apprenticeship Before School is Out: How German Adolescents Adjust Vocational Aspirations When Getting Close to a Developmental Deadline. *Journal of Vocational Behavior, 60*, 199-219.

Jencks, C., Crouse, J., & Mueser, P. (1983). The Wisconsin Model of Status Attainment: A National Replication with Improved Measures of Ability and Aspiration. *Sociology of Education, 56*(1), 3-19.

Kao, G., & Tienda, M. (1995). Optimism and Achievement: The Educational Performance of Immigrant Youth. *Social Science Quarterly, 76*(1), 1-19.

Kerckhoff, A. C. (1976). The Status Attainment Process: Socialization or Allocation? *Social Forces, 55*(2), 368-381.

Kerckhoff, A. C., & Huff, J. L. (1974). Parental Influence on Educational Goals. *Sociometry, 37*(3), 307–327.

Klieme, E., Artelt, C., Hartig, J., Jude, N., Köller, O., Prenzel, M., Schneider, W., & Stanat, P. (2010). *PISA 2009: Bilanz nach einem Jahrzehnt*. Münster: Waxmann.

Lent, R. W., Brown, S. D., & Hackett, G. (1994). Monograph: Toward a Unifying Social Cognitive Theory of Career and Academic Interest, Choice, and Performance. *Journal of Vocational Behavior, 45*, 79-122.

Lloyd, K. M., Leicht, K. T., & Sullivan, T. A. (2008). Minority College Aspirations, Expectations and Applications under the Texas Top 10% Law. *Social Forces, 86*(3), 1105-1137.

Maaz, K., Baumert, J., & Trautwein, U. (2010). Genese sozialer Ungleichheit im institutionellen Kontext der Schule: Wo entsteht und vergrößert sich soziale Ungleichheit? In H.-H. Krüger, U. Rabe-Kleberg, R.-T. Kramer & J. Budde (Eds.), *Bildungsungleichheit*

Revisited: *Bildung und soziale Ungleichheit vom Kindergarten bis zur Hochschule* (pp. 69-102). Wiesbaden: VS Verlag für Sozialwissenschaften.

Morgan, S. L. (1996). Trends in Black-White Differences in Educational Expectations: 1980-1992. *Sociology of Education, 69*(4), 308-319.

Morgan, S. L. (1998). Adolescent Educational Expectations: Rationalized, Fantasized, or Both? *Rationality and Society, 10*(2), 131-162.

Relikowski, I., Schneider, T., & Blossfeld, H.-P. (2010). Primäre und sekundäre Herkunftseffekte beim Übergang in das gegliederte Schulsystem: Welche Rolle spielen soziale Klasse und Bildungsstatus in Familien mit Migrationshintergrund? In T. Beckers, K. Birkelbach, J. Hagenah & U. Rosar (Eds.), *Komparative empirische Sozialforschung* (pp. 143-167). Wiesbaden: VS Verlag für Sozialwissenschaften.

Relikowski, I., Yilmaz, E., & Blossfeld, H.-P. (2012). Wie lassen sich die hohen Bildungsaspirationen von Migranten erklären? Eine Mixed-Methods-Studie zur Rolle von strukturellen Aufstiegschancen und individueller Bildungserfahrung [Special issue]. *Kölner Zeitschrift für Soziologie und Sozialpsychologie,* 111-136.

Reynolds, J., Stewart, M., MacDonald, R., & Sischo, L. (2006). Have Adolescents Become Too Ambitious? High School Seniors' Educational and Occupational Plans, 1976 to 2000. *Social Problems, 53*(2), 186-206.

Rosenbaum, J. E. (1976). *Making Inequality: The Hidden Curriculum of High School Tracking.* New York: Wiley.

Rosenbaum, J. E. (1980). Track Misperceptions and Frustrated College Plans: An Analysis of the Effects of Tracks and Track Perceptions in the National Longitudinal Survey. *Sociology of Education, 53*(2), 74-88.

Schneider, B. L., & Stevenson, D. (1999). *The Ambitious Generation: America's Teenagers, Motivated but Directionless.* New Haven: Yale University Press.

Schwarzer, R., & Jerusalem, M. (1995). Generalized Self-Efficacy Scale. In J. Weinmann, S. C. Wright & M. Johnston (Eds.), *Measures in Health Psychology: A User's Portfolio. Causal and Control Beliefs* (pp. 35-37). Windsor, UK: NFER-NELSON.

Sewell, W. H., Haller, A. O., & Ohlendorf, G. W. (1970). The Educational and Early Occupational Status Attainment Process: Replication and Revision. *American Sociological Review, 35*(6), 1014-1027.

Sewell, W. H., Haller, A. O., & Portes, A. (1969). The Educational and Early Occupational Attainment Process. *American Sociological Review, 34*(1), 82-92.

Vallet, L.-A. (2007). What Can We Do to Improve the Education of Children from Disadvantaged Backgrounds? In M. S. Sorondo, E. Malinvaud & P. Léna (Eds.), *Globalization and Education: Proceedings of the Joint Working Group. The Pontifical Academy of Sciences* (pp. 127-155). Berlin: De Gruyter.

Explaining students' educational expectations 10

The previous sections showed that the variables that were introduced to capture effects of social and ethnic origin, the formal entry requirements for students' future career aspirations and social-psychological variables significantly contribute to the explanation of the variation in students' educational aspirations. Also, the analysis above points to a significantly higher background-adjusted probability of students with a migration background, and specifically of migrants from families with both parents born abroad, to plan to complete the highest level of general education compared to their native peers. As regards students' subjective probabilities to successfully realize their expressed aspirations, however, the descriptive analysis revealed rather high levels of uncertainty on the part of students, in particular among migrants, to eventually translate their aspirations into attainment. Also, the analysis so far provided evidence to suggest that a gap between students' aspirations and expectations cannot be conceived of as the mere result of the opportunity structure by showing that several students do not face constraints in the form of insufficient levels of educational performance but are uncertain to realize their educational plans due to a mere lack of motivation to continue in general education. In consideration of these observations, the subsequent analysis focuses on the identification of the conditions that are associated with students' expected probability to successfully accomplish their educational plans.

As above, the analysis starts off with a base model that is successively extended by variables to capture primary effects of social and ethnic origin and secondary stratification effects (section 10.1). The association between students' future career aspirations and their expected probability of success is investigated in detail in section 10.2. Section 10.3 additionally introduces social-psychological variables. In line with the primary interest in the explanation of the variation in students' expectations to complete the highest level of general education, and in consideration of varying degrees of difficulty that are associated with the implementation of different educational aspirations, the analysis is based on the subsample of students who reported to plan to attain the highest level of general education ($N = 142$). In view of the growing gap between respondent-reported educational expectations and eventual attainment levels that could be observed in many western countries in the last decades (e.g., Domina et al. 2011; Goyette 2008; J. Reynolds et al. 2006; J. R. Reynolds and Johnson 2011; Rosenbaum 2001), a conservative measure of students' educational expectations was chosen that takes on the value 1 for students who reported to be very certain to complete the highest level of general education and 0 otherwise (cf. Goyette 2008; Morgan 1998).[42] The variables utilized in the analysis are summarized in table 10.1.

Table 10.1 Summary of variables used for analysis of students' educational expectations

	Mean	SD	Min.	Max.
Sex (1=male)	0.36	0.48	0	1
Grade 10	0.44	0.5	0	1
Individual and family characteristics				
One parent born abroad	0.11	0.32	0	1
Both parents born abroad	0.32	0.47	0	1
Nr. of books in household > 200	0.61	0.49	0	1
Socioeconomic position (HISEI)	52.98	19.74	14.21	88.7
Cognitive abilities test score	43.54	9.72	26	67
Language test score	34.9	8.93	13.8	55.82
Self-efficacy beliefs	3.02	0.36	2	4
Educational aspirations and expectations				
Student aspiration: highest general qualification	1	0	1	1
Student aspiration: higher education	0.63	0.48	0	1
Student aspiration: VET	0.27	0.45	0	1
Student expectation: highest general qualification	0.27	0.45	0	1
Motive for educational plan: career requirement	0.29	0.45	0	1
Parental aspiration: highest general qualification	0.96	0.2	0	1
Parental aspiration: higher education	0.58	0.49	0	1
Parental aspiration: VET	0.1	0.3	0	1
Occupational aspirations				
Realistic: all jobs require highest qualification	0.18	0.38	0	1
Realistic: no job requires highest qualification	0.13	0.34	0	1
Idealistic: all jobs require highest qualification	0.25	0.43	0	1
Idealistic: no job requires highest qualification	0.12	0.33	0	1

NOTE: Subsample of students who plan to attain the highest level of general education; $N = 142$

---

42 Based on a 4-point scale with the categories very uncertain, rather uncertain, rather certain, very certain.

10.1 Primary effects of social and ethnic origin

In analogy to the analysis above, in a first step a base model is estimated that includes information on students' sex, the grade they attended at the time of data collection and on their migration background (model 1c, table 10.2). As in the analysis of students' educational aspirations, none of the coefficients is significant. Models 2c and 3c (table 10.2) further suggest that neither the family's cultural capital nor its socioeconomic position is significantly associated with students' expectations to realize their educational aspirations.[43] The only variable that is significantly associated with students' probability to expect to complete the highest level of general education is the grade attended at the time of data collection. As discussed above, the positive coefficient for 10th-graders may be explained by the positive selection of this group with respect to level of educational performance and ambition as particularly poor performing or unambitious students may have left the general educational system after grade 9 already. Model 4c shows that students' cognitive abilities are not significantly associated with their educational expectations either, but that the probability to expect to complete the highest level of general education increases with students' productive majority language skills. In fact, students' language skills are the only variable that significantly increased the fit of the model, which is now significant at the 5% level (model 5c).

---

43 See Appendix D on http://www.ew.uni-hamburg.de/de/ueber-die-fakultaet/personen/trebbels.html for bootstrap results.

Table 10.2 Educational expectations, primary effects (one migrant dummy)

Educational expectation	Model 1c	Model 2c	Model 3c	Model 4c
Male	0.277	0.26	0.245	0.592
	(0.401)	(0.402)	(0.405)	(0.45)
10th grade	0.764	0.795 *	0.8 *	0.915 *
	(0.393)	(0.396)	(0.396)	(0.44)
Migrant	-0.108	0.086	0.123	0.535
	(0.391)	(0.437)	(0.447)	(0.484)
Cultural capital		0.447	0.387	0.3
		(0.451)	(0.477)	(0.49)
Socioeconomic status			0.004	0.005
			(0.011)	(0.011)
Cognitive abilities				0.023
				(0.023)
Language skills				**0.062** *
				(0.025)
Constant	-1.404 ***	-1.775 **	-1.981 **	-5.6 **
	(0.348)	(0.517)	(0.742)	(1.719)
Model fit				
Pseudo R²	0.03	0.04	0.04	0.09
LR χ²	5.23	6.24	6.39	14.18
Prob > χ²	0.1555	0.1823	0.2703	0.0481
Bootstrap replicates (est.)	1000	1000	1000	1000
LR test		(vs. 1c)	(vs. 2c)	(vs. 3c)
LR χ²		1	0.15	7.79
Prob > χ²		0.3169	0.6961	0.0203

NOTE: $N = 142$; * $p < 0.05$; ** $p < 0.01$; *** $p < 0.001$. Standard errors in parentheses. Bolt coefficients at least significant at the 5% level based on bootstrap standard errors, generated using STATA 11 to draw (with replacement) 1000 replicated samples of size N. Bootstrap replicates (est.) = number of replicates (out of 1000) where all parameters could be estimated.

While the data reveals a negative coefficient for the binary migrant variable in the base model, the coefficient became positive and successively increased through the introduction of variables to capture primary effects and secondary stratification effects. Yet, opposed to the analysis of students' educational aspirations, it remains insignificant. The reestimation of the model based on a more fine-grained differentiation of the sample by the number of parents born abroad does not reveal any significant differences between either group of migrants and natives either (table 10.3). This observation is in line with the descriptive finding that migrants are more likely to report high educational aspirations under uncertainty than their native peers on the one hand, and the consideration that the variables introduced into the model so far cannot be assumed to fully capture the variation in the preconditions for students' educational success on the other hand. As the bootstrap results point to estimation difficulties when treating students with one

10.1 Primary effects of social and ethnic origin

and both parents born abroad as separate groups, the remainder of the analysis is based on the binary migrant variable to obtain more stable results.[44]

Table 10.3 Educational expectations, primary effects (two migrant dummies)

Educational expectation	Model 1d	Model 2d	Model 3d	Model 4d
Male	0.263	0.252	0.239	0.629
	(0.402)	(0.403)	(0.405)	(0.456)
10th grade	0.771	0.798 *	0.801 *	0.918 *
	(0.394)	(0.396)	(0.397)	(0.441)
One parent born abroad	0.141	0.261	0.28	0.299
	(0.606)	(0.623)	(0.628)	(0.654)
Both parents born abroad	-0.206	0.003	0.044	0.701
	(0.436)	(0.49)	(0.503)	(0.57)
Cultural capital		0.422	0.368	0.328
		(0.455)	(0.48)	(0.493)
Socioeconomic status			0.004	0.006
			(0.011)	(0.011)
Cognitive abilities				0.025
				(0.024)
Language skills				**0.067** *
				(0.026)
Constant	-1.402 ***	-1.752 **	-1.942 **	-5.899 **
	(0.348)	(0.519)	(0.749)	(1.811)
Model fit				
Pseudo R^2	0.03	0.04	0.04	0.09
LR χ^2	5.51	6.38	6.51	14.48
Prob > χ^2	0.239	0.2707	0.3686	0.0701
Bootstrap replicates (est.)	992	993	992	992
LR test		(vs. 1d)	(vs. 2d)	(vs. 3d)
LR χ^2		0.87	0.13	7.97
Prob > χ^2		0.3496	0.7222	0.0186

NOTE: N = 142; * $p < 0.05$; ** $p < 0.01$; *** $p < 0.001$. Standard errors in parentheses. Bolt coefficients at least significant at the 5% level based on bootstrap standard errors, generated using STATA 11 to draw (with replacement) 1000 replicated samples of size N. Bootstrap replicates (est.) = number of replicates (out of 1000) where all parameters could be estimated.

The poor fit of the models estimated so far appears remarkable in view of the comparatively high explanatory power of exactly the same variables in the analysis of students' educational aspirations. This finding may have several explanations and does not necessarily imply that the variables introduced so far are not significant

---

44 See Appendixes E and F on http://www.ew.uni-hamburg.de/de/ueber-die-fakultaet/personen/trebbels.html for (bootstrap) results of the models that include the more fine-grained migrant variable.

predictors of students' educational expectations. Partly, the insignificance of the variables to capture primary effects can be explained by the focus on the positively selected subsample of students who plan to complete the highest level of general education. Assuming that students' expectations are closer related to their eventual attainment outcomes than their educational aspirations, the insignificance of several variables that are assumed to capture primary effects is in line with the findings of the Wisconsin researchers, who showed the effects of social origin and mental ability on attainment levels to be largely mediated through students' educational plans (Sewell et al. 1969; Sewell et al. 1970). Also, the insignificance of the variables to capture primary effects may be attributable to the fact that it is harder to identify statistical significance based on small samples, and to the conservative estimate of what constitutes students' educational expectations (cf. Morgan 1998).

Following these considerations, the finding of a significant coefficient for students' language test scores suggests that a comparatively small proportion of the effect of majority language skills on student expectations is mediated through their educational plans. This observation in turn reassures the particular importance of productive majority language skills as a direct determinant of students' expectations of success on the one hand, and supports the interpretation of majority language skills in terms of ethnic effects on the other hand.

10.2 Future career aspirations

The analysis carried out in the previous chapter revealed several observations to support the notion that the formal educational requirements for students' future career aspirations may not be universally non-causal but matter to the construction of the educational aspirations of at least several students. Yet, the study also provided evidence to support the consideration that students cannot necessarily be assumed to seriously pursue their expressed career plans (Alexander and Cook 1979; Coleman et al. 1966; Jencks et al. 1983; Kerckhoff 1976; Rosenbaum 1976, 1980). For instance, the analysis of the variation in students' educational plans not only revealed students who plan to pursue careers that do not formally require the completion of the highest general educational level to be significantly less likely to plan to attain the highest level of general education than their peers who have career aspirations that are associated with higher formal entry barriers. Also, it was shown that students who are undecided whether to enter higher education or the VET system have a significantly lower probability to plan to attain the highest level of general education than their peers who reported their plans to enter higher education. Similarly, students who expressed a range of occupational as-

10.2 Future career aspirations

pirations that are associated with different formal entry barriers were found to be significantly less likely to plan to complete the highest level of general education than their peers who did not express any career aspirations that require a career in the VET system.

The positive selection of the group of students who plan to complete the highest level of general education in the present analysis rules out the possibility that students do not even aspire to meet the formal entry requirements for their expressed future career aspirations. Yet, several observations in the course of the analysis gave rise to the concern that expressed aspirations may be loosely related only to the courses of actions students will eventually take to translate them into attainment. This also applies to the positively selected subsample of students who plan to attain the highest level of general education. For instance, the descriptive analysis showed that a considerable share of students are not uncertain to realize their educational aspirations due to a concern about their educational performance but merely due to a lack of motivation to continue in general education. This share is as high as 17% in the present subsample. Also, several students who reported to plan to complete the highest level of general education – and some of them their plans to enter higher education – had already applied for a position in VET when the data was collected. In consideration of these findings, and that the likelihood that aspirations are translated into attainment will depend on dimensions such as the degree of specificity and the strength of preference for a particular career (Gambetta 1987; Gottfredson 1981, 2005; Haller and Miller 1963; Lent et al. 1994), the analysis below investigates whether and to what extent students' future career aspirations are associated with their expectations to successfully accomplish their plans in general education.

Opposed to the binary variable that differentiated between students who plan to pursue a career in VET or who exclusively reported future career aspirations that do not formally require the highest level of general education and the remainder of students used in the analysis of students' educational aspirations, the present analysis operationalizes students' future career aspirations in a different way to allow to explicitly take into consideration the mechanisms that are discussed in the literature to explain the existence of a causal effect from students' future career aspirations on their general educational expectations: The new variable takes on the value 1 if students plan to enter higher education or exclusively expressed realistic occupational aspirations that formally require the highest level of general education and 0 otherwise.

Above, it was argued that the extent to which aspirations motivate positive educational behavior, and hence the likelihood that aspirations are translated into eventual attainment, is an increasing function of the strength of preference for a particular career and of the extent to which aspirations are clear and specific (Gambetta 1987; Gottfredson 1981, 2005; Haller and Miller 1963; Lent et al. 1994). The new variable operationalization is based on the consideration that the plan to enter higher education and the exclusive expression of realistic occupational aspirations that formally require the highest level of general education may reflect a comparatively strong preference for careers that require the completion of higher education. Also, the new variable operationalization allows to relax the assumption that students who consider to pursue careers that are associated with different educational requirements necessarily prefer the most prestigious alternatives within this range but face constraints of different intensity in implementing their most preferred aspirations. Instead, as suggested by vocational-psychological perspectives (e.g., Gottfredson 1981, 1996, 2005), it allows to explicitly take into account the possibility that students not only rank their career aspirations by level of prestige but along several dimensions, including sex-type and field of interest. Following the consideration that students may attribute comparatively high importance to dimensions other than level of prestige, assigning students who did not report any realistic occupational aspirations and who are undecided what type of future education to pursue to the reference group allows for the possibility (1) that the respective students equally prefer careers that are associated with different formal entry barriers and are more likely to leave the general educational system early as some of their aspirations can be realized at a lower cost along dimensions such as the time, effort and money associated with additional general education, and (2) that students prefer lower-level careers over alternatives that require the highest level of general education, for instance because they better meet their interests.

Table 10.4 contains the results of the models that include a binary variable to reflect whether students plan to enter higher education or exclusively listed realistic occupational aspirations that formally require this type of education or not. A first observation is that students who plan to enter higher education are not significantly more likely to expect to accomplish their high educational plans than their peers who are undecided what type of future education to pursue or who plan to pursue a career in the VET system (model 5c, table 10.4). Contrarily, model 6c (table 10.4) reveals that students who exclusively reported realistic occupational aspirations that formally require the highest level of general education have a significantly higher probability to expect to obtain this qualification than the remainder of students. The introduction of the latter variable but not information on students' future educational aspirations significantly improved the fit of the model.

A fist implication that arises from these findings is that students' realistic occupational aspirations may be a better predictor of the actions students will eventually take than their future educational plans. In view of the high share of students who reported their plans to enter higher education but who also or even exclusively expressed realistic occupational aspirations that do not formally require this type of education, or who did not report any realistic occupational aspirations, the present findings indicate that students' future educational plans may be more likely to constitute vague preferences than their realistic occupational aspirations.

Table 10.4 Educational expectations, future career aspirations

Educational expectation	Model 5c	Model 6c	Model 7c	Model 8c
Male	0.74	0.742	0.66	0.771
	(0.464)	(0.471)	(0.49)	(0.502)
10th grade	0.834	0.728	0.894	0.749
	(0.446)	(0.454)	(0.473)	(0.481)
Migrant	0.515	0.398	0.481	0.406
	(0.497)	(0.505)	(0.527)	(0.536)
Cultural capital	0.279	0.146	0.109	-0.072
	(0.506)	(0.512)	(0.541)	(0.553)
Socioeconomic status	0.002	0.007	0.01	0.013
	(0.012)	(0.012)	(0.12)	(0.12)
Cognitive abilities	0.02	0.011	0.024	0.016
	(0.024)	(0.025)	(0.026)	(0.027)
Language skills	**0.061** *	**0.063** *	**0.073** **	**0.077** *
	(0.025)	(0.026)	(0.027)	(0.029)
Future career aspirations				
Higher education	0.83		0.426	
(Ref. other)	(0.463)		(0.494)	
All jobs require highest degree		**1.483** **		**1.355** *
(Ref. other)		(0.505)		(0.546)
Motive career requirement			**1.526** **	**1.554** **
(Ref. other)			(0.471)	(0.477)
Constant	**-5.807** **	**-5.271** **	**-6.916** ***	**-6.743** **
	(1.761)	(1.781)	(1.937)	(2.02)
Model fit				
Pseudo R^2	0.11	0.14	0.17	0.21
LR χ^2	17.59	22.99	28.74	34.19
Prob > χ^2	0.0245	0.0034	0.0007	0.0001
Bootstrap replicates (est.)	1000	1000	999	1000
LR test	(vs. 4c)	(vs. 4c)	(vs. 5c)	(vs. 6c)
LR χ^2	3.42	8.81	11.15	11.2
Prob > χ^2	0.0646	0.003	0.0008	0.0008

NOTE: $N = 142$; * $p < 0.05$; ** $p < 0.01$; *** $p < 0.001$. Standard errors in parentheses. Bolt coefficients at least significant at the 5% level based on bootstrap standard errors, generated using STATA 11 to draw (with replacement) 1000 replicated samples of size N. Bootstrap replicates (est.) = number of replicates (out of 1000) where all parameters could be estimated.

The finding of a significant and positive coefficient for the formal educational requirements for students' realistic occupational aspirations is in line with the arguments presented above in favor of the notion of a causal effect from students' future career aspirations on their expectations in general education. Yet, the possibility remains that students who also expressed occupational aspirations that are associated with lower formal educational requirements do not equally prefer lower- and higher-level careers, or even prefer the former over the latter, but that the respective students do so precisely *because* they are not certain to meet the entry requirements for higher education. This interpretation was not only supported by the descriptive finding that the great majority of students who plan to complete the highest level of general education and who do not expect to accomplish their educational plans referred to a concern about insufficient levels of educational performance as the only reason for their uncertainty. Besides, the analysis of students' educational aspirations indicated that majority language skills capture level of (perceived) academic ability to some extent. As such, the decrease in the language coefficient indicates that the formal entry requirements for students' future career aspirations to some extent reflect level of (perceived) educational potential also among the positively selected subsample of students who plan to complete the highest level of general education.

Yet, as in the analysis of the association between students' future career aspirations and their aspirations in general education, several observations suggest that a non-causal interpretation of the coefficient for students' realistic occupational aspirations does not universally apply either. The interpretation of the association between students' future career aspirations and their educational expectations as the result primarily of compromised future career aspirations would suggest that the concern about insufficient levels of educational performance plays the central role in the construction of the educational expectations of students who pursue future careers that are associated with comparatively low educational requirements. However, the respective students indicated a lack of motivation to continue in general education comparatively often and referred to a concern about their grades less often than their peers with realistic occupational aspirations that are associated with higher formal entry requirements. For instance, the share of students who do not expect to complete the highest level of general education due to a lack of motivation to continue in general education is as small as 9% among students who plan to enter higher education and as high as 20% among the remainder of students. Also, even if it was the case that all students who reported career aspirations that are associated with different formal entry requirements do so because they are uncertain to meet the educational prerequisites for their most preferred career options, the question arises why several students who reported

10.2 Future career aspirations

to plan to enter higher education exclusively reported realistic occupational aspirations that do not require this type of education. As discussed above, this observation may, at least partly, result from a lack of knowledge about the formal entry barriers for different types of future careers.

Above, it was discussed that the chosen variable operationalization rests on the strong assumption that students whose future career aspirations do not formally require the highest level of general education are not aware of the existence of informal entry barriers in the VET system. The following models additionally include a variable that allows to relax this assumption: It contains information on the reasons based on which students have primarily constructed their educational plans and takes on the value 1 if students have primarily constructed their educational plans in consideration that they require the highest level of general education to be able to realize their future career aspirations and 0 otherwise (table 10.4, models 7c and 8c). A remarkable observation is the large size and high significance of the coefficient. Students who plan to attain the highest level of general education because this qualification constitutes a prerequisite for them to realize their future career aspirations have a significantly higher probability to expect to realize their educational aspirations than the remainder of students who have constructed their educational aspirations primarily based on other criteria, such as parental expectations or labor market opportunities in general. The observation that the coefficient is significant when the formal entry requirements for students' future career aspirations are controlled for further gives rise to the assumption that instrumentality considerations matter *net* of the formal entry barriers for students' future career aspirations. Put differently, even if all students held the same future career aspirations in terms of the associated formal entry requirements – which may have been subject to compromise –, the probability to expect to complete the highest level of general education will still systematically vary across students depending on the reasons based on which they have primarily constructed their educational plans.

In sum, even though the present data does not allow for causal inference, the observations so far indicate that students' future aspirations are causal for the educational expectations of at least several students. Besides, the selection of the positive subsample of students who plan to attain the highest level of general education the present analysis is based on makes a causal interpretation of the association between students' future career aspirations and their educational expectations more convincing. As discussed above, even though some students may face stronger constraints than others in implementing their most preferred career aspirations, the possibility is ruled out that the respective students had compromised their educational plans when the survey was carried out. Also, the data was collected in the very end of the school year, when the majority of students already knew whether they were admitted to continue in general education or not.

Yet, as discussed in the previous chapter, the results do not constitute conclusive evidence due to several methodological difficulties that cannot be explicitly taken into account based on the present data. For instance, it was discussed that students not only compromise their realistic aspirations but that they also tend to adjust their idealistic career aspirations towards more realistically accessible options as they experience or anticipate barriers in the course of their educational careers (Armstrong and Crombie 2000; Heckhausen and Tomasik 2002). Also, several students may have been falsely assigned due to a lack of information on their precise career aspirations. As in the analysis of students' educational aspirations, however, the risk associated with false assignments relates to an underestimation of the coefficient for the formal entry barriers for students' future career aspirations and does hence not call the present findings into question. Finally, the high significance and large size of the coefficient for the variable that reflects the reasons based on which students have primarily constructed their educational plans, and in particular its significance *net* of the formal entry barriers for students' future career aspirations, strongly gives rise to believe that students' future career plans are not universally non-causal for their educational expectations. In sum, it neither appears to be the case that low educational expectations can be exclusively attributed to students' (perceived) educational ability, nor that future career aspirations that are associated with comparatively low formal entry requirements exclusively result from the fact that students do not expect to meet the entry requirements for more ambitious careers.

10.3   Social-psychological correlates

As in the analysis of students' educational aspirations, parents' aspirations for their children's educational careers and students' self-efficacy beliefs are considered in a last step. As discussed above, parents are not only assumed to influence their children's educational aspirations but also to directly influence their expected and actual probabilities of success, for example by means of providing support with school work or financial and emotional support (e.g., Erikson and Jonsson 1996; Lent et al. 1994). Students' self-efficacy beliefs are assumed to directly influence students' probability of success by means of motivating constructive educational behavior, such as task persistence, effort expenditure and how firmly students remain committed to their aspirations (Bandura 1991; Lent et al. 1994). It was further discussed that these variables are likely to capture some of the variation in the preconditions for students' educational success that is not captured by the variables introduced into the models so far. Also, the possibility can be explicitly considered that the significant association that was identified between students' educational expectations and their future career aspirations is the mere product of a variation in students' self-efficacy beliefs.

The inclusion of a variable that captures parental aspirations for their children's careers in the general educational system is related to methodological difficulties in the analysis of the variation in students' educational expectations. None of the students who perceive that their parents would not like them to obtain the full or restricted entry qualification for higher education expects to accomplish their high educational aspirations. This finding suggests the existence of a particularly strong association between students' educational expectations and their parents' aspirations, and is supportive of the significant role attributed to parental aspirations in shaping students' actual and perceived probabilities of success. Yet, the possibility was discussed that the association between parents' and students' own educational expectations is not of causal nature but the product of the simultaneous consideration and evaluation of the opportunity structure by both parties, and that low educational aspirations in parents are, at least to a certain extent, the product of their appraisals of students' educational abilities (Jencks et al. 1983; Morgan 1998). As all students reported that their parents would either prefer them to obtain an intermediate degree or a qualification that provides access to higher education, no alternative variable operationalization can be used to capture parents' aspirations for their children's general educational qualifications. Hence, the subsequent models include a variable that captures parents' aspirations for their children's future educational careers only (table 10.5). The variable is operationalized in analogy to students' own future educational aspirations and takes on the value 1 if parents would like their children to enter higher education after leaving the general educational system and 0 otherwise.

Table 10.5 Educational expectations, parental aspirations and self-efficacy beliefs

Educational expectation	Model 9c	Model 10c
Male	0.968	0.964
	(0.538)	(0.544)
10th grade	0.592	0.476
	(0.493)	(0.504)
Migrant	0.72	0.64
	(0.569)	(0.58)
Cultural capital	0.177	-0.014
	(0.568)	(0.581)
Socioeconomic status	0.021	0.027
	(0.014)	(0.014)
Cognitive abilities	0.022	0.015
	(0.027)	(0.027)
Language skills	**0.087** **	**0.089** **
	(0.029)	(0.03)
Future career aspirations		
Higher education	0.767	
(Ref. other)	(0.548)	
All jobs require highest degree		1.475 **
(Ref. other)		(0.586)
Motive career requirement	**1.385** **	**1.436** **
(Ref. other)	(0.499)	(0.501)
Parental aspiration higher education	-0.579	-0.389
(Ref. other)	(0.494)	(0.487)
Self-efficacy beliefs	**2.338** **	**2.379** **
	(0.716)	(0.751)
Constant	-15.123 ***	-15.001 ***
	(3.472)	(3.576)
Model fit		
Pseudo R²	0.25	0.28
LR χ^2	41.71	46.20
Prob > χ^2	0.0000	0.0000
Bootstrap replicates (est.)	1000	1000
LR test	(vs. 7c)	(vs. 8c)
LR χ^2	12.97	12.01
Prob > χ^2	0.0015	0.0025

NOTE: $N = 142$; * $p < 0.05$; ** $p < 0.01$; *** $p < 0.001$. Standard errors in parentheses. Bolt coefficients at least significant at the 5% level based on bootstrap standard errors, generated using STATA 11 to draw (with replacement) 1000 replicated samples of size N. Bootstrap replicates (est.) = number of replicates (out of 1000) where all parameters could be estimated.

Opposed to the models to explain students' educational aspirations, parental aspirations for their children's future educational careers are not significantly related to students' expected probability of success. Assuming the validity of the mechanisms hypothesized by the Wisconsin researchers (Sewell et al. 1969; Sewell et al. 1970), this finding may be partly explained by the fact that the variable is causal for and precedes students' own educational aspirations. Then, as was argued to explain the insignificance of several variables that are assumed to capture primary effects, the variable is less likely to be significant in analyses that are based on students who reported the same educational plans.

Model 10c reveals that students' self-efficacy beliefs, which were not found to be systematically associated with students' educational plans in the model that used information on students' future educational aspirations, are positively and significantly associated with the probability that students expect to complete the highest level of general education. First, the significance of the variable is in line with the literature that postulates self-efficacy beliefs as determinants of positive educational behavior (Bandura 1991; Lent et al. 1994). Second, this finding is in line with the results of the descriptive analysis, which indicated that it is students' expectations for success rather than their educational plans that are strongly conditioned by their perceptions of the opportunity structure.

As concerns the association between students' future career aspirations and their educational expectations, both the coefficient for the formal educational requirements for students' realistic occupational aspirations and the reasons based on which students have primarily constructed their educational plans remain stable and significant when parental aspirations and students' self-efficacy beliefs are taken into account. Although the concern was discussed that a general measure of students' self-efficacy beliefs may not fully capture the beliefs that are relevant for the construction of their career aspirations and expectations (Bandura 1986), the present findings are at any rate counter to the interpretation of the variation in students' realistic occupational aspirations as the mere result of a systematic variation in students' self-efficacy beliefs. This, in turn, further supports the notion that the formal entry requirements for students' future career aspirations may not be universally non-causal for the construction of their educational expectations.

References

Alexander, K. L., & Cook, M. A. (1979). The Motivational Relevance of Educational Plans: Questioning the Conventional Wisdom. *Social Psychology Quarterly, 42*(3), 202-213.

Armstrong, P. I., & Crombie, G. (2000). Compromises in Adolescents' Occupational Aspirations and Expectations from Grades 8 to 10. *Journal of Vocational Behavior, 56*(1), 82-98.

Bandura, A. (1986). Human Agency in Social Cognitive Theory. *American Psychologist, 44*(9), 1175-1184.

Bandura, A. (1991). Social Cognitive Theory of Self-Regulation. *Organizational Behavior and Human Decision Processes, 50*(2), 248-287.

Coleman, J. S., Campbell, E. Q., Hobson, J. C., McPartland, J., Mood, A. M., Weinfeld, F. D., & York, R. L. (1966). *Equality of Educational Opportunity*. Washington, D.C.: U.S. Government Printing Office.

Domina, T., Conley, A., & Farkas, G. (2011). The Link between Educational Expectations and Effort in the College-for-all Era. *Sociology of Education, 84*(2), 93-112.

Erikson, R., & Jonsson, J. O. (1996). Explaining Class Inequality in Education: The Swedish Test Case. In R. Erikson & J. O. Jonsson (Eds.), *Can Education Be Equalized? The Swedish Case* (pp. 1-63). Stockholm: Westview Press.

Gambetta, D. (1987). *Were They Pushed Or Did They Jump? Individual Decision Mechanisms in Education*. Cambridge: Cambridge University Press.

Gottfredson, L. S. (1981). Circumscription and Compromise: A Developmental Theory of Occupational Aspirations. *Journal of Counseling Psychology Monograph, 28*(6), 545-579.

Gottfredson, L. S. (1996). Gottfredson's Theory of Circumscription and Compromise. In D. Brown & L. Brooks (Eds.), *Career Choice and Development* (3 ed., pp. 179-232). San Francisco: Jossey-Bass.

Gottfredson, L. S. (2005). Applying Gottfredson's Theory of Circumscription and Compromise in Career Guidance and Counseling. In S. D. Brown & R. W. Lent (Eds.), *Career Development and Counseling: Putting Theory and Research to Work* (pp. 71-100). New Jersey: Wiley.

Goyette, K. A. (2008). College for Some to College for All: Social Background, Occupational Expectations, and Educational Expectations over Time. *Social Science Research, 37*(2), 461-484.

Haller, A. O., & Miller, I. W. (1963). *The Occupational Aspiration Scale: Theory, Structure and Correlates* (AES-TB No. 288). Retrieved September 9, 2011, from http://files.eric.ed.gov/fulltext/ED016712.pdf

Heckhausen, J., & Tomasik, M. J. (2002). Get an Apprenticeship Before School is Out: How German Adolescents Adjust Vocational Aspirations When Getting Close to a Developmental Deadline. *Journal of Vocational Behavior, 60*, 199-219.

Jencks, C., Crouse, J., & Mueser, P. (1983). The Wisconsin Model of Status Attainment: A National Replication with Improved Measures of Ability and Aspiration. *Sociology of Education, 56*(1), 3-19.

Kerckhoff, A. C. (1976). The Status Attainment Process: Socialization or Allocation? *Social Forces, 55*(2), 368-381.

Lent, R. W., Brown, S. D., & Hackett, G. (1994). Monograph: Toward a Unifying Social Cognitive Theory of Career and Academic Interest, Choice, and Performance. *Journal of Vocational Behavior, 45*, 79-122.

Morgan, S. L. (1998). Adolescent Educational Expectations: Rationalized, Fantasized, or Both? *Rationality and Society, 10*(2), 131-162.

Reynolds, J., Stewart, M., MacDonald, R., & Sischo, L. (2006). Have Adolescents Become Too Ambitious? High School Seniors' Educational and Occupational Plans, 1976 to 2000. *Social Problems, 53*(2), 186-206.

Reynolds, J. R., & Johnson, M. K. (2011). Change in the Stratification of Educational Expectations and Their Realization. *Social Forces, 90*(1), 85-110.

Rosenbaum, J. E. (1976). *Making Inequality: The Hidden Curriculum of High School Tracking*. New York: Wiley.

Rosenbaum, J. E. (1980). Track Misperceptions and Frustrated College Plans: An Analysis of the Effects of Tracks and Track Perceptions in the National Longitudinal Survey. *Sociology of Education, 53*(2), 74-88.

Rosenbaum, J. E. (2001). *Beyond College-for-all: Career Paths for the Forgotten Half.* New York: Russell Sage Foundation.

Sewell, W. H., Haller, A. O., & Ohlendorf, G. W. (1970). The Educational and Early Occupational Status Attainment Process: Replication and Revision. *American Sociological Review, 35*(6), 1014-1027.

Sewell, W. H., Haller, A. O., & Portes, A. (1969). The Educational and Early Occupational Attainment Process. *American Sociological Review, 34*(1), 82-92.

Conclusions 11

The following sections provide a summary of the central results of the empirical study and discuss them in relation to previous research and the research questions posed in chapter 6. Sections 11.1 and 11.2 summarize the key findings on the distribution and construction of the educational aspirations and expectations of native and migrant students. Section 11.3 addresses the question of the direction of the association between students' future career aspirations and their aspirations and expectations in general education. Section 11.4 reconsiders the question of the meaning of respondent-reported career plans. Sections 11.5 to 11.7 provide a more general discussion of the theoretical, methodological and interpretative implications the present results give rise to. Section 11.8 concludes the study by discussing its limitation and by pointing out prospects for future research.

11.1 Distribution and construction of educational aspirations

As regards students' aspirations in general education, the majority of about two thirds reported to plan to complete the highest level of general education and a small share to plan to obtain restricted access to higher education. About one quarter plan to obtain the intermediate qualification, and a negligibly small share only to leave the general educational system after the completion of the lowest qualification. Almost half of the students plan to pursue a career the VET system and a comparable share to enter higher education after leaving the general educational system.

In line with the literature, comparatively high educational aspirations were found in migrant families even when background characteristics are not taken into account (e.g., B. Becker 2010; Ditton et al. 2005; Klieme et al. 2010; Kristen and Dollmann 2010). The share of students who plan to complete the highest level of general education is highest among migrants with both parents born abroad and lowest among natives. The aspirations of migrant students in general education slightly exceed those of their native peers only, but comparatively large gaps can be observed with regard to the type of future education students plan to pursue. The majority of natives and students with one parent born abroad plan to enter the VET system after leaving the general educational system. Conversely, more than half of the students from families with both parents born abroad plan to enter higher education.

Parental aspirations for their children's general educational qualifications exceed students' own aspirations in all three groups. A less clear pattern was observed for parents' aspirations for their children's future educational careers. Parents in both migrant groups would like their children to complete higher education much more often than students plan to do so themselves. A reverse pattern was observed in native families.

Labor market-related criteria were clearly shown to play the most important role in the construction of students' aspirations. Adoption and imitation mechanisms are considered comparatively less important. A remarkable observation is the high share of students who have constructed their general educational plans in consideration of the entry requirements for their future career aspirations. A very high share of students reported their need for the planned qualification to be able to realize their future career aspirations as the most important reason both for their general and future educational plans. Also, a considerable share do not plan to complete the highest level of general education as their future career aspirations do not require high levels of general education. The former consideration is comparatively important to migrants, and in particular to students with one parent born abroad, and the latter to natives.

The multivariate analysis confirmed the explanatory power of variables that are discussed in the literature with reference to primary effects of social and ethnic origin. The family's cultural capital and its socioeconomic position, and also students' productive majority language skills were identified as significant predictors of the probability to plan to complete the highest level of general education. The finding that students' language skills and the family's socioeconomic position are not systematically related specifically suggests the interpretation of productive majority language skills as ethnic effects. In line with the significantly lower socioeconomic position and language test scores of migrants with both parents born abroad, their probability to plan to complete the highest level of general education is significantly higher compared to their native peers when variables are introduced that are thought to capture primary effects of social and ethnic origin. No significant differences were observed between natives and students from families with one parent born abroad.

The formal entry barriers for students' future career aspirations were identified as a further significant predictor of the probability to plan to complete the highest level of general education (e.g., Goyette 2008; Looker and McNutt 1989; Xie and Goyette 2003). Students who plan to pursue a career in the VET system or who exclusively expressed occupational aspirations that do not formally require the highest level of general education are significantly less likely to plan to obtain this qualification than the remainder of students. Also, uncertainty on the part of students with regard to their future career aspirations was found to be significantly associated with the probability to plan to complete the highest level of general education (cf. Morgan 2002). Not only students who pursue a VET career but also those who are undecided what type of future education to pursue are significantly less likely to plan to complete the highest level of general education than their peers who plan to enter higher education. Similarly, students who expressed occupational aspirations of which some do and others do not formally require the highest level of general education were found to be significantly less likely to plan to obtain this qualification than their peers who did not express any occupational aspirations that do not formally require the completion of higher education.

In line with the literature, parental aspirations for their children's educational careers are significantly associated with students' educational aspirations (e.g., Behnke et al. 2004; Heath and Brinbaum 2007; Schuchart and Maaz 2007). This applies to parental aspirations both for their children's general and future educational careers. Students whose parents would like them to obtain full or restricted access to higher education have a significantly higher probability to plan to complete the highest level of general education than their peers whose parents have any lower aspirations. Students whose parents would like them to pursue a career in VET are significantly less likely to plan to attain the highest level of general education than the remainder of students, even net of parental aspirations for their children's careers in general education. Data limitations precluded to directly address the question whether students comply with the aspirations of their significant others, or whether they construct their own aspirations based on the same evaluation of the opportunity structure as their parents (Morgan 1998; Sewell et al. 1969; Sewell et al. 1970). Yet, the observation of the simultaneous significance of students' own and their parents' career aspirations, along with the decrease in the former coefficient when parental aspirations are additionally taken into account, indicates that students to some extent but not fully respond to the preferences of their significant others, or construct their educational plans based on the same evaluations of the opportunity structure.

11.2 Distribution and construction of educational expectations

In contrast to students' high aspirations, the study revealed a quite different pattern with regard to their expectations to succeed in the educational system. In all three groups, students reported high levels of uncertainty to eventually accomplish their educational aspirations. Migrants, and in particular those with one parent born abroad, reported to be uncertain to translate their high educational plans into attainment comparatively often. The great majority in all three groups referred to a concern about their level of current and future educational performance as the only reason for their uncertainty to accomplish their plans in general education. Yet, a considerable share in all three groups do not face any such constraints but are uncertain to realize their aspirations merely because they are not sure whether they really want to remain in the general educational system much longer. No differences were observed in this pattern between natives and either migrant group.

Opposed to the models developed to explain the variation in students' educational aspirations, neither the family's socioeconomic position nor its cultural capital is systematically related to the probability that students expect to complete the highest level of general education. At the level of primary effects, productive majority language skills were identified as the only significant predictor of students' educational expectations. Following the positive selection of students who plan to complete the highest level of general education the analysis of students' educational expectations was based on, this observation is in line with the fundamental finding of the Wisconsin researchers, who showed the effects of background variables on level of educational attainment to be largely mediated through students' educational plans (Sewell et al. 1969; Sewell et al. 1970).

While the literature provides mixed evidence for the gross educational expectations of migrants, existing studies point to a relatively clear pattern of significantly higher expectations in migrant families when primary effects are taken into account (Paulus and Blossfeld 2007; Roth et al. 2010; Stanat and Christensen 2006b). No such differences were observed in the present study between natives and either migrant group. Due to the different methodological approach to estimate the probability to expect to complete the highest level of general education of those students only who plan to obtain this qualification, the present findings cannot be directly compared to other studies and are thus not in conflict with available empirical evidence. This aspect is discussed in more detail in section 11.7.

As suggested by the literature, students' future career aspirations were identified as significant predictors of their expectations to translate their educational plans into attainment (Gambetta 1987; Goyette 2008). Students who exclusively expressed realistic occupational aspirations that formally require the completion of the highest level of general education have a significantly higher probability to expect to realize their educational aspirations than the remainder of students. Opposed to the models to explain students' educational aspirations, no significant differences were observed between students who plan to enter higher education and their peers who plan to pursue a career in VET or who reported to be undecided what type of educational career to pursue after leaving the general educational system. The reasons based on which students have primarily constructed their educational aspirations were identified as an even stronger predictor of their educational expectations. Students who plan to complete the highest level of general education to be able to pursue their future career aspirations are significantly more likely to expect to realize their high educational aspirations than students who have primarily constructed their educational plans based on other criteria, such as labor market opportunities in general or the expectations and actions of their significant others.

As attested by the literature, extremely strong associations were observed between parental aspirations for their children's careers in general education and students' expectations to complete the highest level of general education (Erikson and Jonsson 1996; Morgan 1996; Zhang et al. 2011). No student whose parents would not like them to obtain either full or restricted access to higher education expects to accomplish their educational plans. Just like students' own future educational aspirations, parents' aspirations for their children's future educational careers are not significantly associated with their probability to expect to complete the highest level of general education. While students' self-efficacy beliefs were not found to be significantly related to the probability to plan to attain the highest level of general when students' future educational aspirations are taken into account, they were identified as a significant predictor of students' educational expectations (Caprara et al. 2008; Lent et al. 1994).

11.3 Future career aspirations: cause or consequence?

A further research objective was to provide insight into the nature of the association between students' future career aspirations and their aspirations and expectations in general education. Specifically, the question was raised whether the significant association between these variables is merely attributable to the fact that students compromise their educational and hence future career aspirations as they encounter or anticipate barriers in the course of their educational careers (Gottfredson 1996, 2005; Heckhausen and Tomasik 2002), or whether there is evidence that students construct their aspirations and expectations in general education in consideration of the extent to which their future career aspirations will allow them to take full advantage of high general educational qualifications (Gambetta 1987; Goyette 2008; Looker and McNutt 1989). Although the cross-sectional design of the present study does not allow for causal attribution, both the descriptive and the multivariate analysis provided valuable insight into this matter.

Several observations throughout the study indeed support the notion that students compromise their most preferred career options as a result of their low expectations to succeed in the educational system. Among these are the findings that several students would prefer to obtain higher qualifications in general education than the ones they plan to obtain but do not expect to meet the required level of performance, and that students' idealistic occupational aspirations are associated with higher formal entry requirements than their realistic occupational aspirations. The analysis of the variation in students' educational aspirations further revealed the formal entry requirements for students' future educational and realistic occupational aspirations to be systematically associated with the variables that are assumed to capture primary effects.

Yet, there is also evidence to suggest that a non-causal interpretation of the significant coefficient estimated for the formal entry requirements for students' future career aspirations does not universally apply either. As regards the observation that several students would prefer to obtain higher general educational qualifications if their grades were better, an even larger share among those who do not plan to attain the highest level of general education reported their need for the planned educational qualification to be able to realize their future career aspirations, or that the jobs they are interested in do not require any higher levels of general education. Similarly, the great majority of students who plan to enter the VET system after leaving the general educational system primarily do so to be able to attain their dream jobs or because the jobs they are interested in do not require the completion of higher education. Very few students who do not plan to enter higher education would prefer to do so but do not expect to meet the entry requirements. Also, if the assumption held that students who plan to enter the VET system do so exclusively because they do not expect to meet the entry requirements for higher education, a comparatively high share of the respective students who do not plan to attain the highest level of general education should prefer to do so if their grades were better. Yet, the data revealed a different pattern.

11.3 Future career aspirations: cause or consequence

While a comparatively small share reported their preference for a higher qualification, more than twice as many students from this group do not plan to complete the highest level of general education as the careers they are interested in do not require this qualification.

Further evidence against a universally non-causal claim was provided by the observation that not only the formal entry barriers for students' realistic occupational aspirations but also those for their idealistic occupational aspirations are a significant predictor of the probability to plan to attain the highest level of general education. While the possibility was discussed that students may have shifted their idealistic occupational aspirations in the direction of their realistic occupational aspirations in the course of their educational careers (Armstrong and Crombie 2000; Gottfredson 1981, 2005; Heckhausen and Tomasik 2002), several observations gave rise to believe that the former are at any rate compromised to a lesser extent than students' realistic occupational aspirations, or in other words that not all students have compromised their idealistic aspirations. Not only were students' idealistic occupational aspirations found to be associated with higher formal entry barriers than their realistic occupational aspirations. Also, opposed to students' realistic occupational aspirations, they are neither systematically associated with any of the variables that are assumed capture primary effects, nor with parental aspirations or students' self-efficacy beliefs, which the results indicated to capture some of the variation in (perceived) educational potential. Following these considerations, the fact that the coefficients for students' idealistic and realistic future career aspirations remain significant when the latter variables are taken into account further supports the notion that students' future career aspirations matter to the construction of the educational aspirations of at least several students.

As regards the association between students' future career aspirations and their expectations in general education, a causal effect from the former on the latter was hypothesized based on the consideration that students who are more certain what type of career to pursue and who have a stronger preference for a specific career will be more firmly committed to their aspirations than students who have vague career preferences only (Gambetta 1987; Gottfredson 1996; Lent et al. 1994). Assuming that a small range of career aspirations in terms of the associated formal entry barriers reflects a comparatively strong preference for the respective level of career, the finding that students who exclusively expressed realistic occupational aspirations that formally require the highest level of general education are significantly more likely to expect to translate their educational plans into attainment than the remainder of students is in line with this reasoning.

As in the analysis of students' educational aspirations, however, several observations also give rise to the assumption that the association between students' future career aspirations and their expectations in general education is, at least partly, attributable to the fact that students have compromised their future career aspirations in the course of their educational careers. For example, the great majority of students – also among those who plan to complete the highest level of general education – referred to a concern about their educational performance as the only reason for their uncertainty to realize their high aspirations in general education. Following this observation, the possibility was discussed that students also consider to pursue careers that are easier accessible in anticipation that they may fail to meet the formal entry barriers for their most preferred career aspirations. If this interpretation applies, however, the respective students should refer to low educational performance as the reason for their uncertainty to accomplish their educational plans comparatively often. However, the respective students reported a lack of motivation to continue in general education as the only reason for their uncertainty to accomplish their general educational plans more often and a concern about their grades less often than their peers who exclusively listed occupations that formally require the highest level of general education.

A further central observation is that students who aspire to the highest general educational qualification primarily in consideration that this qualification will allow them to realize their future career aspirations have a significantly higher probability to expect to complete their educational plans than their peers who have constructed their aspirations primarily based on other criteria. In particular the finding that the coefficient for this variable is significant when the formal entry barriers for students' future career aspirations are taken into account gives rise to believe that instrumentality considerations matter *net* of the formal entry barriers for students' future career aspirations, which may have been subject to compromise as a result of students' low educational expectations. This finding in turn suggests that instrumentality considerations not only matter to the construction of the educational expectations of students who exclusively reported career aspirations that formally require the highest level of general education but also to students who expressed occupational aspirations that are associated with lower formal entry barriers.

The observation that both career variables remain significant predictors of students' educational expectations when parental aspirations and students' self-efficacy beliefs are additionally taken into account further supports the notion that the association between the formal entry barriers for students' future career aspirations and their general educational aspirations and expectations is not the mere product of compromise. Also, the positive selection of students who plan to complete the highest level of general education in the analysis of students' educational expectations supports this interpretation as none of the respective students had compromised their educational aspirations at the time of data collection. Not least due to the fact that the survey was carried out in the very end of the school year, when the majority of students were informed about whether they were admitted to continue in general education or not, the respective students can be expected to perceive the completion of the highest level of general education as accessible.

The analysis of the association between students' future career aspirations and their aspirations and expectations in general education was discussed to be subject to several methodological difficulties that may impact the present findings. First, it was discussed that several students may have been falsely classified due to a lack of information about their precise career aspirations and the fact that expressed career aspirations may constitute a sample only out of the full range of careers students consider to pursue (Gottfredson 1981, 1996; Haller and Miller 1963). Yet, it was discussed that the associated risk relates to an underestimation of the association between students' future career aspirations and their aspirations and expectations in general education. However, the consideration that students do not only tend to compromise their realistic occupational aspirations but also to adjust their idealistic occupational aspirations in the direction of their realistic occupational aspirations over time (Armstrong and Crombie 2000; Gottfredson 1981, 2005; Heckhausen and Tomasik 2002), which deserves explicit consideration not least due to the use of information on the gap between the two variables to argue in favor of a causal claim, cannot be addressed in more detail based on the present data. Also, even though the present results are in line with the mechanisms that were discussed to theoretically explain the observed association between students' future career aspirations and their aspirations and expectations in general education, they leave alternative interpretations. This difficulty was reinforced by a lack of information on students' knowledge about the entry requirements for different types of careers.

Even though the present study does certainly not provide conclusive evidence, in sum the analysis revealed several pieces of evidence to strongly support the notion that students' future career aspirations may indeed not be conceived of as the mere product of their general educational expectations (Gambetta 1987; Goyette 2008; Looker and McNutt 1989). Rather, the present observations give rise to believe that students' future career aspirations matter to the construction of the educational plans and expectations of at least several students. As such, the present results support the notion that the explicit consideration of labor market-related conditions may significantly improve the explanatory power of traditional socialization models (Morgan 1996, 1998, 2005).

11.4 Meaning of respondent-reported career plans

A further research objective was to shed light on the meaning of respondent-reported career plans. As outlined in the theoretical part of the study, the importance attributed to student aspirations derives from their presumed role in motivating constructive educational behavior and ambitious attainment decisions (Bandura 1986, 1991; Caprara et al. 2008; Lent et al. 1994; Quaglia and Cobb 1996; Rojewski 2005). While the literature indeed consistently attests significant associations between expressed aspirations, expectations and later attainment levels (e.g., Beal and Crockett 2010; Buriel and Cardoza 1988; Jacob and Wilder 2010; Domina et al. 2011; Mau and Bikos 2000; Ou and Reynolds 2008; Rojewski and Kim 2003; Zhang et al. 2011), both the predictive value of aspirations and the notion of a causal effect on attainment levels were shown to be discussed controversially. Considerations that have been brought forward in this context are that educational aspirations may not be value orientations that index motivation but reflections of students' perceptions of the opportunity structure (Alexander and Cook 1979; Bourdieu 1973; Jencks et al. 1983; Kerckhoff 1976), that aspirations may constitute vague preferences that have no salience to adolescents in their everyday lives as they fail to commit to and/ or to take effective action to realize their aspirations (Alexander and Cook 1979; Coleman et al. 1966; Jencks et al. 1983; Kerckhoff 1976; Rosenbaum 1976, 1980), and that expressed aspirations may result from lacking or inaccurate information about the educational system and unrealistic appraisals of students' educational potential (Coleman et al. 1966; Kerckhoff 1977; Kerckhoff and Campbell 1977; Rosenbaum 1976, 1980, 1978).

As regards the concern that respondent-reported educational aspirations may reflect students' perceived chances to succeed in the educational system rather than index motivation, the measurement of aspirations as *plans* and close to an important transition was discussed as a major reason for the urge of the reinterpretation of the fundamental associations identified by the Wisconsin researchers (Alexander and Cook 1979; Kerckhoff 1976). The same approach was adopted in the present study.

The observation that a considerable share of students would prefer to obtain higher qualifications in general education than the ones they plan to obtain if their grades were better indeed supports the hypothesis that students' educational plans, at least to some extent, reflect their perceptions of the opportunity structure. Yet, several observations that were discussed in the previous section give rise to believe that students' educational plans may not be conceived of as mere reflections of the opportunity structure either. For example, a considerable share of students do not plan to complete the highest level of general education as their future career aspirations do not require this qualification. Further, the study revealed that students tend to report high general and future educational plans even under high levels of uncertainty to succeed in realizing their aspirations. These observations not only indicate that that it is indeed not the case that educational plans reflect pure motivation. Also, they are supportive of the hypothesis of variations in the extent to which students adapt their educational aspirations to their perceived chances to succeed (B. Becker 2010; Goyette 2008).

The observation that the great majority of students are uncertain to realize their general educational plans due to a concern about insufficient educational performance specifically gives rise to the interpretation that it is not students' educational plans as much as their expectations for success that are strongly conditioned by their perceptions of the opportunity structure. This notion was further supported by the finding that students' self-efficacy beliefs were identified as a significant predictor of students' educational expectations but not of their plans to complete the highest level of general education when students' future educational aspirations are taken into account. However, the observation of a considerable share of students who reported a lack of motivation to continue in general education much longer as the only reason for their uncertainty to accomplish their educational plans indicates that students' educational expectations cannot be conceived of as mere reflections of their perceived chances to succeed in the educational system either – and hence that a gap between students' educational aspirations and expectations cannot necessarily be interpreted as the product of students' evaluations of the opportunity structure. Although the present data does not allow to investigate the extent to which students' expectations for success reflect their actual probability to succeed in realizing their aspirations, the finding that the majority of students are uncertain to realize their aspirations due to insufficient educational performance further indicates that students are, at least to some extent, aware of the barriers they face in implementing their educational aspirations.

Also, the results are supportive of the notion that expressed aspirations may constitute vague preferences that have no salience to adolescents in their everyday lives. For instance, several students were found to report future career aspirations that are associated with different formal entry barriers. Also, the descriptive analysis pointed to a rather strong mismatch between the future educational and realistic occupational aspirations students reported in the questionnaire. In addition, several students who reported to plan to attain the highest level of general education, also among those who reported their plans to enter higher education, had already applied for a position in the VET system when the survey was carried out. The multivariate analysis further revealed students who are undecided what type of future education to pursue, or who expressed occupational aspirations of which some do but other do not formally require the highest level of general education, to be significantly less likely to even *plan* to obtain this qualification than their peers who did not express any career alternatives that do not formally require the completion of the highest level of general education.

These observations were discussed to not necessarily imply that students equally prefer all of their expressed aspirations. Instead, they may, at least partly, be attributable to the fact that students also consider to pursue careers that are comparatively easily accessible in anticipation that they may fail to realize their most preferred career aspirations (Gottfredson 1981, 2005). If the latter interpretation applies, however, the question arises why several students who reported their plans to enter higher education exclusively reported realistic occupational aspirations that do not require this type of education. Also, it was discussed that a lack of knowledge about the formal entry barriers for different careers may contribute to these observations. Yet, even then the question remains open why a considerable share of students do not expect to realize their educational aspirations merely due to a lack of motivation to remain in general education.

In sum, the results suggest that educational plans can be conceived of as the product of students' perceptions of the opportunity structure in the case of some but not in the case of other students. Also, the study provides evidence to support the notion that both students' general educational and future career aspirations are vague preferences for at least some students, and that students are indeed to some extent opportunistic in seeking and accepting career alternatives (Gottfredson 1981, 1996; Simon 1955, 1957). Further, the finding that the educational plans of some students are related to high levels of uncertainty and appear to constitute idealistic aspirations, while the plans of other students are strongly conditioned their subjective probabilities of success, challenges the notion of the existence of a universal meaning of respondent-reported educational plans – and hence the comparability of expressed educational plans across students (cf. Goyette 2008). In conclusion, even though the data does not allow to investigate the association between students' subjective beliefs and their later attainment levels, the results clearly point to the need for the explicit consideration of the arguments discussed above in the interpretation of subjective data in order to arrive at reasonable conclusions with respect to the role student aspirations play in the attainment process.

11.5 Applicability of traditional approaches to explain ethnic differentials in education

At a theoretical level, the empirical results give rise to several implications with respect to the question of the applicability of traditional models to explain social disparities in educational attainment to investigate the processes that shape ethnic differentials in education.

In line with the literature, the family's socioeconomic position was identified as a significant predictor of the probability that students plan to complete the highest level of general education. Also, the probability of migrants to plan to complete the highest level of general education was shown to increase with the introduction of the variable. Migrants with both parents born abroad were found to be significantly more likely to plan to attain the highest level of general education than their native peers when the family's socioeconomic position is taken into account. The finding that the family's socioeconomic position is not significant in the models to explain the variation in students' educational expectations was discussed to be, at least partly, attributable to the different methodological approach adopted in the present study. More specifically, the insignificance of the variable was discussed to support the hypothesis that the influence of the family's socioeconomic position on attainment is largely mediated through students' educational plans (Sewell et al. 1969; Sewell et al. 1970) and does hence not imply that students' subjective probabilities to realize their educational plans are not influenced by their social background.

These observations indicate that educational aspirations are a function of social origin not only in native but also in migrant families (R. Becker and Schubert 2011; Heath and Brinbaum 2007), and suggest that traditional approaches to explain social disparities in education constitute a useful starting point for the explanation of ethnic disparities in education. Yet, the present findings also emphasize the need for the explicit consideration of migration-specific conditions and the adaptation of conventional measures to obtain deeper insight into the processes that shape ethnic disparities in educational attainment – both at the level of primary and secondary effects.

First, in line with the literature the data not only showed migrants to have a significantly higher background-adjusted probability to plan to complete the highest level of general education but also to report higher gross aspirations than their native counterparts (Heath and Brinbaum 2007). In view of the disadvantaged socioeconomic position of migrant students compared to their native peers, this observation supports the notion that migration-specific conditions, such as the desire for upward mobility in the receiving country, are associated with an investment behavior in migrant families that differs from the educational behavior in native families in a comparable socioeconomic position (Schuchart and Maaz 2007; Vallet 2007). This aspect is addressed in more detail in section 11.7.

Second, the study revealed rather large differences in the absolute and relative importance native and migrant students attribute to different criteria in constructing their educational and future career aspirations. For instance, adoption and imitation processes appear to play a much less important role in the construction of students' educational and occupational aspirations than labor market-related criteria in all three groups. Yet, in particular the opinion and suggestions of students' significant others were shown to be comparatively important to migrants, and specifically to students from families with both parents born abroad. Also, it was shown that migrants construct their career aspirations in considerations of additional aspects that are specific to the migration situation. For example, a considerable share of migrants, in particular among those with both parents born abroad, consider the demand for a given occupation in the heritage country as an important criterion in constructing their occupational aspirations. Further, the multivariate analysis identified students' productive majority language skills as a significant predictor of the probability to plan and expect to attain the highest level of general education and specifically gave rise to the interpretation of majority language skills as effects of ethnic origin.

Yet, it was discussed that the interpretation of the present data requires considerable caution. Following the consideration that conventional measures of the family's socioeconomic position may not reflect the educationally-relevant resources in migrant families to the same extent as in native families, and that the educational outcomes of migrants are influenced by additional conditions that are specific to the migration situation, both the coefficients for migrants and the family's socioeconomic position may be systematically biased. The migrant coefficients were discussed to be most likely underestimated due to an insufficient control for primary effects. As regards the interpretation of productive majority language skills as ethnic effects, the possibility cannot be ruled out that the family's socioeconomic position and students' productive majority language skills are in fact systematically related, but that this association remained unobserved in the present analysis. Data on parental level of education was not used in the present study as the great majority of students whose parents completed their educational careers in a foreign country could not report their parents' level of education. Also, it was discussed that level of parental education may not reflect the educationally-relevant resources in migrant families to the same extent as in native families either due to the restricted transferability of origin-specific human capital to the educational setting in the receiving country (Kristen and Granato 2007; Kristen et al. 2011; Schuchart and Maaz 2007).

11.6 Measurement of aspirations

At a methodological level, the present findings give rise to several implications with regard to the measurement and interpretation of student aspirations.

First, the observation that the gap between students' educational aspirations and their expectations to succeed cannot be conceived of as the mere product of the opportunity structure, but that students' motivation to continue in general education plays a central role in determining their educational expectations (see section 11.4), suggests that conventional survey instruments do not capture the difference between students who are seriously thinking about certain types of careers and who commit to their aspirations and students who report vague preferences that have no salience to their educational behavior (cf. Goyette 2008; Morgan 2002).

Second, the findings of the study are clearly supportive of vocational-psychological perspectives, which suggest that career aspirations may be more appropriately conceptualized as a range with rough upper and lower boundaries rather than as a single point (Gottfredson 1981, 1996, 2005; Haller and Miller 1963). For instance, several students reported high plans in general education but had already applied for a position in VET when the survey was carried out. Also, a considerable share who reported their plans to enter higher education expressed realistic occupational aspirations that vary in terms of their formal entry barriers. These patterns were discussed to not necessarily imply that students' aspirations are interests or vague preferences that do not matter to their everyday behavior as the possibility remains that students lack knowledge about the formal entry barriers for different types of careers, or consider alternative careers in anticipation that they may fail to realize their most preferred career aspirations. However, the analysis also showed that several of the respective students reported to be uncertain to realize their educational plans merely due to a lack of motivation to continue in general education. Even though the present data does not allow to investigate the association between students' educational plans and their later attainment levels, these observations at any rate suggest that students respond to measures that conceptualize aspirations as a single point even if they in fact consider to pursue a range of career alternatives that are associated with different formal entry barriers.

Opposed to the variation in the formal entry requirements for students' realistic occupational aspirations, a very small share of students reported to be undecided whether to pursue a career in VET or to enter higher education after leaving the general educational system. Yet, only the formal entry barriers for students' realistic occupational aspirations but not their plans to enter higher education were identified as a significant predictor of their expectations to realize their educational plans. Independent of the question whether students equally prefer all of their expressed occupational aspirations or not, the latter finding at any rate suggests that measures that explicitly allow for the assumption that students may entertain a range of aspirations with upper and lower boundaries may predict their expectations for success better than commonly used single-point measures.

Finally, the considerations above point to the additional difficulties that arise in the attempt to assess aspirations for transitions in the distant future. This concern regards both the likelihood that students will eventually pursue their expressed career aspirations and the extent to which their expressed aspirations are based on realistic appraisals of their educational potential. The findings that students tend to have a range of occupational aspirations, and that a considerable share who do not face constraints such as low levels of educational performance are not certain whether they want to continue in general education or not – even among those who reported to plan to enter higher education –, render the assumption that students had indeed already decided what type of future career to pursue at the time of data collection rather questionable. The observation that students not only tend to report high general educational plans under uncertainty to be able to realize these plans, but that they also tend to express ambitious future career aspirations in the presence of high levels of uncertainty to meet the formal entry barriers, indicates that students' future career aspirations are conditioned by their expectations of success to an even lesser extent than their general educational plans.

11.7 Secondary effects of ethnic origin

Finally, the question remains to be addressed in how far the significant coefficient that was estimated for students from families with both parents born abroad in the models to explain students' educational aspirations indicates the existence of secondary effects of ethnic origin. First, the findings of the study are discussed with respect to the mechanisms the literature discusses to explain the existence of secondary effects of ethnic origin. Second, several difficulties are addressed that were outlined in the previous sections and need to be considered to arrive at reasonable conclusions with respect to the meaning of the high aspirations expressed by migrants, some of which are specific to the present study and some of which relate to the interpretation of significant migrant coefficients in models that estimate differences in the aspirations, expectations and transition probabilities of natives and migrants in general.

The finding that migrants express comparatively high educational aspirations when background characteristics are not taken into account was discussed to support the notion that the educational behavior in migrant families from lower social backgrounds does not conform to the behavior of native families in comparable social positions (Relikowski et al. 2012; Schuchart and Maaz 2007; Vallet 2007). As regards the mechanisms the literature discusses to explain the existence of secondary effects of ethnic origin, the results of the study further support the hypothesis that the desire for upward mobility, which is perceived as accessible through high educational qualifications obtained by the children, is a central explanation for the high educational aspirations in migrant families (Gresch 2012; Heath and Brinbaum 2007; Heath et al. 2008; Kao and Tienda 1995; Stanat et al. 2010; Vallet 2007). On the one hand, the data not only shows migrants to have higher general educational aspirations than their native peers, but also to express more ambitious future career aspirations. This applies in particular to the group of students from families with both parents born abroad, who plan to enter higher education and expressed occupational aspirations that are associated with comparatively high formal entry requirements much more often than natives and students with one parent born abroad. On the other hand, migrants were shown to construct their general educational plans more often in consideration of the need for a specific qualification to be able to realize their future career aspirations. As regards the construction of students' occupational aspirations, migrants were further shown to attribute comparatively high importance to aspects like income prospects and chances for job promotion – both in comparison to other criteria, such as the expectations and actions of their significant others, and to native students. As above, this is particularly true for the group of migrants with both parents born abroad.

The upward mobility argument further assumes that parental aspirations are transmitted to the children (Heath and Brinbaum 2007). The finding that not only migrant students themselves but also their parents expressed comparatively high educational aspirations indirectly supports this hypothesis. As in the case of students' own aspirations, particularly large discrepancies can be observed with respect to the future educational aspirations native and migrant parents hold for their children. Parents in migrant families would like their children to complete higher education more often than students plan to do so themselves. A reverse pattern can be observed in native families. The investigation of the criteria based on which students construct their occupational aspirations further supports the notion that the high aspirations in the group of students from families with both parents born abroad are, at least partly, attributable to the transmission of parental aspirations: The opinion and suggestions of the family and social network strongly matter to the construction of the occupational aspirations of migrants with both parents born abroad but were rated as relatively unimportant by students from the other two groups.

The theoretical part of the study discussed the concern that the membership of migrants in relatively homogenous networks in terms of low socioeconomic positions and lower-prestige positions in the labor market may not only reinforce the effects of an unequal distribution of resources across native and migrant families at the level of primary effects but also shape educational disparities at the level of secondary effects (Kao and Thompson 2003; Nauck 2011; Roth et al. 2010). Mechanisms such as the orientation toward an inner-ethnic career or toward occupations attained by students' significant others, which are associated with comparatively low prestige in the majority society (as indicated by the lower socioeconomic positions of migrant families in the present sample), are discussed in the literature to potentially lead to a systematic underinvestment in education of migrant students (Diefenbach 2010; Wiley 1967, 1970). The present study provided evidence against this notion: Not only were migrant families shown to report comparatively high educational and future career aspirations. Also, students from families with both parents born abroad were found to attribute high importance to the opinion and suggestions of the family and the social network in constructing their educational and occupational aspirations. Conversely, imitation processes were revealed to play a minor role in the formation of students' aspirations. Along with the finding that migrant students consider aspects such as income prospects and the societal valuation associated with a given occupational alternative in Germany as very important in constructing their occupational aspirations, the present results are clearly counter to the notion that adoption processes in the migrant population go hand in hand with mechanisms that lead to an underinvestment in education.

Opposed to the models to explain students' educational aspirations, neither migrant group was found to have significantly higher background-adjusted educational expectations than their native peers. Partly, this finding may be attributable to the insufficient control of primary effects. Further, the methodological approach to focus on the subsample of students who plan to attain the highest level of general education and the conservative measure of what constitutes students' expectations may contribute to the insignificance of the background-adjusted coefficients. The descriptive analysis indicated that it is students' educational expectations rather than their aspirations that are conditioned by their perceptions of the opportunity structure. Given that migrants were shown to report their plans to complete the highest level of general education more often under uncertainty than their native peers, the insignificance of the migrant coefficients does not appear surprising in view of the positively selected subsample of students who plan to obtain this qualification the analysis of students' educational expectations was based on. The comparability of the present results with findings from other studies is further limited by the fact that empirical studies most often investigate the transition from primary into secondary education, and sometimes the transition into higher education, and that it is in both cases typically parental aspirations but not students' own aspirations that are assessed (e.g., B. Becker 2010; Ditton et al. 2005; Kristen and Dollmann 2010; Paulus and Blossfeld 2007; Roth et al. 2010). At any rate, the present results are not in conflict with studies that attest significantly higher educational expectations in migrants when primary effects are controlled for based on samples of students that vary in level of educational aspiration (e.g., Stanat and Christensen 2006b).

As outlined in the theoretical part of the study, the observation of significantly higher aspirations, expectations and more favorable transitions in migrant families when background characteristics are taken into account are often discussed with reference to secondary effects of ethnic origin (Heath and Brinbaum 2007; Kristen and Dollmann 2010). Also, it was discussed that the expression of comparatively high aspirations in the migrant population has led several researchers to conclude that ethnic disparities in education may not be the product of lower ambition among migrants as much as of less favorable preconditions for success in migrant families (Gresch et al. 2012, p. 65; Klieme et al. 2010, p. 202). Yet other researchers have suggested that migrants may be positively selected for their educational ambition and drive due to the existence of migration-specific conditions such as their desire to achieve upward mobility in the receiving country (cf. Heath and Brinbaum 2007). So far, the results of the study appear to be supportive of these notions. Yet, some final considerations deserve to be addressed which relate to methodological difficulties on the one hand, and to the question of the theoretical meaning of respondent-reported career aspirations on the other hand.

At the methodological level, the question arises to what extent models to explain students' educational aspirations, expectations or transition probabilities sufficiently control for the variation in the preconditions for educational success in native and migrant families and for secondary stratification effects. First, this concerns the use of conventional measures of the family's socioeconomic position that are based on information on parental level of education and occupation. In view of the consideration that these characteristics may not reflect the availability of educationally-relevant resources in migrant families to the same extent as in native families due to the limited transferability of origin-specific human capital, the coefficient for the family's socioeconomic status – and hence the coefficients for both migrant groups – may be systematically over- or underestimated. Given a comparable educational background of native and migrant parents, the migrant coefficients are likely to be upward biased if migrant parents occupy comparatively unfavorable labor market positions, and underestimated if they occupy labor market positions comparable to those of their native counterparts due to aspects such as the limited transferability of origin-specific human capital to the educational setting in the receiving country. Second, and partly independent of measurement difficulties that are associated with the assessment of the family's socioeconomic position, it is unlikely that the variables in the models to explain the variation in students' educational aspirations and expectations fully capture differences in the preconditions for educational success in native and migrant families. As regards the existence of conditions that specifically affect the educational outcomes of migrant students, productive majority language skills were explicitly taken into account and identified as a significant predictor of both students' educational aspirations and expectations. However, considerations such as lacking knowledge about the educational system in the receiving country in migrant families could not be explicitly considered. Assuming that primary effects of ethnic origin negatively influence the educational performance of migrants, and in view of the observation that empirical studies consistently attest comparatively low test scores in different educational domains for mixed migrant samples, the omission of conditions that specifically affect the educational performance of this group is most likely associated with an underestimation of both migrant coefficients.

While an insufficient control for primary effects will affect the results of any models to estimate differences in the background-adjusted aspirations, expectations or decisions in native and migrant families, this consideration may be particularly important with regard to the interpretation of the present results due to the omission of a direct performance measure apart from students' productive language skills. Most commonly, studies on secondary effects include information on teacher-assigned grades or standardized performance tests scores students achieve in different educational domains. In the present study, information on students' grades was not used as they attended courses of different levels of difficulty so that a comparison of their grades does not appear appropriate. Although teacher-assigned grades and other performance measures cannot be expected to fully reflect students' educational abilities and preconditions for success either, for instance due to different levels of motivation or teacher preferences, they may still predict students' probabilities of success better than the measures used in the present analysis to the extent that it is school performance which will eventually determine whether students are admitted to continue in general education or not (Harlen 2005; Stocké 2007). Also, to arrive at more parsimonious model specifications, the analysis of students' educational aspirations and expectations used several imprecise measures to capture primary effects, such as the binary variable to reflect the number of books in the household.

Besides the methodological difficulties that are inherent to the estimation of secondary effects of ethnic origin, in view of the controversy surrounding the meaning of respondent-reported educational aspirations the question further arises to what extent higher aspirations in migrant families will eventually lead to more favorable educational decisions and attainment levels.

First, it was discussed that the interpretation of high aspirations as indicating high motivational potential and ambition relies on the assumption that students indeed commit to their expressed aspirations and take actions for their enactment. Not least the finding that discrepancies between students' educational aspirations and expectations cannot necessarily be conceived of as the result of students' evaluations of the opportunity structure clearly suggests that this assumption cannot be assumed to be universally met. As regards the comparability of aspirations across the sample, however, no differences were found with respect to this pattern between native and migrant students. The hypothesis that migrants tend to express unrealistically high aspirations as a result of the limited transferability of origin-specific human capital (e.g., Gresch et al. 2012; Relikowski et al. 2010; Stanat and Christensen 2006a) cannot be investigated based on the present data. Also, it was discussed that comparatively large gaps between the aspirations, expectations and attainment levels in the migrant population do not necessarily imply that migrants are less firmly committed to their aspirations than natives as these observations may as well be attributable to the fact that they fail to effectively deal with the barriers they face in implementing their aspirations.

Second, and independent of the question to what extent students are able to realistically appraise their educational potential, the analysis provided evidence to support the notion of variations in the extent to which students adapt their educational aspirations to their *perceived* probabilities of success (Goyette 2008). Thus, the possibility remains that the comparatively high aspirations in migrant families, at least partly, result from their lesser adjustment to their expectations of success. Even though the data does not allow to investigate the extent to which students' expectations reflect their actual probabilities of success, the study provides evidence in favor of this notion by showing that both migrant groups are more likely to express high general educational plans under uncertainty to realize their aspirations than their native peers. As regards students' plans to enter higher education, this pattern is particularly pronounced in the group of students from families with both parents born abroad, who reported their plans to enter higher education much more often than their peers from the other two groups. Yet, more than one third of migrants with both parents born abroad who plan to enter higher education reported to be rather or even very uncertain to meet the formal entry barriers. This applies to a quarter of students in the other two groups only. In view of these observations, it appears to be an open question to what extent the observation of comparatively high aspirations of migrants from families with both parents born abroad can be interpreted as implying lower levels of ambition in native students.

A last consideration relates to the question whether the extremely high educational and future career aspirations in migrant families, and of students with both parents born abroad in the present study specifically, necessarily promote successful transitions in the educational system. The share of students who plan to enter higher education but who also reported realistic occupational aspirations that do not require this type of education is much higher among natives compared to migrants. The majority of students from all three groups expressed one single idealistic occupational aspiration only, but natives expressed a much larger number of realistic occupational aspirations than migrants, and especially than migrants with both parents born abroad. The share who did not express any realistic occupational aspirations was found to be highest among migrants with both parents born abroad and lowest among natives.

On the one hand, these observations may reflect a stronger preference for higher-level careers of migrants and their higher willingness to invest time and effort to realize their most preferred career aspirations, and is in line with the hypothesis that migrants are positively selected for their educational ambition due to their desire to achieve upward mobility (cf. Heath and Brinbaum 2007; Kao and Tienda 1995). On the other hand, the possibility was discussed that students may not equally prefer all of their expressed career aspirations but consider to pursue alternative careers that they perceive as more realistically accessible in anticipation that they may fail to meet the formal entry barriers for their most preferred career aspirations (Gottfredson 1981, 2005). Then, even if it was true that students seriously attempt to realize their expressed aspirations, in view of the comparatively high levels of uncertainty reported by migrants to successfully accomplish their educational plans, their lower tendency to seek career alternatives that are easier accessible may as well be an obstacle to their successful transition into the VET system in case they fail in general education (cf. Goyette 2008; Reynolds et al. 2006; Rosenbaum 2011).

In sum, the present results are in line with the hypothesis that the attainment gap is the product of different preconditions for educational success across native and migrant families rather than of lower levels of ambition among the latter (Gresch et al. 2012; Klieme et al. 2010). More specifically, the empirical findings support the notion that the desire to achieve upward mobility in the receiving country constitutes a central explanation for the observed patterns of aspirations in native and migrant families (Kao and Tienda 1995; Vallet 2007; cf. also Heath and Brinbaum 2007). Even though the data indicates that the aspirations of migrants may be looser associated with their attainment outcomes compared to native students, the results neither give reason to believe that educational disparities emerge and persist as a result of systematically lower investments in education in migrant families, nor that migrant students are less firmly committed to their aspirations than their native peers. In conclusion, the results clearly point to the need for combined data on students' subjective beliefs, the actions they take to realize their aspirations and on their eventual attainment outcomes to tackle the question of the meaning and comparability of the educational aspirations and expectations expressed by natives and migrants, and to assess the extent to which the attainment gap is a matter of lacking commitment or of ineffective courses of action students take to realize their expressed aspirations.

11.8   Limitations and prospects for future research

The present study investigated the distribution of the educational and future career aspirations and expectations as well as the belief-formation processes of native and migrant students at the end of compulsory full-time education. On the one hand, the data provided insight into the absolute and relative importance students attribute to different dimensions in the construction of their educational and future career aspirations and expectations, and clearly showed these patterns to differ across the groups of natives and migrants with one and both parents born abroad. Further, the study shed light on the meaning of respondent-reported educational aspirations and into the nature of the association between students' future career aspirations and their aspirations and expectations in general education. On the other hand, the results give rise to important implications with regard to the applicability of models to explain social disparities in educational attainment to the explanation of ethnic differentials in education, the measurement of subjective data in the form of respondent-reported aspirations, and the interpretation of the significantly higher background-adjusted educational aspirations that are consistently attested for migrant families. The study certainly contributes to the understanding of the educational behavior in native and migrant students, but several questions could not be answered based on the present data and remain to be addressed.

The cross-sectional design of the study constitutes a first major limitation. Even though the data allows for a plausible interpretation of the results that were derived from the analysis of students' educational aspirations and expectations, causal attribution is not feasible. As regards the question of the direction of the association between students' future career aspirations and their aspirations and expectations in general education, the present findings provide tentative support for the hypothesized mechanisms that may lead to a causal effect from the former on the latter variables. Yet, as discussed above, the results leave alternative interpretations. These difficulties are reinforced by the lack of information on students' knowledge about the formal and informal entry barriers for different types of careers. Similarly, the question to what extent students comply with the aspirations of their parents or carry out the same evaluations of the opportunity structure remains to be addressed.

Also, the cross-sectional design does not allow to take into consideration the dynamic nature of educational aspirations and expectations. As such, the data neither allows to address the question to what extent students had adjusted their realistic future career aspirations to their (perceived) educational potential at the time of data collection, nor whether they had shifter their idealistic occupations in the direction of their realistic occupational aspirations in the course of their educational careers (Armstrong and Crombie 2000; Hanson 1994; Heckhausen and Tomasik 2002). Yet, these considerations are of particular importance not least due to the use of information on the gap between the two variables to argue against a universally non-causal interpretation of the effect from students' future career aspirations on their aspirations and expectations in general education. Further, the consideration could not be taken into account that educational aspirations and expectations may not be conceived of as the mere result of past experiences of success and failure, but that they may have shaped past performance outcomes themselves (Lent et al. 1994). For instance, the finding that several students would prefer to obtain higher qualifications in general education if their grades were better does not necessarily imply that the respective students indeed tried to achieve higher in the past. Finally, it remains an open question how firmly students are committed to their expressed aspirations, and to what extent their aspirations and expectations are associated with eventual attainment levels.

Further, the data does not allow to use methods that take into account the potential endogeneity of the predictors used in the multivariate analysis. For instance, there is evidence that students not only comply with the aspirations of their parents but that the latter also adjust their aspirations toward their children's own aspirations (Jencks et al. 1983; Zhang et al. 2011). Similarly, the empirical results suggest that future career aspirations are causal for students' educational aspirations and expectations in general education in some cases but not in others. Following these considerations, both the coefficients and standard errors that were estimated for students' future career aspirations and parental aspirations must be expected to be biased.

Besides, the comparatively small sample size led to estimation difficulties at several points throughout the analysis and does not allow to draw generalized conclusions. Perhaps most important to the present research question, the consideration could not be taken into account that the effects of migration-specific conditions may vary in their direction and intensity depending on the precise migration situation (Diefenbach 2010; Heath and Brinbaum 2007). As regards the present data, the migrant subsample is extremely heterogeneous and comprises students from 44 countries. On the one hand, treating migrants as a homogenous group may have precluded the identification of conditions and mechanisms that matter to some immigrant groups only but not to others, or that have a reverse effect on the educational outcomes of different groups of migrants. On the other hand, it is likely that the differences that were observed between students from families with one and both parents born abroad are, at least partly, attributable to a different composition of the two groups in terms of their migration biographies.

Despite these methodological difficulties, the study provided valuable insight into the patterns of belief-formation in native and migrant students at the point of decision to remain in general education or to leave and enter the VET system. Not only do the present results point to the need for the explicit consideration of migration-specific conditions to better understand the emergence and persistence of ethnic differentials in education. Also, they strongly confirm the notion that the transition at the end of compulsory full-time education is a critical point in students' educational careers, and encourage further research on the belief-formation and transition processes of the age group under consideration. Even though the results revealed severe difficulties that are related to the measurement and interpretation of respondent-reported aspirations and expectations, and certainly challenge their value to predict attainment levels, they clearly point out the value of subjective data to test the strong assumptions of revealed preference approaches that are based on objective transition data. For instance, the finding that students' educational expectations not only fall short of their aspirations due to students' concern about insufficient levels of educational performance but also because they tend to be uncertain what careers to pursue suggests that observed differences between expressed aspirations and expectations cannot necessarily be conceived of as the product of the opportunity structure on the one hand, and supports the notion that students are not rational decision makers but to some extent opportunistic in seeking and accepting careers on the other hand (Gottfredson 1996, p. 201; Simon 1955, 1957). In conclusion, the study strongly points to the need for the combined analysis of subjective and objective data in a longitudinal perspective to allow for the explication and empirical testing of behavioral assumptions, and encourages an increased interdisciplinary discourse to provide more fine-grained insight into the processes that generate the attainment gap between natives and migrants.

References

Alexander, K. L., & Cook, M. A. (1979). The Motivational Relevance of Educational Plans: Questioning the Conventional Wisdom. *Social Psychology Quarterly, 42*(3), 202-213.

Armstrong, P. I., & Crombie, G. (2000). Compromises in Adolescents' Occupational Aspirations and Expectations from Grades 8 to 10. *Journal of Vocational Behavior, 56*(1), 82-98.

Bandura, A. (1986). Human Agency in Social Cognitive Theory. *American Psychologist, 44*(9), 1175-1184.

Bandura, A. (1991). Social Cognitive Theory of Self-Regulation. *Organizational Behavior and Human Decision Processes, 50*(2), 248-287.

Beal, S. J., & Crockett, L. J. (2010). Adolescents' Occupational and Educational Aspirations and Expectations: Links to High School Activities and Adult Educational Attainment. *Developmental Psychology, 46*(1), 258-265.

Becker, B. (2010). *Bildungsaspirationen von Migranten: Determinanten und Umsetzung in Bildungsergebnisse* (MZES Working Paper No. 137). Retrieved Febuary 5, 2012, from http://www.mzes.unimannheim.de/publications/wp/wp-137.pdf

Becker, R., & Schubert, F. (2011). Die Rolle von primären und sekundären Herkunftseffekten für Bildungschancen von Migranten im deutschen Schulsystem. In R. Becker (Ed.), *Integration durch Bildung: Bildungserwerb von jungen Migranten in Deutschland* (pp. 161-194). Wiesbaden: VS Verlag für Sozialwissenschaften.

Behnke, A. O., Piercy, K. W., & Diversi, M. (2004). Educational and Occupational Aspirations of Latino Youth and Their Parents. *Hispanic Journal of Behavioral Sciences, 26*(1), 16-35.

Bourdieu, P. (1973). Cultural Reproduction and Social Reproduction. In R. K. Brown (Ed.), *Knowledge, Education, and Cultural Change: Papers in the Sociology of Education* (pp. 71-112). London: Tavistock.

Buriel, R., & Cardoza, D. (1988). Sociocultural Correlates of Achievement Among Three Generations of Mexican American High School Seniors. *American Educational Research Journal, 25*(2), 177-192.

Caprara, G. V., Fida, R., Vecchione, M., Del Bove, G., Vecchio, G. M., Barbaranelli, C., & Bandura, A. (2008). Longitudinal Analysis of the Role of Perceived Self-efficacy for Self-regulated Learning in Academic Continuance and Achievement. *Journal of Educational Psychology, 100*(3), 525-534.

References

Coleman, J. S., Campbell, E. Q., Hobson, J. C., McPartland, J., Mood, A. M., Weinfeld, F. D., & York, R. L. (1966). *Equality of Educational Opportunity*. Washington, D.C.: U.S. Government Printing Office.

Diefenbach, H. (2010). *Kinder und Jugendliche aus Migrantenfamilien im deutschen Bildungssystem: Erklärungen und empirische Befunde* (3rd ed.). Wiesbaden: VS Verlag für Sozialwissenschaften.

Ditton, H., Krüsken, J., & Schauenberg, M. (2005). Bildungsungleichheit – der Beitrag von Familie und Schule. *Zeitschrift für Erziehungswissenschaft, 8*(2), 285-304.

Domina, T., Conley, A., & Farkas, G. (2011). The Link between Educational Expectations and Effort in the College-for-all Era. *Sociology of Education, 84*(2), 93-112.

Erikson, R., & Jonsson, J. O. (1996). Explaining Class Inequality in Education: The Swedish Test Case. In R. Erikson & J. O. Jonsson (Eds.), *Can Education Be Equalized? The Swedish Case* (pp. 1-63). Stockholm: Westview Press.

Gambetta, D. (1987). *Were They Pushed Or Did They Jump? Individual Decision Mechanisms in Education*. Cambridge: Cambridge University Press.

Gottfredson, L. S. (1981). Circumscription and Compromise: A Developmental Theory of Occupational Aspirations. *Journal of Counseling Psychology Monograph, 28*(6), 545-579.

Gottfredson, L. S. (1996). Gottfredson's Theory of Circumscription and Compromise. In D. Brown & L. Brooks (Eds.), *Career Choice and Development* (3 ed., pp. 179-232). San Francisco: Jossey–Bass.

Gottfredson, L. S. (2005). Applying Gottfredson's Theory of Circumscription and Compromise in Career Guidance and Counseling. In S. D. Brown & R. W. Lent (Eds.), *Career Development and Counseling: Putting Theory and Research to Work* (pp. 71-100). New Jersey: Wiley.

Goyette, K. A. (2008). College for Some to College for All: Social Background, Occupational Expectations, and Educational Expectations over Time. *Social Science Research, 37*(2), 461-484.

Gresch, C. (2012). *Der Übergang in die Sekundarstufe I: Leistungsbeurteilung, Bildungsaspiration und rechtlicher Kontext bei Kindern mit Migrationshintergrund*. Wiesbaden: VS Verlag für Sozialwissenschaften.

Gresch, C., Maaz, K., Becker, M., & McElvany, N. (2012). Zur hohen Bildungsaspiration von Migranten beim Übergang von der Grundschule in die Sekundarstufe: Fakt oder Artefakt? In P. Pielage, L. Pries & G. Schultze (Eds.), *Soziale Ungleichheit in der Einwanderungsgesellschaft: Kategorien, Konzepte, Einflussfaktoren* (pp. 56-67). Bonn: Friedrich-Ebert-Stiftung.

Haller, A. O., & Miller, I. W. (1963). *The Occupational Aspiration Scale: Theory, Structure and Correlates* (AES-TB No. 288). Retrieved September 9, 2011, from http://files.eric.ed.gov/fulltext/ED016712.pdf

Hanson, S. L. (1994). Lost Talent: Unrealized Educational Aspirations and Expectations among U.S. Youths. *Sociology of Education, 67*(3), 159-183.

Harlen, W. (2005). Trusting Teachers' Judgement: Research Evidence of the Reliability and Validity of Teachers' Assessment Used for Summative Purposes. *Research Papers in Education, 20*, 245-270.

Heath, A. F., & Brinbaum, Y. (2007). Guest Editorial: Explaining Ethnic Inequalities in Educational Attainment. *Ethnicities, 7*(3), 291-304.

Heath, A. F., Rothon, C., & Kipli, E. (2008). The Second Generation in Western Europe: Education, Unemployment, and Occupational Attainment. *Annual Review of Sociology, 34*(1), 211-235.

Heckhausen, J., & Tomasik, M. J. (2002). Get an Apprenticeship Before School is Out: How German Adolescents Adjust Vocational Aspirations When Getting Close to a Developmental Deadline. *Journal of Vocational Behavior, 60*, 199-219.

Jacob, B. A., & Wilder, T. (2010). *Educational Expectations and Attainment* (NBER Working Paper No. 15683). Retrieved January 26, 2013, from http://www.nber.org/papers/w15683

Jencks, C., Crouse, J., & Mueser, P. (1983). The Wisconsin Model of Status Attainment: A National Replication with Improved Measures of Ability and Aspiration. *Sociology of Education, 56*(1), 3-19.

Kao, G., & Thompson, J. S. (2003). Racial and Ethnic Stratification in Educational Achievement and Attainment. *Annual Review of Sociology, 29*, 417-442.

Kao, G., & Tienda, M. (1995). Optimism and Achievement: The Educational Performance of Immigrant Youth. *Social Science Quarterly, 76*(1), 1-19.

Kerckhoff, A. C. (1976). The Status Attainment Process: Socialization or Allocation? *Social Forces, 55*(2), 368-381.

Kerckhoff, A. C. (1977). The Realism of Educational Ambitions in England and the United States. *American Sociological Review, 42*(4), 563-571.

Kerckhoff, A. C., & Campbell, R. T. (1977). Social Status Differences in the Explanation of Educational Ambition. *Social Forces, 5*(3), 701-714.

Klieme, E., Artelt, C., Hartig, J., Jude, N., Köller, O., Prenzel, M., Schneider, W., & Stanat, P. (2010). *PISA 2009: Bilanz nach einem Jahrzehnt*. Münster: Waxmann.

Kristen, C., & Dollmann, J. (2010). Sekundäre Effekte der ethnischen Herkunft: Kinder aus türkischen Familien am ersten Bildungsübergang. In B. Becker & D. Reimer (Eds.), *Vom Kindergarten bis zur Hochschule: Die Generierung von ethnischen und sozialen Disparitäten in der Bildungsbiographie* (pp. 117-144). Wiesbaden: VS Verlag für Sozialwissenschaften.

Kristen, C., Edele, A., Kalter, F., Kogan, I., Schulz, B., Stanat, P., & Will, G. (2011). The Education of Migrants and their Children Across the Life Course. *Zeitschrift für Erziehungswissenschaft, 14*(2), 121-137.

Kristen, C., & Granato, N. (2007). The Educational Attainment of the Second Generation in Germany: Social Origins and Ethnic Inequality. *Ethnicities, 7*(3), 343-366.

Lent, R. W., Brown, S. D., & Hackett, G. (1994). Monograph: Toward a Unifying Social Cognitive Theory of Career and Academic Interest, Choice, and Performance. *Journal of Vocational Behavior, 45*, 79-122.

Looker, D. E., & McNutt, K. L. (1989). The Effect of Occupational Expectations on the Educational Attainments of Males and Females. *Canadian Journal of Education, 14*(3), 352-367.

Mau, W.-C., & Bikos, L. H. (2000). Educational and Vocational Aspirations of Minority and Female Students: A Longitudinal Study. *Journal of Counseling & Development, 78*(2), 186-194.

Morgan, S. L. (1996). Trends in Black-White Differences in Educational Expectations: 1980-1992. *Sociology of Education, 69*(4), 308-319.

Morgan, S. L. (1998). Adolescent Educational Expectations: Rationalized, Fantasized, or Both? *Rationality and Society, 10*(2), 131-162.

References

Morgan, S. L. (2002). Modeling Preparatory Commitment and Non-Repeatable Decisions: Information-Processing, Preference Formation and Educational Attainment. *Rationality and Society, 14*(4), 387-429.

Morgan, S. L. (2005). *On the Edge of Commitment: Educational Attainment and Race in the United States.* Stanford, CA: Stanford University Press.

Nauck, B. (2011). Kulturelles und soziales Kapital als Determinante des Bildungserfolgs bei Migranten? In R. Becker (Ed.), *Integration durch Bildung: Bildungserwerb von jungen Migranten in Deutschland* (pp. 71-93). Wiesbaden: VS Verlag für Sozialwissenschaften.

Ou, S.-R., & Reynolds, A. J. (2008). Predictors of Educational Attainment in the Chicago Longitudinal Study. *School Psychology Quarterly, 23*(2), 199-229.

Paulus, W., & Blossfeld, H.-P. (2007). Schichtspezifische Präferenzen oder sozioökonomisches Entscheidungskalkül? Zur Rolle elterlicher Bildungsaspirationen im Entscheidungsprozess beim Übergang von der Grundschule in die Sekundarstufe. *Zeitschrift für Pädagogik, 53*(4), 491-508.

Quaglia, R. J., & Cobb, C. D. (1996). Toward a Theory of Student Aspirations. *Journal of Research in Rural Education, 12*(3), 127-132.

Relikowski, I., Schneider, T., & Blossfeld, H.-P. (2010). Primäre und sekundäre Herkunftseffekte beim Übergang in das gegliederte Schulsystem: Welche Rolle spielen soziale Klasse und Bildungsstatus in Familien mit Migrationshintergrund? In T. Beckers, K. Birkelbach, J. Hagenah & U. Rosar (Eds.), *Komparative empirische Sozialforschung* (pp. 143-167). Wiesbaden: VS Verlag für Sozialwissenschaften.

Relikowski, I., Yilmaz, E., & Blossfeld, H.-P. (2012). Wie lassen sich die hohen Bildungsaspirationen von Migranten erklären? Eine Mixed-Methods-Studie zur Rolle von strukturellen Aufstiegschancen und individueller Bildungserfahrung [Special issue]. *Kölner Zeitschrift für Soziologie und Sozialpsychologie,* 111-136.

Reynolds, J., Stewart, M., MacDonald, R., & Sischo, L. (2006). Have Adolescents Become Too Ambitious? High School Seniors' Educational and Occupational Plans, 1976 to 2000. *Social Problems, 53*(2), 186-206.

Rojewski, J. W. (2005). Occupational Aspirations: Constructs, Meanings, and Application. In S. D. Brown & R. W. Lent (Eds.), *Career Development and Counseling: Putting Theory and Research to Work* (pp. 131-154). New Jersey: Wiley.

Rojewski, J. W., & Kim, H. (2003). Career Choice Patterns and Behavior of Work-Bound Youth During Early Adolescence. *Journal of Career Development, 30*(2), 89-108.

Rosenbaum, J. E. (1976). *Making Inequality: The Hidden Curriculum of High School Tracking.* New York: Wiley.

Rosenbaum, J. E. (1978). The Structure of Opportunity in School. *Social Forces, 57*(1), 236-256.

Rosenbaum, J. E. (1980). Track Misperceptions and Frustrated College Plans: An Analysis of the Effects of Tracks and Track Perceptions in the National Longitudinal Survey. *Sociology of Education, 53*(2), 74-88.

Rosenbaum, J. E. (2011). The Complexities of College for All: Beyond Fairy-tale Dreams. *Sociology of Education, 84*(2), 113-117.

Roth, T., Salikutluk, Z., & Kogan, I. (2010). Auf die „richtigen Kontakte" kommt es an! Soziale Ressourcen und die Bildungsaspirationen der Mütter von Haupt-, Real- und Gesamtschülern in Deutschland. In B. Becker & D. Reimer (Eds.), *Vom Kindergarten bis zur Hochschule: Die Generierung von ethnischen und sozialen Disparitäten in der Bildungsbiographie* (pp. 179-212). Wiesbaden: VS Verlag für Sozialwissenschaften.

Schuchart, C., & Maaz, K. (2007). Bildungsverhalten in institutionellen Kontexten: Schulbesuch und elterliche Bildungsaspiration am Ende der Sekundarstufe I. *Kölner Zeitschrift für Soziologie und Sozialpsychologie, 59*(4), 640-666.
Sewell, W. H., Haller, A. O., & Ohlendorf, G. W. (1970). The Educational and Early Occupational Status Attainment Process: Replication and Revision. *American Sociological Review, 35*(6), 1014-1027.
Sewell, W. H., Haller, A. O., & Portes, A. (1969). The Educational and Early Occupational Attainment Process. *American Sociological Review, 34*(1), 82-92.
Simon, H. A. (1955). A Behavioral Model of Rational Choice. *The Quarterly Journal of Economics, 69*(1), 99-118.
Simon, H. A. (1957). *Models of Man: Social and Rational – Mathematical Essays on Rational Human Behavior in a Social Setting.* New York: Wiley.
Stanat, P., & Christensen, G. (2006a). *Schulerfolg von Jugendlichen mit Migrationshintergrund im internationalen Vergleich: Eine Analyse von Voraussetzungen und Erträgen schulischen Lernens im Rahmen von PISA 2003.* Berlin: Bundesministerium für Bildung und Forschung.
Stanat, P., & Christensen, G. (2006b). *Where Immigrant Students Succeed: A Comparative Review of Performance and Engagement in PISA 2003.* Paris: OECD Publishing.
Stanat, P., Segeritz, M., & Christensen, G. (2010). Schulbezogene Motivation und Aspiration von Schülerinnen und Schülern mit Migrationshintergrund. In W. Bos, E. Klieme & O. Köller (Eds.), *Schulische Lerngelegenheiten und Kompetenzentwicklung* (pp. 31-58). Münster: Waxmann.
Stocké, V. (2007). *Strength, Sources, and Temporal Development of Primary Effects of Families' Social Status on Secondary School Choice* (SFB504 Working Paper 07-60). Retrieved Januar 5, 2013, from https://ub-madoc.bib.uni-mannheim.de/2508/1/dp07_60.pdf
Vallet, L.-A. (2007). What Can We Do to Improve the Education of Children from Disadvantaged Backgrounds? In M. S. Sorondo, E. Malinvaud & P. Léna (Eds.), *Globalization and Education: Proceedings of the Joint Working Group. The Pontifical Academy of Sciences* (pp. 127-155). Berlin: De Gruyter.
Wiley, N. F. (1967). The Ethnic Mobility Trap and Stratification Theory. *Social Problems, 15*(1), 147-159.
Wiley, N. F. (1970). The Ethnic Mobility Trap and Stratification Theory. In P. I. Rose (Ed.), *The Study of Society: An Integrated Anthology* (pp. 397-408). New York: Harper & Brothers.
Xie, Y., & Goyette, K. A. (2003). Social Mobility and the Educational Choices of Asian Americans. *Social Science Research, 32*(3), 467–498.
Zhang, Y., Haddad, E., Torres, B., & Chen, C. (2011). The Reciprocal Relationships Among Parents' Expectations, Adolescents' Expectations, and Adolescents' Achievement: A Two-Wave Longitudinal Analysis of the NELS Data. *Journal of Youth and Adolescence, 40*(4), 479-489.

Glossary

The terms below are used in my empirical study as follows:

Migration background, migrant:
Students who migrated to Germany themselves and/or who have at least one parent born abroad.

Students' aspirations in general education, general educational aspirations:
Highest level of general education student plans to complete.

Students' expectations in general education, general educational expectations:
Subjective probability to realize expressed aspirations in general education.

Students' future educational aspirations, aspirations for future education:
Type of educational career student plans to pursue after leaving the general educational system.

Students' idealistic occupational aspirations:
Dream occupation(s).

Students' realistic occupational aspirations:
Occupation(s) student plans or can realistically imagine to attain.

Parents' aspirations in general education, general educational aspirations:
Highest level of general education parents would like student to complete, as perceived by student.

Parents' future educational aspirations, aspirations for future education:
Type of education parents would like student to pursue after leaving the general educational system, as perceived by student.

The manufacturer's authorised representative in the EU is Springer Nature Customer Service Centre GmbH, Europaplatz 3, 69115 Heidelberg, Germany. If you have any concerns regarding our products, please contact ProductSafety@springernature.com

Printed and bound by CPI Group (UK) Ltd, Croydon, CR0 4YY

23/03/2026

02076676-0001